The Dawn From On High

Light For the Path

DEACON
PETER HODSDON

First Edition

Published by Aventine Press
55 East Emerson St.
Chula Vista CA 91911
www.aventinepress.com

ISBN: 978-1-59330-901-5

Library of Congress Control Number: 2016901690
Library of Congress Cataloging-in-Publication Data
The Dawn From On High/ Deacon Peter Hodsdon

Printed in the United States of America

Contents

In the tender compassion of our God, the dawn from on high shall break upon us, to shine on those who dwell in darkness and the shadow of death, and to guide our feet into the way of peace.
(Luke 1:79)

Acknowledgments

Any creative work owes a debt of gratitude to the Creator, first and foremost. Not a single one of these homilies would be possible without the guidance of the Holy Spirit. In truth, the Spirit prompts through many different forms, and I likewise thank those who listened and guided: my wife Katie, innumerable parishioners who greeted me after Mass with a comment or a question, my incredibly supportive pastor, Fr. John Howard, CJM, and all of you who said, "Keep it up!"

I am further grateful to authors and teachers who have inspired me, including Richard Rohr, OFM, Meghan McKenna, Robert Spitzer, SJ, John Shea, and the inimitable William Barclay. I have made every attempt to credit any of their ideas I have borrowed in these writings. If I have somehow missed such an accreditation, I beg forgiveness!

Chapter 1 – Who Am I?

Our identity seems to be a forgone conclusion. We seek titles that flatter us; we are given labels that reflect how the world views us; but neither really get to the heart of who we are. One of the key teachings of Jesus, in accord with most other spiritual masters, is that our true identity is who we are in God, our *true self* according to Merton.

A key step in our spiritual journey is to discern our true self. Sometimes the best way to find that core identity is by stripping away the false self, that build-up of worldly titles and responsibilities, and do some *shadow work.* It can be painful, but the payoff is immense, since once found, the true self can never be lost or broken by anyone or anything. It is who we are, our deepest reality, as revealed by God.

Late Bloomers

Scripture Referenced: Luke 9:18-24

Once when Jesus was praying in solitude, and the disciples were with him, he asked them, "Who do the crowds say that I am?".

When I was in my late teens and early twenties, I remember having conversations with friends, usually fueled by a pitcher of beer, around the subject of identity. All too aware of the fact that our lives to date were largely directed by others – parents, school teachers and the like – we all struggled to answer the question, "Who am I?" We would try to answer the question by ticking off our good qualities and achievements, but inevitably one of us would challenge such a list by asking with blunt force, "But who are you *really*?"

As years go on, the question of identity seems to be answered for us. We acquire titles, some desirable, others not so. I remember how proud I was to get my first business card with my title on it – *programmer analyst*. Other titles are bestowed on us whether we like it or not –adult, or taxpayer, or illegal alien. Some we are proud to take – husband, wife, father, mother, deacon, grandma. Some we are not – addict, thief, liar, loser, old man. Do these titles describe us? To some degree, yes. But we know that such labels are at best approximations, and even the sum of every title we passively receive does not answer the question, "But who are you *really*?"

Our gospel today features Jesus trying to answer that question. Note that the reading starts with him "praying alone". The scene is quiet, reflective, with the disciples nearby. Jesus, coming out of his reverie, asks a simple question – "Who do the crowds say that I am?" Is Jesus confused about his identity? John's gospel would say no, never. But this is Luke, and like the other synoptic gospels, a key element of the narrative is Jesus coming to awareness of who he is and what he is called to be. So the question is thoughtful and provocative. His disciples answer honestly, perhaps eagerly – this is an interesting question because they're not really that sure themselves. John the Baptist, Elijah, one of the ancient prophets – you can hear the crowd debating among itself.

These aren't bad answers – they're just incomplete. So Jesus stops them with an appeal, at once pointed and poignant – who do *you* say that I am?

Peter answers quickly and forcefully: "You are the Messiah of God." But Jesus, although he doesn't dispute the answer, does not seem to embrace it either. Why not? Because what Peter means by the Messiah is not a spiritual leader but a worldly savior, a king like David who will bring about a new kingdom. It's partially true and on the right track – a lot better than a resurrected prophet – but it's insufficient and ambiguous. This is why Jesus sternly warns them against spreading this title around. The crowds will certainly leap to the incorrect conclusion and miss the point of who Jesus really is. And who is he? He promptly reveals his identity – Jesus is the "Son of Man" who will suffer, be killed, and raised on the third day. You can picture Jesus poring over the scroll of the prophet Isaiah and coming to the horrifying yet compelling conclusion that he is the suffering servant prophesied, saving his people through the ultimate sacrifice. Talk about an "aha moment"! That's a cup that's hard to drink from…

Note how much time it takes Jesus to come to this realization of his true identity. In an era when life expectancy was maybe 45 years, Jesus takes two thirds of his potential life span to come to this understanding. But the really interesting message of this gospel is *how* Jesus comes to understand who he is. Although he may have had an inkling that he was called to be someone very special, it is the act of living that reality of healing, preaching, teaching, and prayer that he comes to the truth, the essence of his being. He shares the secret with the disciples in one of the most quoted and misunderstood sayings in the Scriptures: "If any want to become my followers, let them deny themselves and take up their cross daily and follow me. For those who want to save their life will lose it, and those who lose their life for my sake will find it."

So who are you *really*? The irony is that the more you seek to find yourself, the more likely you are to miss the mark. To the extent that we seek affirmation and a desirable label from the outside world, we are setting ourselves up for a major letdown. Just as bad labels don't really describe us well, neither do good labels. Part of us desperately seeks those good labels and is so quick to take offense when that label is tarnished or threatened. Just last week, I forgot to make an important delivery to a customer, and he was pretty upset with me. I was tempted to get defensive and make up excuses, but in the end I simply agreed with him that I had dropped the ball. By the way, that's a good practice – if you screw up, admit it. It totally disarms the situation! One of the reasons I could make that admission of error is that I'm not bought into the label of "an excellent project manager". I am sometimes, and I'm not sometimes. That's called being human.

But who are you *really*? Jesus tells you how to find out. Get out of yourself. Stop focusing on me, me, me. Stop seeking how to save your life and start giving it away. Be careful – don't give it away to someone who can pay you back. Don't give it to someone so you can gain a new label. Philanthropist, major donor, sponsor, member of the inner circle. Pointless. Give it in such a way that your right hand doesn't know what your left hand is doing. Give it away and don't crow about it. Do you know how much fun it is to give something anonymously? Have you ever left a waitress a ridiculous tip? Or bought a meal for a family that clearly could use an extra dollar? Have you ever donated clothing or furniture that is in great shape? Or does it have to be thoroughly used? Have you ever thought, "Gee, if I could start over, I'd do *that*…" So what's stopping you?

When you start giving yourself away, the best of who you are begins to shine through. All of the stuff we carry around falls away. All of our precious labels are exposed for the silly ego trips that they are. We realize as St. Paul tells us that we are not Greek nor Jew nor male nor female nor slave nor free person – we are simply one in Christ. I'm completely convinced that no one finds their true vocation until much later in life. If you're before the age of 45, you're probably not in your true vocation yet. Just this week, the parish sponsored a talk on the mystic Hildegard of Bingen. She did the vast majority of her writing and ministry between the age of 50 and 80. What's your excuse?

Someone told me the other day that I was "a born deacon". I laughed out loud – why didn't anyone tell me until I was 47 years old? Brothers and sisters, we're all late bloomers, and thankfully so. It takes a bit of life under our belt to see the truth of our mistaken identity and grow the courage to redefine ourselves by giving our lives away. Yes, it can be painful. Yes, it can mean wearing different clothes and learning new ways. But the reward is a life *that is found*. Find out who you are *really*.

True Self, False Self

Scripture Referenced: Mark 8:27-35

> He summoned the crowd with his disciples and said to them, "Whoever wishes to come after me must deny himself, take up his cross, and follow me. For whoever wishes to save his life will lose it, but whoever loses his life for my sake and that of the Gospel will save it."

There's an old Rolling Stones song that has always resonated with me, and no, it's not *Honky Tonk Woman*. The song I'm thinking about is *You Can't Always Get What You Want*. Maybe we can have it as our recessional hymn? Maybe not! Anyway, the title came to mind while I was reading today's Scriptures, especially the Gospel. Here's Jesus asking the disciples in a very casual way as they stroll down the road, "Who do people say that I am?" It's a very simple question, at least, on the surface. By this point, Jesus' fame has spread, but as anyone who reads *People* magazine knows, there's the public persona and the real person. Jesus is curious – do the crowds understand who he is? Well, you can't always get what you want. The crowd sort of gets it – John the Baptist and Elijah are famous prophetic figures. To be compared with either of them is quite a feather, but still a misidentification.

But then, to everyone's astonishment, including Jesus I suspect, Peter gets it right. Four simple words: You are the Christ. The other Gospels have Peter saying more, but I like this simple pronouncement. You are the Christ. "Christ" means the anointed one, a reference to royalty with a religious twist, typically translated as the Messiah. So Jesus runs with it, describing his role as the Messiah as he sees it, carefully drawing parallels to the suffering servant of Isaiah in our first reading. Peter, however, is appalled.

Last February, up in Los Angeles, I heard a talk given by a Jewish rabbi about how Jews view Christianity, particularly Jesus. There were many interesting observations, but the one I most remember was his answer to the question, "Why don't Jews accept Jesus as the Messiah?" He was quite matter of fact in his response. He said, "We don't accept

Jesus as the Messiah, because Jesus didn't act like the Messiah." At our puzzled expressions, he described how the Jews understand the Messiah: fully human being, a political or military ruler, nothing to do with the redemption of sin, and certainly not God in any sense. This is the Messiah that Peter is thinking about when he takes Jesus aside and rebukes him. Can you imagine rebuking Jesus? Anyway, Jesus loses his temper at Peter and blasts him – Get behind me, Satan! Poor Peter. You can't always get what you want.

And now we come to one of the most challenging, provocative statements made by Jesus in the Gospels. *For whoever wishes to save his life will lose it, but whoever loses his life for my sake will save it.* Saving, losing, losing, saving. It's confusing, isn't it? I don't think that there's a sane human being who wouldn't say yes to the question, "Do you wish to save your life?" So Jesus clearly doesn't mean our physical life – it goes beyond this to a deeper level. And that is a question worth pondering. You see, brothers and sisters, each of us, every day, is employed in the work of "saving ourselves". We seek food, shelter, rest, social interaction, meaningful work. We care for our families and encourage them to "save themselves" with good decisions and a similar focus. Isn't that sensible? What's wrong with that? Nothing is wrong with it, and yet, everything is wrong with it. Living only to save yourself is no better than what any animal does. It's instinctual, it's basic, and it's a life of meaningless existence. It's a waste. We're made for so much more, and somehow, to tap that "so much more" we have to lose!

Now, to "lose" in this context does not mean to lose a job or some money, or a loved one. What are we losing then? Thomas Merton probably had the best term – he said that we had to lose our *false* self. Others have called it the *small* self. St. Paul calls it the *flesh*. It's all the same. The false self is that "person" we put on for the sake of others. The false self is our own design, carefully constructed over the years, emphasizing our best qualities as we see them, and carefully hiding those aspects of ourselves we'd rather not share. It's a mask, an illusion. False selves love titles and honors, love to be respected and admired, and preen before the cameras. So here I am before you, a deacon (great title – my small self loves that), a successful business man (more polish for the mask), and a published author. Woohoo! But are those characteristics really who I am deep inside? In the eyes of God?

Contrast the false self to the *true* self. The true self is the deepest reality of who we are – it's our naked, bleeding body – no illusions, no masks, no games. It's that part of us that screams for God's help when we're down, that hurts the most, that loves the deepest, that responds from the gut. Have you ever seen someone who you thought you knew do something that completely shocked you? I usually see it in two different circumstances. Put a person in front of a baby or a puppy and see what happens. The true self tends to pop open when faced with the unconditional love shown through a puppy or a baby. To see the flip side, the false self, note how often a person is offended. The more frequently a person feels slighted or expresses anger at how the world treats them always reveals just how engrained the false self is in that person.

Jesus wants us to lose our false selves. Period. Oh, is that all? Take note. Losing your false self *is not easy*. It's going to feel like death. Why? Because the false self is not only an illusion, it is the source of sin in our lives. As long as I strive to live up to the ideals of our society (the false self) I am denying the God-part of who I am. Denying God is sin. Let me share a simple example from my life. Five years ago, I was challenged to start putting in 60 hours/week at work if I wanted to be recognized as successful and by the way, earn a pile of money. My false self was saying, "No problem! Let's go! Money, possessions, security!" My true self said *no*. If I put those kinds of hours in, I couldn't do prison work, write homilies, visit with people in need, or be spiritually grounded. So I said no and took a big demotion. Hurray for me, right? Now I'm really happy, right? For weeks after that decision, I slept horribly, second-guessed myself every day, and more than once, planned on how to resurrect my now failing career. It felt like I was dying. And it was true – my false self was really ticked off. What got me through it? Jesus. If he could allow himself to be stripped and tortured to reveal his true self to the world, couldn't I do a little of that too?

Breaking away from the false self takes honesty, prayer, and time. It's the dark night of the soul, as John of the Cross called it. But that is exactly what Jesus means by losing your life for His sake – that's the only way to save yourself. By the way, do you remember the last chorus of that Rolling Stones song?

You can't always get what you want. But if you try some time, you just might find, you just might find, you get what you need!

The Shadow Self

Scripture Referenced: Mark 1:21-28

> In their synagogue was a man with an unclean spirit; he cried out, "What have you to do with us, Jesus of Nazareth? Have you come to destroy us? I know who you are – the Holy One of God!"

Who is the focal point of this story? No, not Jesus. Yes, the demon.

Don't you find it rather odd that the demon, a decidedly evil creature, is given the role of the prophet? Listen to what he says: "What have you to do with us, Jesus of Nazareth? Have you come to destroy us? I know who you are – the Holy One of God!" Unlike the good people who are listening to Jesus preach, it is the demon-possessed man who stands up and names the truth of Jesus' identity!

How can evil speak truth? Doesn't evil speak in lies? It certainly would be nice if the world were that black and white, wouldn't it? But we know that life is not so clear. We know that life is often a contradiction. We know that even though our life may be a pillar of rectitude in the sunlight, that pillar casts a shadow. Our nature as human beings is one of flaw and brilliance. There's not a perfect diamond out there anywhere. Mark is highlighting that the beginning of the spiritual journey involves facing demons!

I work with a lot of people who are discovering God, often for the first time. When the realization of God's love for them sinks in, it is a moment of sheer exhilaration. It's like a huge crush. The person is genuinely sorry for the life they've led up to then, and in the midst of their conversion, they feel that life is now on the right track and everything is going to come up roses from now on. But…it doesn't work like that. Inevitably, they must come down the mountain and face the person in the mirror who, omigosh, sins again! The same old addictions beckon, the same old habits reappear, and some of these new converts decide that Christianity is just not for them. How could it be? The same old mess is in the same old sink.

Ever feel that way? As horrible as it may sound as I say it, our journey requires us to listen to the demon! That demon, that dark side of us, that part of us we would prefer not to show, has a way of calling us out. The demon loves to show us as hypocrites, loves to expose us for the liars we sometimes are. That's why the demon doesn't have any trouble speaking the truth. Because, brothers and sisters, to quote Jack Nicholson, we can't handle the truth! But we need to learn how to deal with it, to understand what this shadow, this dark side of us, looks like.

Ironically, the best part of us, the ideal part of us, is often dancing ever so close to the worst of us. Let me give you an example from my life. Those of you who know me well, know that I am an analytic person, someone who loves to study a situation carefully, loves to read and think things through. All good stuff for the most part. That personality trait has done well for me over the years, leading to good grades in school, and a good job. So what's the downside? That same tendency also leads to a sense of separation from the world, a sort of observer from the sidelines, a disconnected, aloof way of being. That's not healthy, nor does it go over well with spouse, friends, and family. That is the shadow side, the place that needs redemption, the place that needs constant awareness.

There are many other examples. People who have a strong sense of justice in the world, but cannot abide anyone disagreeing with them. People who help other people selflessly, until you realize that they actually need to be needed. People who are oriented to success and achievement who cannot ever just relax and stop doing, doing, doing. People who love a debate, but cannot ever lose a debate. People who love to be different, until you realize that their entire life is built as a reaction to what others think of them.

In the world of spiritual direction and growth, the realization of our darker side and the necessity to do something about it is called "shadow work". I know it sounds kind of new age, but in reality this practice goes back many hundreds of years. Many people avoid this part of the spiritual journey because it can be painful. We must allow the demon to speak, and you may be surprised to learn that one of the meanings of the word Satan is "the accuser." Understand that the aim of Satan is not to make you do bad things. The aim of Satan is to discourage you from doing good things, to bring you to a sense of hopelessness and despair, to move you to the point of believing that you are no good, that God could not possibly love you. Because, brothers and sisters, if you buy that, then you'll never cooperate with God's grace, you'll simply walk in the shadow, unredeemed and blind, wallowing in your misery.

This is why Jesus is so relentless in his healing ministry, so intent on showing everyone that God is primarily concerned with making us whole, even if it means "re-creating" us as new human beings. Notice how many of Jesus' miracles have Him not only fixing something physical (blindness, lameness, speech, hearing) but also forgiving sins and restoring the individual to a real human life. Do you get the good news here? Jesus, our brother in humanity and divinity, accepts the fact that we are often in the shadow, in fact, seem to somehow get stuck in the shadow, the darkness. When he invites us to come into the light, he is saying that we need to recognize two critically important things. The first is that yes, we need to acknowledge our darkness, our shadow side, and become aware of its influence in our lives. Do not ignore it! Develop the humility and awareness to acknowledge it.

And secondly, most importantly, as sad as that shadow self is, God loves us regardless of the darkness. He loves us in spite of ourselves. He loves us through that shadow. As astonishing as it seems, God won't wait for us to become perfect. It'll never happen anyway. He simply asks us to become aware, to not become discouraged by our failings, and to cooperate with His grace. If you do that, you'll *never despair*, and lo and behold, if you keep cooperating with God, that shadow side of you will become lighter and lighter, until it is barely discernible. So come, enter into the light, hear the demon speak, and then tell your demon to be gone! Now, as Mark tells us, you're ready to follow Jesus…

You Are the Salt of the Earth!

Scripture Referenced: Matthew 5:13-20

> Jesus said to his disciples: "You are the salt of the earth. But if salt loses its taste, with what can it be seasoned? It is no longer good for anything but to be thrown out and trampled underfoot. You are the light of the world."

When people come to me for spiritual direction, the conversation typically begins to circle around one main point of confusion, one deceptively simple yet profoundly important query. At root, every one of us wants to know, "who am I?" Who am I – *really,* deep down? How do I go out into the everyday world and be the best Christian man or woman that I can be? What image can I grasp that makes sense to me?

As we heard last week, we're in that portion of Matthew's gospel called the Sermon on the Mount. Matthew depicts Jesus as the new Moses, bringing to his followers a new way of looking at life, not inscribed on stone tablets, but written on our hearts. Last week it was the Beatitudes, next week it is about the law, the week following about love of enemies. The Sermon on the Mount is probably the heart of Jesus' teaching from Matthew's point of view, so it's no wonder the Church takes four weeks to ponder it all.

Today's excerpt is intensely personal – the presentation style has moved from the somewhat mystical language that make up the Beatitudes to simple declarative statements. It's as if Jesus has been asked a question, a question we all have. *Jesus, who am I?* Here's his answer: "You are the salt of the earth." It's a startling statement actually. Is it a compliment? A challenge? A little of both? Consider what salt meant to first century people of Palestine. It is not simply a nice-to-have, it is a critical substance! Salt is the only known way to preserve food, to have the lamb you slaughtered or the fish you caught last more than a few hours before rotting completely. Salt gives simple food a special zing, a zest of flavor, that is highly prized. It's no different today, of course, salt is as popular as ever! Maybe too popular!

So Jesus tells us that we are like salt – we are critical to the earth. We somehow preserve the goodness of things. We add zest to life. We are sought after by all the world. So yes, this is a compliment and a challenge. For if we aren't being salt-like, then something has been wasted, hasn't it? Might as well throw it in the dirt.

Now picture another person addressing Jesus with the same question. Jesus, who am I? Another startling answer: "You are the light of the world!" A beacon in the night. A person who not only lights up the house, but lights up the world to the benefit of everyone. Wow, what a compliment, and what a challenge! The logical question of course, is how? How do we light up the world? Jesus sums it up nicely: "…let your light shine before others, so that they may see your good works…" Apparently, the question of *who we are* is tightly bound up in *what we do*.

One of my favorite sayings from Richard Rohr illustrates this key point: "You don't think yourself into a new way of acting. Rather, you act yourself into a new way of thinking." Essentially, what this means is that the answer to who we are is contained in the ordinary and everyday actions of life. At the risk of oversimplifying things, if you want to be more like Christ, you don't get there by sitting in the corner and murmuring prayers of petition. What you do is to start acting in a Christ-like way! Good psychology will tell you this very same thing. You want to feel better about yourself? Start doing things for others who are in need. Your actions begin to inform your mind in new and interesting ways, and suddenly, you are not simply a candle in the darkness, but a beacon in the night. Something wondrous occurs. We become who we emulate.

Those of you who are active in our Church and community know this intrinsically. You deserve a pat on the back. But be sure to heed the warning in Jesus' words today as well. If you've been doing the same ministry for the past umpteen years, you need to ask yourself if the salt is getting a little flat and tasteless. If your ministry is only inside the Church building on Sunday mornings, then realize that this building is kind of shaped like an upside down bushel basket, isn't it? Is your light only shining in here?

Whether you're seeking that first ministry to join, or perhaps a change of scene, how do you discern what God wants you to do? How do you figure it out? Ironically, you start with a better understanding of who you are. Before you can exercise that human *doing*, you need to get hold of the human *being*. We're back to that original question, "who am I?" Here's a few ways to figure that out:

- As a member of the body of Christ, you are unique and connected at the same time. Sometimes we don't see our own unique qualities, however, and that's why it's important to simply ask a good friend what they see as *your* gift. It often surprises us, because what someone else sees as our special gift feels totally simple and mundane to us! When someone first asked me to give a speech, I thought, "Well, OK. What's the big deal about that?"
- It's OK to try out a new ministry and see what happens. You may find it the best fit or you may find it an absolute chore. The key is to try. I have a friend who decided he wanted to try prison ministry mostly because of my glowing reviews. He went through all of the prep work, walked into the jail and after one visit, walked away. He just couldn't handle it -- the bars, the close quarters – it was kind of claustrophobic for him. I told him it was OK, try something different. He agreed, and said that the best thing about trying prison ministry was the realization that he *could not do* jail time. He said, "I'll never break a law again – ever!"
- But here's the most important thing. You'll know that the ministry is a fit for you if you begin to experience *the fruits of the Spirit*. You see, the Holy Spirit works best by working through the gifts that God gave you, and when the Spirit has moved through you, the Spirit always leaves something behind, a trail marker or two. The two markers I see the most often are joy and peace.
- If you're curious about a ministry, talk to someone who is already working in that ministry. Ask the questions, dig into to it a bit. What do they love about it? What don't they care for? If their stated positives ring loudly with you, listen to that. If their positives leave you a little ho-hum, then look somewhere else. If you're still not sure, ask someone on the St. James staff. We have lots of ideas!

In closing, I'd like to mention one ministry that is uniquely Catholic and always in need of good-hearted people with the Spirit within them. That ministry is Eucharistic ministry – the sharing of the Body and Blood of Christ. We've had an unfortunate loss of people in this ministry lately, due to various reasons – mostly folks getting sick, some dying, or moving away. It's a simple ministry, as simple as giving out communion at Mass. But it's also contains an element of profound power, especially when you carry Christ to the sick and homebound who can't come to Mass on Sunday. When you feed the spiritually hungry with the body of Christ, you'll be fed as well. As Isaiah tells us, "If you bestow your bread on the hungry and satisfy the afflicted, then light shall rise for you in the darkness, and the gloom shall become for you like midday." You'll be salt of the earth and light of the world at the same time! Now *that's* a ministry! Come and join us.

Group Identification

Scripture Referenced: Luke 10:25-37

> But because he wished to justify himself, he said to Jesus, "And who is my neighbor?" Jesus replied, "A man fell victim to robbers as he went down from Jerusalem to Jericho."

Have you ever noticed how many different groups you belong to? It's actually kind of startling. When my wife and I go on vacation, especially overseas, you know it goes something like this. Where are you from? The U.S. Oh, that's nice, where? California. Oh, where in California? San Diego? Really? Do you know so and so? Well, I'm in Encinitas, actually. Oh, where's that? You get the picture. So, let's see, I'm a San Diegan, a Californian, and an American. Oh, did I mention that I'm part Irish, a Santa Clara alumnus, a Padre fan when they're playing well, and work in the high tech world? And oh yes, I'm a Roman Catholic too. Why do we have all of these group memberships? What is the point?

Social scientists will tell us that group membership and identification are critical for the human species. We all start out as part of a family, perhaps the most important group in our lives. After all, our family defines our ethnicity and our cultural background. Through the family, we are often handed membership in other groups, such as a neighborhood, or a religious identification, or a civic organization. Groups are protective, they form our social identity, they feed us and clothe us, and of course, they provide a shared vision of the world, a lens through which we see the world and perceive how the world sees us. Without group membership, we would grow up as sociopaths, people unable to relate to others.

With group identification, however, comes a risk. The risk is that we so identify with *our* group that we see others outside the group as lesser beings, as somehow defective humans. You may be thinking that you would never think that way, but consider what happens when you go to a sports game and you see a fan rooting for the opposing team. Don't you wonder, "what's wrong with that guy? He must have a screw loose." The more we identify with a particular group, the stronger this insider/outsider thinking gets. It's often the most severe and potent when it comes to religion. Why? Because religion is probably the most powerful group identification that we acquire, often more important than family. Religion, after all, is about God, about proper behavior, about spiritual power, about inner peace, about eternity. If someone is not of our religion, we wonder what makes them tick, we may feel threatened, and as the Jews were taught in the time of Jesus, we may ignore or worse yet, persecute these "others".

Jesus uses this story of the Good Samaritan to get right at the heart of this group identification problem. As the Chosen People, dedicated to the One God, the Jews rightfully considered themselves special. They had special rituals, they circumcised their males, they had washing rituals, and purity rites, they had the Law. Their identity as Jews defined who they were, how they were to act, even how they were to think. The Law of Moses was very clear – your "neighbor" was a fellow Jew. No one else matters very much. The scholar of the law in the Gospel is attempting to engage Jesus in a debate about the nature of this term "neighbor" within the Jewish community. For example, is a Levite more of a neighbor than a Pharisee? Jesus totally shocks him by utterly breaking this constricted notion of a neighbor and expanding the definition beyond the group, expanding the definition of neighbor to people in other groups, even (gulp) to your enemies!

We've heard this Good Samaritan story so many times that I fear that it has lost its punch. We tend to think about the nice person who stopped to help change your flat tire. That's way too simple!! Jesus challenges us to look at our group identification and actively seek ways to break out of our membership "in-thinking" and help someone who is "other". Like what? Like bringing food to a hungry Mexican laborer without consideration for his legal status. Like visiting a mosque to better understand what it means to be a Moslem. Like visiting a prisoner without asking yourself what got him in jail. Like breaking out of our usual clique of friends and making a special effort to befriend someone who doesn't quite fit in. That's the challenge Jesus throws down. Get beyond the external, the group think, and see the person who God loves. Because God loves the good and the wicked both, his rain falls on us all. The question is not, "who is my neighbor?" but "who ISN'T my neighbor?"

These past couple of months, many people have expressed concern about the direction our country seems to be heading. The ongoing secularization of our society seems to be a slap in the face to what have been cherished beliefs about the right path, the Christian path, that has to date influenced much of our American history. How do we respond to these concerns? In the light of today's gospel, what would Jesus say? Here's a few pointers that may help:

1. First and foremost, Jesus was ardently *un-political*. To him, systems of government were distractions, human constructs that had value only to the extent that the widow and the orphan were cared for. Shows of power and military might were disdained – give to Caesar what is Caesar's and to God what is God's. What matters to Jesus is the state of the human heart – each of us individually.
2. Jesus never condemned anyone who was a sinner, especially if they were an admitted sinner. He only condemned hypocrites, and mostly because hypocrites gave God a bad name by claiming to speak for Him. As religious people, our hypocrisy is the very fuel that our foes thrive on. How do we avoid such pitfalls?
3. The best response to evil in the world is the practice of what is good. Note that I don't say *preaching* what is good. Ask yourself why our Pope Francis has caught the world's attention. Is it because of what he has said? To a small degree, yes. But what has really stood out is what he has done, and *not* done. The lesson is simple. Unless we speak from a life of compassion actually lived out, we will not be heard, regardless of how truthful our words are.
4. So do we ignore evil and risk its spread? No, not at all. But ask yourself what kind of response is appropriate. If your temptation is to castigate the "other side", you're no different than the lawyer in today's gospel. If your temptation is to label them, to group them in a simple box, you're embarking on a dangerous road. Labeling people is always overly simplistic and unhelpful. Just as none of us is a perfect embodiment of a Catholic, neither are our foes a perfect embodiment of their label. We change the world one person at a time, by *attracting them to our lives*, not condemning theirs. Are you attracting others by your life? That's a much harder path, doggone it. But that is exactly what Jesus asks of us.

As Catholics, we have been gifted with a wonderful faith – and we should relish our membership in this family we call Catholic. However, if we *ever* feel that somehow we are better than others, Jesus tells us that we need to see the world as God does – with everyone as a member of only one group – *God's children.* Your job this week is to help one of God's children who needs your help, in whatever way you can. That's the meaning of the good Samaritan. He didn't care that the guy by the road was a Jew or a Greek or fellow Samaritan. He saw one of God's children in need. That's our challenge as well. They'll know we are Christians by our love, not by our membership cards.

Testify

Scripture Referenced: John 1:6-8, 19-28

> A man named John was sent from God. He came for testimony, to testify to the light, so that all might believe through him. He was not the light, but came to testify to the light. And this is the testimony of John.

Last week we heard Mark's depiction of John the Baptist. He is called a messenger, preparing the way for someone "mightier than he". Today we hear John's depiction, and although there are many similarities, there is a different word used by John to describe the Baptist's role. Listen again:

A man named John was sent from God. He came for testimony, to testify to the light, so that all might believe through him. He was not the light, but came to testify to the light.

Did you hear the new word? Yes, *testify*. Other translations use the term "bear witness". What does it mean to testify? To bear witness? Let's get a little more contemporary, shall we? A reporter comes up to you and says, "I've been told that you are a Catholic." You nod your head. He begins to ask you questions about Catholic beliefs, and you gamely attempt to answer them as best you can. He asks about sacraments, and the Mass, and the afterlife, and the place of Mary in the Church. The questions get tougher, about Papal authority, the immaculate conception, Church history and politics, and you find yourself a bit swamped. Your struggle is clear to the reporter, and he finally stops, smiles grimly, and says, "Obviously, you can't answer all of my questions. Why do you even claim to be a Catholic? What do you have to say for yourself?"

Ever find yourself in that position?

Our friend John the Baptist is facing a similar inquisition in today's Gospel reading. The priests, Levites, and Pharisees, all come down from Jerusalem full of questions. Who are you? What are you? Are you Elijah, a Prophet, the Messiah? No, no, no. The questioners are trying to figure out what box to put John in, and John won't play along. It's only when the key question is asked, "what do you have to say for yourself?" that John finally *testifies*. "I am the voice of one crying out in the desert, 'Make straight the way of the Lord.'"

Do you see the difference? Answering a bunch of questions is simply an intellectual exercise in memory management. What the Church teaches is good to understand, don't get me wrong, but it isn't the same as testimony. Testimony is an intensely personal statement of who you are and how you got to be who you are. It always points to a higher truth, a greater good, something above and beyond you that you know through your own personal experience to be completely true, even if difficult or impossible to adequately describe.

When we teach our children about the Catholic Church, we often struggle to find the right approach. After all, there's lots of stuff about the Church that seems important to know. The prayers, the Mass, the sacraments, the priests, the nuns, the holy days, what mortal sin is. But if that's all we teach our children about the Catholic faith, then we've missed the boat. If we haven't given our testimony to them, if we haven't started a story to our children with the words, "this is why I'm a Catholic", then we've missed the boat. Because, as you well know, kids see through us. *Testimony*, brothers and sisters, is not about *what* you know, but *Who* you know.

Now, I'm not saying this to give you a guilty feeling. Because, I for one could not have answered that question properly for much of my life. It wasn't my parents fault, nor my Catholic grammar school. I had plenty of informative teachers. I had the information part down pretty well, but to be honest, I was a Catholic in name only. I had no relationship with Jesus to speak of. I was frankly quite terrified of God the Father, the scary judge in the sky eyeballing my every move. Church on Sunday was simply a matter of keeping God off my case, or as a friend of mine put it, "fire insurance". Not much of a testimony, huh?

Notice how when John the Baptist gives his testimony, he states two critical facts. He claims an important identity and he puts himself in proper context. He says that he is the voice crying in the wilderness (his role), and humbly places himself beneath the one who is coming. It is this identity and role that gives him the power to speak in public without fear, regardless of the consequences. He is a dangerous man.

My identity and role were a long time coming. It took God a long time to break through to me. Not God's fault. My pride, my intellect, my success, my scientific mind, all conspired to block God's efforts to love me into relationship. I simply couldn't accept it. And then, as my carefully constructed life began to fray at the edges, and I did not have the answers, I finally learned how to pray. And Jesus rushed in. Oh, I had a hard time at first with this new relationship. I tested it, I challenged God, I set Him up to fail me, and he didn't fail. He didn't always answer as I expected, and I would find myself open-mouthed in astonishment at the way he would answer. And do you want to know what finally, finally allowed me to open the door wide? God's sense of humor. He loves to laugh. Not at us, but with us. Partnering with God is a lot more smiles than tears, I'll tell you that without hesitation.

What I just gave you was a testimony. Notice the complete lack of Church teaching. It's a "who" statement, not a what statement. But look where it takes me. Knowing deep inside who God is, and how God thinks, and how God loves, gives me an immense feeling of stability and humility. I'm not afraid of God at all, but I utterly respect and bow before Him, because without God I'm nothing.

I know that many of you have your own testimonies. I've heard them. Many of you, especially you young people, are still seeking what testimony means for you. Here's a few tips. Suffering is an incredible door opener to God. Whether you yourself are suffering, or you witness and walk with another who is suffering, it doesn't matter. God doesn't cause suffering, but he takes advantage of it to break through our puny human defenses. Tip two: pray. Or better stated, converse with God as you understand God. It can be frustrating, but stick with it. Third tip, as Jesus stated last week, wake up! Look around you for the evidence of God's action in the world. It's hidden in plain sight. It permeates this Church this evening, but we don't see it until we *look* at it. Jesus is being born. Again. In eleven days. Is your manger ready? Are you ready to bear witness? Ask for *that* present from God and your Christmas will be complete.

Chapter 2 – Who Is God?

Simple question, but oh so difficult to answer! God places a spark of Himself in our souls at conception, and that spark draws us into relationship with Him. Why do we fight it so? Probably because we're so in love with our autonomy, our precious free will. Compounding the difficulty is that many of us are in great fear of God, especially if we've led less than exemplary lives. But God keeps calling, calling, calling.

The Scriptures give us various clues about the nature of God, clues that can often sound contradictory. God, realizing this, did something pretty amazing. He made himself small, ridiculously small, and became a human being. Jesus is the living image of God in human form, showing us how God thinks and acts and loves. It's simple. You want to understand God, get to know Jesus.

God is Love

Scripture Referenced: Colossians 1:12-20

> He is the image of the invisible God, the firstborn of all creation. For in him were created all things in heaven and on earth, the visible and the invisible, whether thrones or dominions or principalities or powers; all things were created through him and for him. He is before all things, and in him all things hold together.

The feast of Christ the King always startles me for a number of reasons. It marks the end of our Church year, which begs the question "Where did the year go? Wasn't Easter like last month?" It also means that Advent starts next Sunday, and although I really enjoy the build-up to Christmas, I always feel like the race has started while I'm still tying my shoelaces! Finally, on a purely theological basis, I struggle with the notion of Christ as a King. The term "king" connotes all sorts of analogies and imagery, steeped in mythology and lore, not to mention government and politics. The feast was named by Pope Pius XI specifically as a response to the rise of fascist governments in Europe in the 1920's, so there was an undeniable political purpose to this feast.

But it does raise an interesting question that is worth considering in our faith journey, one that the readings invite us to ponder. The question is a simple one – how does one define God? Is "king" a good definition? Let's see how our Scriptural Tradition attempts to answer that question.

How did the Hebrew people define God? It doesn't take long to recognize that the seminal event in Hebrew history is the Exodus, when God is revealed to them as a fearsome warrior, leading the Hebrews from bondage to freedom, destroying their enemies without a single loss of Hebrew life. This warrior God continues to support the Hebrew people as they enter the promised land, leading the armies into one battle after another, allowing the Hebrews to mow down anyone who stands in their way. Let's call this warrior, God *Version One*.

It doesn't take long however, for the Hebrew people to realize that God, Version One doesn't seem content to be a simple warrior God like the gods of the neighboring tribes. Speaking through the prophets, the warrior God begins to make some interesting demands on the Hebrews. The demands are surprising, because rather than demanding human sacrifices, which all the other gods seems to want, this God asks the Hebrews to care for the widows, the orphans, and the aliens in their midst. This is indeed puzzling, and the people struggle with this notion of God, a God that's more like a shepherd than a warrior. Let's call this God, *Version Two*.

The first reading today perfectly illustrates this point in time when God Version 1 and God Version 2 are in uneasy alliance. God picks out David from among the people as someone who seems to understand the heart of God. In fact, David is the first ruler of Israel to "get it", and you'll note in this coronation reading the dictate of David's dual responsibility to be both a shepherd and a commander. David is uniquely expected to show Israel how this warrior/shepherd God operates. So, how did David do? Overall, not too bad for a human being – he did some things wonderfully well, mostly on the warrior side, but he also showed the shepherd side as well, ruling the people with justice and wisdom. For years after David, the Hebrew people struggle to balance these two versions of God. Israel strives to become a major player in the Middle East, asking God to be the warrior God they remember so fondly, and God telling them that the way of war is not the answer – that He will take care of them if they simply live the covenant, live the way of justice and care. God clearly prefers Version Two, and the Hebrews can't get beyond Version One.

Now Jesus arrives on the scene and with him, a new commandment, a new version based on what? Love. Compassion. Forgiveness. God, *Version Three*. Jesus acknowledges his role as the Son of God, the very image of God in human form. No one comes to the Father except through me, he tells the people. And if Version Two was hard to accept, Version Three is darn near impossible. This God is not a warrior God at all! He's not going to smite the Romans. He's going to (gasp) forgive them! The gospel shows us the depth of God's love through Jesus, willing to give up his life for others. It's mind boggling, and so impossible to believe that Jesus must be resurrected to show his followers that yes, not only does Version 3 better describe God than the earlier versions, it is *the way, the truth, and the life*.

St. Paul's letter to the Colossians takes us one step further, exalting Jesus the Christ as the image of the invisible God, the firstborn of all creation. This amazing hymn from the early days of the Church that Paul quotes goes on to place Christ as the keystone of the cosmos, where everything is created for him, through him, and reconciled in him for all time. Wow. It wouldn't be inaccurate to call this God, Version 4, because it brings us to the understanding of God as three persons, of God as a Relationship, God as intimately engaged in our lives. Once we see that reality, everything changes. Suddenly we know God intimately from within, and we know that God is immensely other and beyond. Both at the same time.

Now we circle back to Christ the King. Is this somehow Version 5? No, I don't think so. The label of "king" is simply another attempt to describe how to reconcile all of these other versions. A good king is a commander, a shepherd, a lover of justice, and the ultimate authority on everything. It's good for us to recognize that God is God, and we are not. In fact, the moment you think that you have God figured out, you have made the cardinal error of your life. God is immensely beyond anything that you think.

Does that mean that all of these versions are somehow wrong? Misleading? Is God completely unknowable? I find it useful to recall when faced with such seeming inconsistencies about God to remember the key definition of God that comes to us from the pen of the beloved apostle, John. *God is love.*

Consider love. Consider what love compels us to do. Does love drive us to care for those who need our attention? To engage the world, at least our small part of it, and shepherd our people? Does love lead us to stick up for the downtrodden? Does love move us to defend the innocent, to stand bold in the face of injustice? Ask the mother of child being bullied, or a veteran who fought for his country. Yes, love can bring out the warrior in us, love can bring out the shepherd in us, love can bring out the compassionate in us. Love is the most compelling force in our lives and the one that leaves us the most vulnerable.

Do you remember the first time you told another person that you loved them? No, I don't mean your mother. I mean that first crush, that first out-of-control feeling that was undeniable, a little terrifying, and yet, oh so right. Do you remember the sheer fright of the moment you stared into that person's eyes, and said, "I love you"? That moment of terror when you wondered if the love would be returned? It's a moment of supreme vulnerability, as if our soul was laid open. Is it any wonder that this moment is the stuff of more movies and novels than practically anything else?

Jesus is God's invitation to love, the embodiment, the image of God in human form. Commander, shepherd, compassionate one. We hear this so often, we miss the power and the poignancy. Jesus tells us that there is no greater love than to lay down your life for your friends. Jesus takes it one step farther. He lays down his life for everyone, friends and enemies. There he is, up there on the cross, saying to the world three simple words. *I love you.* And he waits for our response. And waits. And waits. He waits in agony to hear our answer. Every person has the opportunity to answer. What's your response?

God, version 1 through 5, is defined in the end by a simple and profound word. Love. None of us totally understand love, do we? We simply experience it. God is the same way. Don't put God in a box – simply open yourself to the experience of God loving you. In fact, God *rejoices* in you!

God Chooses

Scripture Referenced: John 15:9-17

> It was not you who chose me, but I who chose you and appointed you to go and bear fruit that will remain, so that whatever you ask the Father in my name he may give you. This I command you: love one another.

If there's one word that gets to the heart of the American creed of individualism, it would have to be the word "choice". After all, what does it mean to be independent if it doesn't mean to have a choice? Our founding fathers, from the get-go, made sure to encapsulate within our Constitution fundamental tenets such as freedom of the press, freedom of religion, freedom from unreasonable search and seizure, freedom of speech, and freedom of movement. At the heart of these freedoms is the simple word choice – I can choose where I live, how to worship, what I would like say and write, all without concern that a government agency will stop me. These assumptions of choice are so prevalent that we can hardly imagine life without them, and shake our heads when we hear about foreign governments who restrict their citizens.

Sometimes this emphasis on freedom of choice leaks into a dangerous fallacy, a fallacy that proclaims that the freedom to choose is a right in and of itself, regardless of what the choices are. This is most obvious in the corrupted rhetoric of the pro-abortion lobby in America, who have taken the cherished freedom to choose our life path and made that ability to choose more important than the selected outcome. The argument is intentionally refocused from the morality of abortion in itself to a debate on whether or not the government should restrict a person's right to choose – whatever they want! Anything goes apparently, as long as we don't take away your *choice*.

Our readings today are all about choice, although many would say that they are all about love. It's easy to see why -- the word love is mentioned fifteen times when counted among the second reading and the gospel. So, where does choice come into the matter? Let's take a closer look. From the second reading, "In this is love: not that we have loved God, but that he loved us…" From the gospel, "It was not you who chose me, but I who chose you…" Wait a second, who's doing the choosing here? I thought that we choose our religion. I thought that we choose our life path. I thought that we are the ones with the freedom to choose. What does it mean that God *chose us*? Don't we get a say in the matter? Who does God think he is?

There's a young man I know who is struggling to find his purpose in life. Let's call him John in honor of our gospel writer. John moves from crisis to crisis, finding a good path for a while and just as quickly tossing it aside as the next pretty girl or glossy job opportunity comes his way. John has so many choices that it would make your head spin. All of these choices have not helped him in the least – he's completely at sea, drifting with the currents, and desperately unhappy. John doesn't know what to do next, and he's wondering why he's even here in the first place. Know someone like that in your life? Here's the interesting thing. God keeps calling John. I know this because I know what it means to have God call you. I'm not being elitist here, I'm simply stating a fact. When you experience God choosing you, you see the signs in others. You see the way God pursues – he's really good at it, and persistent too!

What do I see? I see invitations. John tells me that this movie really moved him. It features a man who follows his heart to a foreign land and finds love, although it is a difficult path. Hmmm, I say. Or he suddenly pipes up and says, wasn't that earthquake in Nepal awful? Where is God in all of that? I just look at him. God didn't cause the earthquake, I tell him. God is in the response. Look for him in the rescuers, in the donors, in the people who fly to their aid, in the legislators who mandate new building codes. That's where God is. I look at his youth and energy and ask myself, doesn't he see the invitation?

What does it mean to be chosen by God? Does that seem scary to you? Does it seem like you're losing something? This is one of the great fallacies in spiritual direction. Somehow, people think that doing God's will for them is a zero-sum game. In order for me to do what God wants, I must eliminate some options from my life. I lose some *choices*. This is absolutely true.. But here's the really interesting thing. Those choices you must eliminate are not good choices to begin with. God's will for me next Wednesday is to visit the state prison and discuss the Scriptures with a bunch of criminals, losers one and all. My other choice that day is to sit around the house after dinner, watch the Padre game, and do the NY Times crossword puzzle. That seems like a pretty obvious choice, doesn't it? Why would you choose a prison? John's gospel: "It was not you who chose me, but I who chose you and appointed you to go and bear fruit that will remain, so that whatever you ask the Father in my name he may give you." In short, the choice is between a *happy* evening at home or a *joyful* night in the prison. Give me joy over happiness any day. As Ricardo, one of the inmates, said to me a couple of weeks ago, "When I leave Bible study, the prison yard with all of its barbed wire and ugly buildings becomes a *beautiful park*." That's joy. That's how you know God chose you.

God's invitation is actually pretty easy to discern, when you get right down to it. Here's what you'll see. The invitation is intriguing to you – it's *interesting*. But, second point, the invitation has an apparent cost to it. It's not easy to say yes. Something else will have to give. Third characteristic: you know deep down inside that you'll be a better person for it; i.e., it's *good* for you. Final characteristic – you've probably heard this invitation before. You've said no to a similar invitation in the past. It keeps coming up, like a bad penny, like a persistent lover, like a "hound from heaven," as the poet Francis Thompson wrote.

God is patient, God is kind, God is not pompous or rude, God bears all things, believes all things, hopes all things, endures all things. Wait, that's not how it goes, right? Paul wasn't writing about God, he was writing about love. Oh, wait. What did we just hear from St. John? God is love. So, of course – interchangeable terms. Love is patient, God is patient. Love is kind, God is kind. You get the point. How does Paul end his ode to love? Ah yes. Love never fails. Saying yes to God's invitation does indeed remove choices from your life. But rather than a diminishment, the amazing irony is that choosing God's path bursts you into fire, into life. You are now the full embodiment of who you are meant to be. You and God together are an unbeatable pair, a completeness, a fullness of life. That's what "bearing fruit" means! You become a life giver rather than a life taker. That's why a woman who accepts God's invitation could never in a million years have an abortion. That's why a young man who enters a life of service doesn't miss the night life. That's why a prisoner can see flowers, trees and sunlight in a prison yard. That's why life with God cannot possibly compare with the life offered by this world. That's what it means to say yes to the invitation. That's what Moses meant when he said to the people, "I put before you life and death, the blessing and the curse. Choose life!" (Deuteronomy 30:19b)

A girl of sixteen is pregnant. But she seems totally unconcerned, totally accepting of this new challenge in her life. Where does she get such strength? Her future is uncertain, her impending marriage doubtful, yet she is at peace. Why? I think you know. Her name was Mary, and through the simple words of the angel Gabriel, she understood that she had been chosen by God. She is to bear fruit, the fruit of her womb, the Christ. On this Mother's Day, I invite all of the mothers in this congregation to ponder your children. Whether you think you chose them or not, I invite you to consider that perhaps God chose you to bear these children at the appointed time. You were loved first. Thank you for loving us.

The invitations never stop, however. For you mothers, for all of us actually, what is God inviting you to today? How are you being chosen? Most importantly, what is your answer?

Depicting God

Scripture Referenced: John 14:1-12

> Philip said to him, "Master, show us the Father, and that will be enough for us." Jesus said to him, "Have I been with you for so long a time and you still do not know me, Philip? Whoever has seen me has seen the Father."

I think that the older we get, the more familiar this Gospel reading is. Why? It's a favorite at most funeral liturgies! It's no surprise really. Jesus is at his loving, caring best, trying to reassure the Apostles that although He is facing death and physical separation soon, it is not the end of their relationship; in fact, there is much more to come. But the part of this reading that I really love is Philip's seemingly reasonable request, "Lord, show us the Father, and we will be satisfied". Don't you have that desire too? God, just show us your face, that's all we need. Wouldn't it be great to see God face to face?

A number of years ago, a movie came out called "Oh God". Do you remember it? It starred George Burns as a slightly quirky supreme being who appears to John Denver the grocery store manager. I remember getting a lot of good chuckles throughout the movie, as "God" performs some silly miracles and poor John Denver tries to convince people that he's not crazy or on drugs. Which is ironic, since John Denver was on drugs fairly often in real life, but... I digress! The movie, after many plot twists, finally allows God to address the human race by answering a bunch of religious questions, and the result is, well, kind of flat. I remember being disappointed, and then puzzled by my own reaction. Here's Hollywood giving Philip what he wants, giving us what we want, a picture of God we can all relate to – and it doesn't work.

What's a better vision of God? Go back in time. How about the sun, or the ocean, or a volcano? How about Zeus or Apollo? Any better? Not really. These depictions of God are all partly accurate – mostly focused on God's power, but again, incomplete at some basic level. The fundamental problem with any human depiction of God is that we always aim far too low. In the words of theologian John Shea, we need an understanding of God that blows our mind.

St. Anselm gave it a try. He said that God is that than which nothing greater can be thought. (repeat) Try it out. Think of the most grandest notion of who and what God is, and realize that God is more than that. So go bigger, grander. Still not enough. And so on. You can't get there. We're too small and God is too big. You see, brothers and sisters, the more you get to know God, the more awe inspiring God turns out to be, the more clear it becomes that we puny humans can never get our heads around the immensity of God.

God, realizing this, did something pretty amazing. He made himself small, ridiculously small, and became a human being. Jesus is the living image of God in human form, showing us how God thinks and acts and loves. It's simple. You want to understand God, get to know Jesus. And this, of course, is exactly the answer Jesus gives Philip, "Whoever has seen me has seen the Father."

You're in the grocery store, and the manager, who looks a lot like John Denver, comes over to you and asks, "how do I get to know Jesus?" How would you answer him?

Well, if you're a good Evangelical Christian, you'd toss him a bible, and encourage him to accept Jesus in his heart as his Lord and Savior. It's a good answer – Jesus can certainly be discovered in the Word, but that's not an easy road to navigate. Having taught Bible study over the years, I can tell you that the image of God is not uniformly presented as you move from book to book. The New Testament is a bit better, but even here, Jesus the Christ is often portrayed in contradictory ways.

If you're a good Catholic, you might say, "Find Christ in the Eucharist!" Taste and see the body and blood of Christ in the Eucharist. Spend an hour in prayer in front of the Blessed Sacrament. Another good answer! But also challenging. Contemplative prayer implies a relationship with Christ that is already fairly mature. I'm not sure that a beginning seeker will find this an easy and practical approach to getting to know Jesus.

Is there a better answer? How about this? "Well, mister grocery store manager, why don't you come have a cup of coffee with me and we'll talk it over?" The truth, brothers and sisters, is that what draws people to Jesus is not the Bible or the Eucharist, but *other people*. That's where it starts. Virtually every conversion story I've heard, and it's quite a few, begin with a simple one-on-one conversation. The best way to get to know Jesus is by spending time with his followers. That's the root of missionary work. Read the lives of the great missionaries. They go to the ends of the earth with a simple agenda. Be Christ-like to the people – feed them, heal them, teach them – and you will attract converts as Jesus himself did. Jesus is made known by the Body of Christ – all of us!

Back in the early 90's, as I began to take my faith journey seriously, I realized one day that the type of friends I had was changing. I remember remarking to my wife that all of our friends seemed to be associated with St. James Parish, or the wider Diocese. Was this a good thing? We laughed about it a bit, but in the end, the simple truth was that we enjoyed you people. We saw the world in similar ways, but most importantly, we realized that you people were friends we could count on no matter what happened in our lives. You were like Jesus to us. I see so many of you individually out here today. I want to say thank you for loving me. Thank you for loving us. You're the reason I'm a deacon.

Who do you hang out with? Do you surround yourself with God-like people? There's nothing wrong with that, as long as you realize that it can't stop there. The body of Christ takes nourishment and strength from its members, as we are doing right this moment at Sunday Mass. We take nourishment from the Eucharist, we take nourishment from the Word. Coming together is as necessary as breathing in, as long as we then go out there and exhale the Spirit into the world. Breathe in, and breathe out.

If you want to see God, don't bother with Hollywood. If you want to see God, don't spend a lot of time in the library. If you want to see God, look for Jesus. His followers are all around you. And just like a married couple that has lived together over dozens of years, the more you surround yourself with the body of Christ, the more you'll look alike. It's Jesus everywhere you look. And if you see Jesus, you're seeing God!

Christ, the Stumbling Block

Scripture Referenced: 1 Corinthians 1:22-25

> Jews demand signs and Greeks look for wisdom, but we proclaim Christ crucified, a stumbling block to Jews and foolishness to Gentiles, but to those who are called, Jews and Greeks alike, Christ the power of God and the wisdom of God. For the foolishness of God is wiser than human wisdom, and the weakness of God is stronger than human strength.

Most of the time when you hear one of us preach, we'll focus on the Gospel. It's not surprising why – there is wonderful depth to our Gospel readings, often featuring the very words of Jesus, and as has been stated so often, the words of Jesus are the very bread of our existence. So, of course we'll talk about the Gospel! But today's reading from Paul is worth a closer look.

It's two sentences long – or should I say, two *long* sentences. Paul mentions three groups of people – Jews, Greeks, and Gentiles. The first distinction is between Jews and Greeks – which represent the two competing cultures of the time, each with a different philosophy of life. To Paul, Jews are always looking for the signs of God's action on behalf of their race, very logically so, since the Jews see themselves as God's chosen people. The Greeks, on the other hand, are the philosophers who ask the difficult meaning of life questions, as seen in the writings of Plato and Aristotle. The last group, the Gentiles, are everyone in the world who isn't Jewish, who isn't specifically one of God's chosen ones. Now that groups are clear, what does Paul say? Listen carefully: *"Jews demand signs and Greeks look for wisdom, but we proclaim Christ crucified..."*

I hope you can hear the jarring tone of that sentence. In essence, Paul is saying that both groups are missing the point – and missing it badly. He goes on to say that Christ crucified is "*a stumbling block to Jews and foolishness to Gentiles*," emphasizing that no one really gets it, really understands the amazing action of God.

Why doesn't the world get it? Because it's not what anyone would expect. If you were God, and you desired to save the world, what would you do? Seriously, think about it. I suspect you'd say something like, "do away with evil" or "end poverty and disease" or "make everyone Christian" or "stop all war". Am I right? Those are certainly good actions, one and all. But God didn't do that. Instead He came down here in the form of a human being, walked the earth in perfect solidarity with all human beings, acted in a completely God-like way through his preaching and healing, and then allowed himself to be killed in the most painful and humiliating way possible. God could have shown us "superman", but instead he showed us "loser man". Is it any wonder that Paul calls this a stumbling block and an obstacle? Who wants to follow a loser?

I was chatting with a co-worker the other day, a person who doesn't know me very well, and he asked me what I liked to do in my spare time. So I told him I did a lot of charity work, which always gets a supportive smile and the follow-up question – oh really? What do you do? Well, I'll answer, one of my favorite activities is bringing Christ into the prison. The eyes get really big then, and if we're walking, the person will literally stop and say, "What?" The stumbling block, the obstacle, is smack dab in their way. You can almost hear the conversation in their heads – "Wait, he doesn't look like a fanatic. Did I hear that right? He seems so normal."

The conversation takes one of three paths after that. The person asks a lot more questions and is sincerely interested in hearing about prison work; OR, they quickly change the subject (that's interesting, I like to mountain bike), OR they get defensive (I'm spiritual but not religious, which apparently means I don't need to think about these things).

Why is God's solution so much better than yours and mine? It's an important question, on every level. Yes, God could have done away with evil, stopped war, and cured every disease and illness. But he didn't. Apparently, God wanted to do something much more subtle and much more potentially effective, if we can see past the obstacle of a crucified loser.

First of all, God wants to preserve our free will. The truly daring creative act of God is that God allows us to reject his grace and mercy entirely. We can decide if we want to walk this life with Him or not. God doesn't want to hand the world over to us on a silver platter and win our fleeting gratitude. No, God wants us to freely give ourselves to His embrace, to say, yes, Lord, I'll follow you because I *choose* to follow you. Which leads to the second subtle, yet critically important point, the meaning of "following the Lord." That means following the path of Jesus wherever it takes us. The irony is that the path of Jesus is always very clear – the path of Jesus is always the path of compassion, the path into the pain of the world.

If you want to follow Jesus, simply look to where the pain of the world is calling you right now. It's usually not very far from your own door. It's a hurting neighbor, a beggar on the street, a child in need of tutoring, a prisoner who hasn't had a visitor in 8 years, a dying old man in a hospice center. Do you see the secret plan of God? Rather than God doing all of the work to save the world, he wants us to do it! What a radical, amazing plan! But, you might think, it still seems like a dumb idea. We're not that strong, we're not that wise.

Paul lays it out for us: *Christ* is the power and wisdom of God. And to stress the point even further, Paul tells us that the weakest and most foolish tools of God far exceed any human-based wisdom and strength. Like many of you, I was taken by the tragic story of Kayla Mueller, the American aid worker who was killed by ISIS three weeks ago. Several people I conversed with about her told me how crazy Kayla was to put herself in harm's way. Without saying it right out loud, the message was clear – as sad as it is, she got what was coming to her. In the wisdom of the world, she was downright foolish, wasn't she? Whatever possessed her to go into Syria like that?

Maybe it was Christ leading her into the pain of the world. Kayla wrote: "This really is my life's work, to go where there is suffering. I suppose, like us all, I'm learning how to deal with the suffering of the world inside myself... to deal with my own pain and most importantly to still have the ability to be proactive." During her last weeks of captivity, Kayla wrote: "I remember Mom always telling me that all in all, in the end, the only one you really have is God. I have come to a place in experience where, in every sense of the word, I have surrendered myself to our Creator because literally there was no else…and by God and by your prayers I have felt tenderly cradled in freefall." Those are words of power and wisdom if I've ever heard any. What a foolish yet wise, weak yet strong person Kayla was. The world is a better place for her belief and utter reliance on Christ – yes, *regardless of the cost*. May we be so foolish!

Lost and Found

Scripture Referenced: Luke 15:1-32

> Coming to his senses he thought, 'How many of my father's hired workers have more than enough to eat, but here I am, dying from hunger. I shall get up and go to my father and I shall say to him, "Father, I have sinned against heaven and against you. I no longer deserve to be called your son; treat me as you would treat one of your hired workers."' So he got up and went back to his father. While he was still a long way off, his father caught sight of him, and was filled with compassion. He ran to his son, embraced him, and kissed him.

There are so many directions one can take in exploring this beloved Gospel story of the Prodigal Son. But before we go there, let's look at the context of this parable among today's readings. Note that in the first reading from Exodus we are presented with a God who is rightfully angry at the Hebrew people. After all he has done for them in leading them from slavery and providing manna in the desert, as soon as Moses is away, they create a golden calf, a metallic idol, and worship it. The Lord God tells Moses to step back and let these stiff-necked people feel his wrath, after which he'll work with Moses on a new chosen people. The Lord God only relents when Moses reminds him of his promises, basically shaming God into backing down.

Now let's pretend that you are a first century Jew and someone asks you how God deals with sinners. What is your response? I suspect that you'd say something like, "The Lord God gets angry with sinners and unless you have someone making sacrifices and soothing God down, you're very likely to take a pretty severe beating, perhaps total destruction!" The converse is true as well. If you've come into some bad luck, say an illness or a poor crop or a business deal gone wrong, ipso facto, you must be a sinner! The punishment reveals the crime, so to speak. So is this God who judges so exactly and harshly a *lovable* God?

With this understanding of God as your context, here comes Jesus who claims an intimate understanding of God and what does he do?

He welcomes sinners to dinner! He seeks them out. It's outrageous to the good and holy people of the time. So, the gospel states, *to them* he addresses three parables. In each case, something is lost. The stakes grow higher in each story. A sheep, a dumb animal, is the first lost object. It represents 1% of the shepherd's flock; in fact, it is likely the audience would this story a little ridiculous. The shepherd is going to leave 99 sheep in the desert and go find one lost lamb? Apparently so. The second story is more challenging. A widow loses 10% of her entire wealth and turns her home upside down to find it. Now the heads nod. Yes, that's worth celebrating – we've all lost coins in the dust. Now the third story is told and the stakes are the highest yet. The Father loses not only half his wealth, he loses one of his sons as well. Worse yet, the son who leaves is clearly an immature brat who shows his Father no respect whatsoever. The audience must be thinking to themselves, "Well, good riddance!"

But now comes the first surprise. If this were the God of the book of Exodus, Jesus would have gone on to say that the Lord God became angry with this impudent boy and smote him a good one. But that's not what happens. The son carries on in his own idiotic way, throwing money away on a life of dissipation. Doesn't sound like a smiting to me. Predictably, the money runs out and the prodigal son, having lost his inheritance and, by extension, his parasitic friends, suddenly has a moment of self-awareness. Gosh, the world doesn't revolve around him after all. He has been a complete fool – his father's servants eat better than he does now. Note carefully. Is this silly boy a sinner? Yes. Did God punish him? Well, no, not exactly. The boy kind of punishes himself through his own stupid decisions, doesn't he? But isn't that what life is? It's not God who is doing the rewarding and punishing here, it's our own choices and free will. Sin, in much the same way as virtue, brings its own outcomes, its own rewards. Jesus, in telling this story, brings this impudent boy to life, and dares his audience to not see that this boy is just like all of his listeners.

But now the punch line, the true surprise, awaits. The sadder and wiser boy decides to go home, tail between his legs, and beg for a job from his father. The audience is nodding their heads now, sure that this is where the boy gets his deserved outcome. But again, Jesus throws them a curve. The Father not only seeks out the boy, he runs to him, embraces him, and brings him back into the family fold without hesitation. If he ended the story right here, it would be shocking enough. But remember that Jesus is speaking to the scribes and Pharisees, the righteous ones. So he puts *them* into the story in the person of the older son, and describes their reaction to this whole business perfectly. Resentment. Anger. Jealousy. Pettiness. The Father pleads with him, *pleads with them*, to fight these feelings and enter into the joy of a kingdom where everyone belongs, not just a few righteous ones. The story ends, as all of Jesus' parables do, with an invitation and a challenge.

The author Thomas Wolfe wrote a famous book called *You Can't Go Home Again*. For those of us who have lived a few years, we know this is true. The first time I went home was after 5 years of graduate school, married with a baby son, looking to get a new start after years of grad school poverty and debt. My parents graciously opened their home to us in Boston, and we moved in for a year. It was a mixed blessing – having a break from financial worries was wonderful, as was the built-in baby sitters, but my wife and I became restless quickly, and we were happy to finally get our own place and re-engage life again. It was good to go home but better to find our own home. Sound familiar?

A few years ago, I took my wife back to visit my home town in upstate New York. After nearly 40 years away, it was great to see old friends and visit old haunts, each the same as I remembered and yet, subtly different and foreign too. The place was saying "Hello again", and in the next breath, "This isn't home for you anymore. You need to leave."

Did the prodigal son stay home? I don't think so. Somehow, I don't think so. He was not the boy who had left the first time. In his growth, as painful as it was, he could no longer play the role of the younger son. He needed to leave. You parents out there know this – your children need to leave home at some point. It may not be far geographically, but it is significant and important that life be lived according to one's own wits, for better or for worse. This time of year, the fall, is the time of new beginnings and new ventures. For young people, it's exciting and scary. For parents, especially the Moms, it's just scary. But it needs to happen.

You see, the parable of the Prodigal Son applies to us all. Our roles change as we age – younger son, older son, loving parent – it speaks to us differently every 3 years. But the truths are universal. We are compelled to follow our urges, which takes us away from our home and often, our God. We plunge into life and make 3 mistakes for every 2 good choices it seems. Then, as experience sets in and we find loving companions on the journey, the ratio shifts and we begin to realize that what is really important is love, forgiveness, generosity, and patience. The hard knocks of life forge wisdom, and although we can't go home again, it also true that we create a new home, and an understanding that a final home awaits us in the distance. It's out there, far on the horizon, and if you look closely, you'll see Father God anxiously awaiting our arrival. You can count on it.

Wherever you are on the journey, whether waiting to go, just starting out, thrashing away at the challenges and difficulties of life, or easing into retirement and dispensing wisdom to the masses, know that God is present in every stage. If we don't see Him, it's not because he's gone away. If you wonder where God is, ask yourself, "Who moved?" Above all, don't fear the journey. Whatever happens, you are a child of God, and He doesn't forget his children. Ever.

Chapter 3 – Truth

We all desire to know the truth. As human beings, we seem to have a very well-tuned sense of truth, an almost intuitive appreciation for the reality of things. Some think it is hard-wired into our psyches, this innate sense of right and wrong, of honesty and falsehood. A good measure of the truth of something is how our gut reacts when we hear a claim. Falsehood can confuse us momentarily, either due to the skill of the liar, or the clever way it misleads us. But in the end, our gut will tell us whether it is true or not.

What does God think? I have learned that God is not going to give us a perfectly clear and concise description of his nature and intentions. Again and again in Scripture, God clearly states that God is so beyond us, that attempting to fully understand God is pointless. But God doesn't slam the door on the subject either. In fact, God entices us to enter the mystery, to dig deeper, to not accept anything on "blind faith". Oddly enough, the more we dig in, the more we learn, and eventually, we get to the point where we realize that as much as we understand, there's still more to understand. And we try and struggle and muddle and consider, and God applauds. He's like a parent of a one year old encouraging those first steps across the living room floor. You can do it!!

Reflecting the Light

Scripture Referenced: John 9:1-41

> As Jesus passed by he saw a man blind from birth. His disciples asked him, "Rabbi, who sinned, this man or his parents, that he was born blind?" Jesus answered, "Neither he nor his parents sinned; it is so that the works of God might be made visible through him."

Quite some while ago, back when I was a teenager, I went camping with some friends one summer weekend in the Adirondack mountains of upstate New York. Half the fun of camping is sitting around a fire, telling stories into the night, mesmerized by the dancing light. After a while, finally tired enough to sleep, we let the fire gradually burn out so we wouldn't have to worry about it. The area where we were was so remote that there was virtually no light to be seen anywhere. We nervously clicked on our flashlights until one of us (not me) said, "hey, turn off your flashlights". We did, and the darkness was utterly complete, descending on us like a blanket. It's as if we were blind. It was a very unsettling moment.

John's gospel of the man born blind is as much a metaphor as it is a story of healing. We're invited to peel back the superficial layer of the story and look for the connection John invites us to consider. The hero of the story, the blind beggar, is not given a name. This is a sure signal from John that we are supposed to put ourselves in his shoes, just as we did last week with the unnamed Samaritan woman. So, let's see if the metaphor works.

First key point, we are *all* born blind. This alludes to original sin, and Jesus immediately deals with that issue as the disciples ask him who sinned such that this man was born blind? Another way of asking the question is, who sinned such that *we* are born blind? Whose fault is it? Jesus' answer is unequivocal – it's not a matter of fault, it's so that God can be made visible through him, through *us*! The original sin of Adam and Eve is not something to be depressed about, it is actually a door opener to the work of God – a God who will break through the crack in our heart. Original sin is a distressing reality that God can use! It is the key to the door into awareness.

Now Jesus acts – note that his action is taken without the blind man's permission or request -- and a physical healing occurs. Let's stop a moment. How were you brought into the Church? If you are like 90% of the people here, you were baptized as an infant. Did your parents ask your permission? Not likely! Now if you were baptized as an adult, I can guarantee that you can trace your eye opening event back to some person who worked themselves into your consciousness, your awareness, without you realizing what was happening. Just like Jesus, this person acted in your life, perhaps in spite of you. And just as the water is poured onto you in baptism, so is the blind man told to wash in the pool of Siloam, a word that means "sent", as John tells us with a smile.

So now you're baptized. As is the blind man. So what? What happened to Jesus in John's story? Where did he go? The blind man (who can now see) returns to his old haunts. You can almost picture him, opening and closing his eyes, comparing the input his newly acquired sense of sight gives him and how it is enhanced by hearing, smell, taste, and touch. Intriguing to realize, however, is that the formerly blind man is hardly complete – he's simply re-created. In the next 30 verses that describe the rest of his day, John gives us a brilliantly conceived predictive roadmap of our journey as well. Look at how this poor man is treated. First of all, no one believes that it is really him, just someone who looks like him. On his insistence that he is the same guy, at least on the outside, the crowd questions him and then takes him to the authorities. The Pharisees, the top of the Jewish social and religious pyramid, refuse to accept the man's account, refuse to accept that he has been healed, even going so far as to have his parents identify him.

The message for us? Expect to be challenged by claiming Christ as your healer, as your focus. In particular, if you have been leading a life that has been totally marked by sin, don't expect *anyone* to buy your story that you have seen the light. We see this today, don't we? If a convicted murderer on death row claims to have discovered Jesus, we act with cynicism and eye rolling. The irony is that I can't think of a *more* suitable place for a person to find Jesus then when facing death! But even if our lives are not so markedly converted as a great sinner's would be, the point is that we will be challenged regardless.

Notice carefully how the once blind man reacts to this very pointed questioning and prodding by the Pharisees. Rather than discouraging and depressing the man, the questioning ironically strengthens him! At first, the blind man names his healer "the man called Jesus". On further prodding, the blind man calls his healer "a prophet". At the third questioning, "a man from God". The language is growing ever more expansive, ever more aware, until finally, the former blind man worships Jesus at His feet. John's point is that rather than fear questioning, welcome it! It will force you to dig deeper, to understand more fully your fragile faith, and as you strive to understand who this Jesus is, you will be pulled inexorably into understanding the glory of God.

That night in the woods, in the utter darkness, was quite frightening at first. We fingered the switches on our flashlights, but my friend said, "wait, just wait". So we did. And slowly and gradually, as our eyes adjusted, we began to notice that there was indeed light, the light of a million stars. The fear ebbed away, replaced by awe and wonder. I was reading in the news just the other day that scientists have come to realize that their estimate of the number of stars in our universe has been wildly inaccurate. It's not that they've over-estimated the number of stars – it's quite the opposite. They've under-estimated the number of stars. They used to say that you could count a star for every person alive on the planet. Now, it appears that there is a star for every person *who has ever lived* on the planet since the dawn of time. And then some. Perhaps our ancestors are lighting our way in the darkness. But more so, there is light to be accessed, even when it appears on the outset that there isn't any at all. We just need to be patient.

St. Paul tells us that we are light in the Lord. We cannot shine on our own, of course. We can only shine by reflecting the light of God, who by definition is beauty, goodness, and truth. So how clean is your mirror? Do you reflect God clearly and brightly? Do you need some spiritual Windex? We're right at the apex of Lent today – we began 20 odd days ago, we have 20 to go. Fasting, prayer, and alms giving, the three "mirror polishers" of Lent, are still available. Pick them up and keep polishing. The light of the world needs bright mirrors to pierce the darkness. That's you and me, that's *us*!

Authentic Christianity

Scripture Referenced: Matthew 23:1-12

> Then Jesus spoke to the crowds and to his disciples, saying, "The greatest among you must be your servant. Whoever exalts himself will be humbled; but whoever humbles himself will be exalted."

At a recent church meeting a very wealthy man rose to tell the rest of those present about his Catholic faith. "I'm a millionaire," he says, "and I attribute it all to the rich blessings of God in my life. I remember that turning point in my faith. I had just earned my first dollar and I went to church that Sunday. The speaker was a missionary who told us about his work. I knew that I only had a dollar bill and had to either give it all to God's work or nothing at all. So at that moment I decided to give my whole dollar to God. I believe that God blessed that decision, and that is why I am a rich man today." He finished and there was an awed silence at his testimony as he moved toward his seat. As he sat down a little old lady sitting in the same pew leaned over and said to him: "I dare you to do it again."

The gospel we've just heard is from the 23rd chapter of Matthew, verses 1-12. Jesus has some strong words for the Scribes and Pharisees who interpret the law in such a black and white fashion as to lay heavy burdens on the people. Furthermore, they act as if they are above the law, violating its spirit in every action they take. The next 24 verses (after this Gospel) in the chapter continue the diatribe, with each paragraph starting with the words, "Woe to you, scribes and Pharisees…" It's interesting to compare this section with the other two synoptic gospels, Mark and Luke. They each devote two verses to this scene, and that's about it. Why does Matthew go on and on – 36 verses altogether? The answer, as you probably can guess, is the community to which Matthew writes. The time is about 80 AD, the temple has fallen, and the scribes and Pharisees are desperately trying to hold on to their authority. They do that, of course, by picking on any who are not following Jewish tradition precisely, and that means followers of The Way, the early Christians. So Matthew extends Jesus' criticism of their hypocrisy in excruciating detail, thereby reinforcing the early Christian community as they fought to keep a foot in both Jewish and Christian camps.

You see, hypocrisy takes two forms – the most common form is when the person preaching good moral behavior continually shows everyone that his words are empty, that practice does not line up with preaching. But the other form is just as irritating – the puffing up of oneself beyond the reality of the situation, as in our wealthy man story. There's a simple arithmetic formula at work here: words not equal to actions.

Words are important, aren't they? Words can inspire us, beguile us, enthrall us, and yes, hurt us badly. When I preside at a wedding and help the couple through their vows, I am always touched by the moment of truth, the moment of promise. You can see it in their eyes – each person suddenly realizes that this is it – this is the precise moment of commitment. It's a rare man or woman who doesn't take a deep gulp at that point and visibly steady themselves. Words are important.

Actions, however, are even more important. Some years ago, I remember being asked the simple question, "If you were accused of being a Christian, would the evidence find you guilty?" It's still a jarring question, because it gets to the heart of what it means to live a life of authentic Christianity. You can say, "OK, I'll try not to be a hypocrite," that is, avoid a negative, or you can approach it from a positive viewpoint: "I need to strive to be authentic, to really treat my faith with serious attention, to answer the question about who Jesus is and why I am a follower. And…to act on it." Do you hear the difference?

What does a life of authentic Christianity look like? Here's three things I've noticed.

An active prayer life: This may not be what you think. It's not about how many Our Fathers and Hail Marys one says each day, nor whether one is a daily Mass attendee. These prayer forms are certainly useful, but what I see in authentic Christians is an ever-present awareness of God operating around them all of the time. It is a pervasive connection with God, like a light plugged into a socket, or a battery that never dies. Every aspect of life is imbued with the Spirit, and the authentic Christian now only knows this, but utterly relies on that connection.

A sense of compassion: The authentic Christian sees the world through the eyes of God. Fueled by an active prayer life, compassion is almost guaranteed to flower. I was in the state prison for the Kairos retreat last weekend and saw this first-hand. I was giving a talk on forgiveness and the need for the men to open themselves to the embrace of God. One of the inmates on the retreat suddenly began to weep out loud, clearly in incredible emotional pain. As all eyes turned to him, five guys suddenly leaped up and ran to him, embracing him, soothing him, and leading him to another room to compose himself. Every one of those five guys was another inmate just like him, except for one difference. The five were all Kairos graduates from an earlier weekend, and they had acquired a new sense of the world, a sense that is rarely seen in a dark and barren prison, a sense of compassion. It was an amazing display of the power of Christianity. Because at its best, Christianity teaches us how to deal with our pain.

Action: The authentic Christian cannot stand by and watch. It is utterly impossible. Fed by God's persistent love as experienced through prayer, seeing the world through God's compassionate eyes, there is a fire that begins to burn deep within, a fire that demands to be channeled into action. The actions can be simple, the actions can be heroic, but whatever the label, the Christian must act. At the end of the last full day of the retreat, one of the inmates came forward and spoke to the group. He was a large African-American man, quite imposing. He looked out at the sea of faces, white, Hispanic, Asian, and black, and spoke to his fellow inmates. He said, "Out there, the races are kept separate. In here, in this chapel, we are all mixed together. I want to say that I consider all of you my Christian brothers, and from now on, whatever the cost, I will greet you as my Christian brothers out there as well. Racism must end, one brother at a time." The fire was burning in him, and he needed to *act*.

Hypocrisy: words not equal to actions. Authenticity: words and actions blend seamlessly.

I'm sure that it comes as no surprise that every one of these traits of the authentic Christian is quintessentially present in Jesus Christ. So if you're wondering further how it "should look" to be an authentic Christian beyond my words here today, turn to the Lord. Be real, keep seeking the truth, don't ever believe you know it all. Ask Jesus to walk the path with you – I promise that if you do, you'll be quickly found guilty of being a Christian. And as St. Paul tells us, if you're going to boast of anything at all, boast of being a follower of Jesus Christ. That's the path of life.

Wake Up!

Scripture Referenced: Mark 1:12-15

> The Spirit drove Jesus out into the desert, and he remained in the desert for forty days, tempted by Satan. He was among wild beasts, and the angels ministered to him. After John had been arrested, Jesus came to Galilee proclaiming the gospel of God: "This is the time of fulfillment. The kingdom of God is at hand. Repent, and believe in the gospel."

There's little doubt we're in Mark's gospel! It takes Luke a whole chapter to tell us about Jesus' temptation in the desert. Mark summarizes the entire episode in two brief sentences. It's so easy to miss the important words, the true depth of the reading. Let's start with the end of the reading, the first words spoken by Jesus in Mark's gospel: "This is the time of fulfillment. The kingdom of God is at hand. Repent, and believe in the gospel." Everything Jesus says sounds very positive – a time of fulfillment, the kingdom of God at hand, believe in the gospel, translated as the "good news". But right in the middle is that word "repent," which always throws us for a loop because it has acquired such a negative connotation. It's hard not to say that word without taking on an accusatory tone. Repent! Wagging our finger in the face of all of you sinners. No wonder we discount the rest of what Jesus says. The good news is trumped by that accusation.

Let's rewrite that word, shall we? Rather than "repent", how about "wake up"? It fits the rest of what Jesus says much better. The kingdom of God is at hand. *Wake up*, and believe in the good news! So what's the good news, and why do we need to wake up to believe it? First of all, the good news – simple and profound – God loves us and wants us to live in communion with him here and now. Not just in heaven, but here and now. Think about the amazing implications of that statement. God, the creator of the universe, is on your side. God wants nothing but good for you. What a wonderfully secure feeling that is, don't you agree? But here's the hard question, why do we have such a tough time believing it? Because the world, ruled by Satan and the "wild beasts" speaks a very different series of messages. Do these sound familiar?

Happiness is being beautiful, healthy, rich, and skinny – preferably all four. Or, it's a zero-sum game – someone's got to lose and someone's got to win. Or, trust no one, especially those in power or authority. Everyone's got a hidden agenda. Or, some people are just meant to be poor. And my favorite, "If it sounds too good to be true, it's probably a lie." In the face of all of this cynicism, can you see why the notion that God loves us unconditionally seems far-fetched? We've been lulled into a sense of tired depression, and that is exactly Satan's goal. This is why Jesus is crying, "Wake up!" How do we wake up? What does it take?

Notice in today's gospel the interesting phrase that leads off the reading, "The Spirit *drove* Jesus out into the desert…" There's a clue, right there. We've got to remove ourselves, even if temporarily, from the noise of the world, from the constant badgering negativity. Let the Spirit drive you out into a quiet place. Note that the devil is still present there, but also notice the wonderfully comforting line that "angels ministered to him". We can and should expect the same treatment!

When I was in my final year of Diaconate formation, my entire class of 12 guys with our wives were sent to a retreat house for a four-day silent retreat. We each had our own separate rooms, but there was no TV, no radio, no phones, no Internet, no newspaper. Just a Bible and a journal to write in. No talking except for two 20 minute sessions/day with a spiritual advisor. We certainly saw each other frequently, but our communication was strictly with hand gestures and facial expressions. I walked a lot, read the Bible readings recommended by my advisor, took naps, wrote in my journal, and simply listened for God's voice. It was amazing how easily God entered my buzzing brain when the buzzing was toned down. Nature was somehow more beautiful. The food tasted wonderful – probably because we had nothing to do but simply savor it. My prayer throughout the four days was simple – show me how to be a good servant of God. His return message over and over was equally simple – tell the people the good news. God loves you and wants you to live in communion with him. I hope that makes you smile – it's pretty good to hear!

Often, when I'm in the prison or the jail talking to the guys, I tell them that they're lucky. God has put them on a "forced retreat". It's not a very attractive retreat setting, to be honest, but hey, they have a room, they're being fed, and they have some spare time, so why not accept it as a retreat? The purpose of Lent, quite simply, is to force us into "retreat mode" so that we can experience the movement of the Spirit. The first Sunday of Lent always presents Jesus in the desert. Lent is a time of prayer, almsgiving, and fasting. Why? The best way to shut off the world's noise is to reject its so-called gifts. I don't need money, I don't need fancy food, I don't need the distractions of the media, I simply don't accept it. We're saying, in quite stark terms, "You, Satan, do not own me!"

Bishop Dolan said it well at the beginning of Mass, didn't he? We find ourselves off the path for reasons that are usually minor and insignificant. An angry, hurtful word. A snap judgment, a refusal to give someone the benefit of the doubt. A moment of selfishness. These little wrong turns, when totaled up, can lead us into the deep woods of confusion, depression, and despair. Jesus says to wake up! Look up! He's waving at you – here's the right path, come on over! That's what Lent is for – getting back on the path. Now just maybe you ate bacon on Friday morning (oops), or you decided that one cookie isn't really dessert, or your best Lenten intention is still waiting for you to act. Don't be discouraged. Lent is 40 days – that's a long time. Start over today if you need to. But start!

The Paschal Journey

Scripture Referenced: John 13:1-15

> So, during supper, fully aware that the Father had put everything into his power and that he had come from God and was returning to God, he rose from supper and took off his outer garments. He took a towel and tied it around his waist. Then he poured water into a basin and began to wash the disciples' feet and dry them with the towel around his waist.

I'm sure you know that this day is called Holy Thursday, but did you know that this evening's celebration has a special name as well? It's called the Mass of the Lord's Supper, an obvious allusion to Eucharist, to the great gift of Jesus at the Last Supper, his body and blood. But for such a celebration, doesn't it seem odd that the gospel reading chosen has nothing to do with bread and wine, nothing to do with body and blood? Wouldn't you think that on this day of all days we'd have the account of Jesus instituting Eucharist to his disciples?

When John wrote his gospel, it is likely that he had access to the accounts of Matthew, Mark, and Luke, as well as the letters of St. Paul. As you well know, John's gospel features a Jesus who is in total control, very God-like, seeing into people's minds and hearts, and knowing his future. While the synoptic gospels use the Last Supper as a way to show the divine nature of Jesus in his gift of himself in the Eucharist, John does just the opposite and brings us a Jesus who performs a thoroughly human, even debasing action, washing his disciples' feet as if he was a lowly slave. What a delicious irony! Why does John present this story?

What we do know is that John's community was very sophisticated theologically and philosophically. There were many Greek converts in the community who brought a very scholarly approach to "The Way", and we have to believe that at some level, this was not all good. John the evangelist must have seen this and decided to wake everyone up. I can relate personally. A number of years ago, I had just completed a weekend retreat and was walking back to my car, my head full of lofty principles and theological musings, when a homeless man came up to me and asked me for a dollar. I was jarred by the request, and a little annoyed, so I brushed past him with barely a word and got in my car. Then it hit me as it must have hit the first readers of John's gospel. Oh, is that what it means to follow Jesus? Oops.

Eucharist, in the Greek, means thanksgiving. Clearly, John wants us to take it one more step. Thanksgiving apparently means service. To be thankful is to give as you have received. In fact, it is the only way to truly show your gratitude. As Jesus says, "as I have done for you, you should also do." How thankful are you? Does it show only in the pew as we're piously praying after Communion? Or does it extend out there? That's John's challenge.

The other important aspect of today's celebration is that it is only part 1 of 3 parts. Yes, it's a trilogy, and doesn't end until the Vigil of Easter arrives on Holy Saturday night. We leave our service tonight unfinished, incomplete, only partially understood. The great theme of these 3 nights is the Paschal mystery, the archetypal journey of Jesus from the high of tonight to the bitter anguish of Good Friday to the resurrection joy of Easter Sunday. Tonight as we complete our service, we accompany Jesus from the table of the Last Supper, out of the Church and, in a symbolic fashion, walk with him and his disciples to the Garden of Gethsemane where he will encounter his executioners. Does Jesus know his fate? Is he confident? Confused? Terrified? Maybe a swirl of all of these emotions?

There are people right now, tonight, who are facing their Paschal journey, poised for the slide. They are in hospitals facing life threatening surgery tomorrow. They are on death row, counting the days until the state, in our name, kills them. They are sitting on the border between Mexico and the United States deciding whether or not they should attempt to cross. They are sitting in a foxhole in Afghanistan, nervously scanning a dangerous ridge, dreading the bark of gunfire or the explosion of an IED. They are looking at a bottle of sleeping pills, considering if anyone would care if they swallowed them all. All of these people are looking for Jesus, all of these people are equal parts confident, confused and terrified. But where is Jesus?

"I have given you a model to follow, so that as I have done for you, you should also do."

The Paschal journey, as difficult and as dreadful as it feels to be on that road, has a great ending. It always does for those who have faith. It's up to us to deliver the good news to those who are on that downward slide, to let them know that Resurrection awaits. We can *speak* that good news, as I am now, but there's a much better way. We can *model* that good news through our service and comfort. That's the Christian Way.

So tonight, in our very safe, warm environment of St. James Church, we model the action of Jesus, washing each other's feet. Many of you are perhaps reluctant to take part, but I can't think of a better place to practice than right here. As you do so, reflect. If you're in good shape this Holy Thursday night, the world needs you to wash some feet out there. If you're not in good shape this night, perhaps somewhere on that downward leg of the Paschal journey, will you let us help you? Will you let us wash your feet and be Jesus to you? We're all in this together.

Beauty, Goodness, and Truth

Scripture Referenced: Matthew 28:1-10

> The angel said to the women, "Do not be afraid! I know that you are seeking Jesus the crucified. He is not here, for he has been raised just as he said. Come and see the place where he lay."

On this most blessed day of our Church calendar, as we ponder the mystery of the Christ, the astonishing news of a tortured dead man apparently resurrected, we must face the question every Christian faces at some point in their lives. What do we believe? What do *you* believe?

It's somewhat fashionable among elite and scholarly circles these days to claim a certain type of atheism, an intellectually derived claim that God is unimportant, indeed irrelevant to our human existence. In fact, with breathless bravado, we are told that God is not simply irrelevant, he is non-existent. What do *you* believe? Our own spiritual belief system has to start here, for without a belief in God, why bother with a belief in anything else?

Now this is when most theologians will launch into various intellectual arguments for the existence of God, and to a certain degree, these discussions are interesting and fruitful. At another level, however, they are less than optimal, for it is far too easy to fall into the trap of trying to use scientific methods and logical syllogisms to prove that God exists. The stark truth of the matter is that you will never get to a convincing proof of the existence of God by using your head. You need *faith.*

Now before you tune out because of that vague word, *faith*, allow me to define this term in a perhaps unusual way. First, what faith is *not*. Faith is not the same thing as belief, or adhering to some dogma, or obeying some command from the pulpit. Faith has nothing to do with the Pope or even for that matter the Catholic Church. Belief, dogma, the Pope, and the Church are all *responses* to faith – they are dependent on faith. They follow faith. So what is faith? Faith, brothers and sisters, is simply accepting *what you already know to be true.*

What do you know to be true? Let me suggest four very unscientific concepts that I bet you know very intimately and from deep within.

The first is *beauty*. Beauty is hard to define, but we can try. It's the combination of qualities that make something pleasing and impressive to look at, listen to, touch, smell, or taste. Beauty is soothing to the soul and a delight to experience. Each of us knows beauty when we see it, don't we? You know beauty.

The second concept is *goodness*. Goodness embodies virtue and kindness, high qualities that attract us and impress us. Someone who is good is always in high demand, for goodness is like a light shining in the darkness. It's hard to measure goodness scientifically, isn't it? But just like beauty, we know it when we see it, know it when we encounter it.

The third concept is *truth*. As human beings, we all seem to have a very well-tuned sense of truth, an almost intuitive appreciation for the reality of things. Some think it is hard-wired into our psyches, this innate sense of right and wrong, of honesty and falsehood. A good measure of the truth of something is how our gut reacts when we hear a claim. Falsehood can confuse us momentarily, either due to the skill of the liar, or the clever way it misleads us. But in the end, our gut will tell us whether it is true or not.

Let's pause a moment. I said that faith is simply accepting what you already know to be true. You know beauty. You know goodness. You know truth itself. Well guess what? If you know beauty, goodness, and truth, you know God. Because beauty, goodness, and truth define who God is. How do I know this? Because beauty, goodness, and truth are the lures, the bait, that God tosses out to lead us all to him. God gives us a beautiful creation, with sunsets and roses and the smell of baking bread. We're attracted. Then we explore some more and we see that the world has good and bad in it, and we are drawn to the good, to the virtuous, to the people who exhibit this quality. You all know at least one person like that, right? I hope so! And when your senses are full of beauty and your heart is impressed by goodness, only then do you engage the brain and seek the ever-present truth. The search for truth is the lifelong journey we call the spiritual path.

Now to the fourth concept (for those who were counting and wondered why I stopped). You see the fourth concept that you know to be true is simply the combination of beauty, goodness and truth. We have a word for it – *love*. In the end, it's simple. If you believe in beauty, goodness, and truth, you certainly believe in love. And if you believe in love, you believe in God. Because St. John, in his amazingly profound insight, said it simply and perfectly. God is love. Love is God.

If you believe in love, then you believe in God. You have faith. You are simply accepting what you already know to be true. How does that feel? Isn't it great to have faith? Isn't it great to know that you've had it all along?

Today is Easter. Today Jesus shows us the final truth, the final expression of God's beauty, goodness, and love. Jesus shows us that death, our greatest fear, is not the end, but somehow the beginning of something profoundly exciting and new. It's available to all of us who have faith. I guess that's all of us! You already know it to be true. You know that this world can't be the end of everything; it's just not possible. Our gut doesn't buy it.

One last question. Do you ever get tired of beauty, goodness, and truth? Do you ever think, oh gosh, if I see one more beautiful flower or hear one more moving piece of music, or learn one more truth about the world, I'll just have to go hide? I don't think so. Our whole life is a day to day search for more beauty, goodness, and truth. Take a guess what heaven is all about. For some strange reason, I don't think we'll be bored when we get there. How could we? Beauty, goodness, truth, love, the very essence of who God is, will permeate heaven.

So the next time someone tells you, "I don't believe in God" ask them, "Oh? You don't believe in love? Or beauty? Or truth? Or goodness? What a sad and frightening world this must be for you!" Then tell them some good news…whether or not you believe in God, God most certainly believes in you. And he's dangling this bait…

Knowing Versus Understanding

Scripture Referenced: Matthew 28:16-20

> Then Jesus approached and said to them, "All power in heaven and on earth has been given to me. Go, therefore, and make disciples of all nations, baptizing them in the name of the Father, and of the Son, and of the Holy Spirit, teaching them to observe all that I have commanded you. And behold, I am with you always, until the end of the age."

Nearly nine years ago, on the Sunday after I was ordained a deacon, I was asked to preach the Masses here at St. James. It happened to be Trinity Sunday. I remember thinking that it wasn't very fair to be handed the most profound mystery of our faith as a homily topic, especially a first homily. But somehow I got through it, mostly quoting from a paper I wrote for one of our classes. Now here I am, much older and wiser, and I'm sure you're anxious to hear how much I've learned in the past years about this deeply complex subject. Perhaps I should pull out a three-leafed clover and quote some of the latest theological writings, but I would probably get lost in the logical structures before long, not to mention bore you to tears. So let's not go in that direction.

When I was a kid, the good nuns of Sacred Heart School taught us that the Trinity was a mystery, and we really weren't expected to understand it. However, we *were* expected to *believe* it, because the Church taught it, and the Church always taught the truth. Even at the age of nine, I found this to be a singularly unhelpful statement, but as I was a good Catholic altar boy, I decided it was better to just go along with it, and add it to the other mysteries of the faith, like the Virgin Birth and the Resurrection and the Nature of Jesus, the God - man. Many good people are content to stay in this place of faithful acceptance throughout adulthood, my mother a notable example. Her faith was deeply personal, and mysteries such as the Trinity were simply accepted truths, so why waste a lot of brain cells on asking how and why?

As I moved through my decidedly scientific education, I was taught that blindly accepting anything was intellectually embarrassing. This refocused my attention on the mysteries of the Church and I began to delve ever deeper into the whys and how's of Church teaching. I wanted proofs and evidence and clarity and logical constructs that moved me from A to B to C to heads nodding in satisfaction and a satisfying QED at the end. A well-meaning friend of mind, noting my frustrating quest, told me that when I entered Church I really should just "check my brain at the door". Is it any wonder that so many scientists struggle with Church teachings? No one with a big ego wants to hear that something is beyond their intellect.

Why aren't religious truths clear and clean and obvious? That would sure make the world a better place, wouldn't it? It's been tried, of course. Back in the early twentieth century, a group of Protestant theologians got together and summarized the entire Christian faith into a small number of "fundamentals", among them the literal inerrancy of the Bible. Accept these truths, accept Christ as your personal savior, and just relax – you're in! There's a certain appeal to that, isn't there? But for me, it wouldn't be enough. I kept going back to St. Augustine, one of our most brilliant theologians, who wrote that the purpose of theology was "faith seeking understanding". This is a critically important observation. Augustine no more believed in "blind assent" than any scientist today, and he was happy to tackle any and all of the mysteries of the Church.

What does God think? I have learned that God is not going to give us a perfectly clear and concise description of his nature and intentions. Again and again in Scripture, God clearly states that God is so beyond us, that attempting to fully understand God is pointless. But God doesn't slam the door on the subject either. In fact, God entices us to enter the mystery, to dig deeper, to not accept anything on "blind faith". Oddly enough, the more we dig in, the more we learn, and eventually, we get to the point where we realize that as much as we understand, there's still more to understand. And we try and struggle and muddle and consider, and God applauds. He's like a parent of a one year old encouraging those first steps across the living room floor. You can do it!!

And then one day I realized that there was a difference between *knowing* something and *understanding* it. And that recognition was the key. For example, we can look at a scene in nature and agree that it is beautiful. But *why* is it beautiful? The colors, the symmetry, the peaceful atmosphere? Yes, but why do we in particular label this beautiful, but not a garbage dump? We know beauty, but we don't understand it. We likewise know truth when we hear it, don't we? Something inside of us responds to truth like a drink of cool water on a hot day. It simply satisfies and makes sense. We don't even need to understand it. Love is the same way. We know love, but understanding it drags us down into chemical composition and biological imprints and pheromone reactions, and we know that love is much bigger than this.

Now back to the Trinity. (Finally!) I'm not going to explain the Trinity so that you *understand* it. Let's go in a different direction. What do you *know* about the Trinity? How do you interact with the Trinity? Why does it *matter*? Here are some questions:

- Who do you pray to? The Father, the Son, or the Spirit? I'm talking about the dialog in your heart, not the canned prayers at Mass. Who do you pray to *the most*? This reveals one of the key facets of the Trinity. Just as we all have different learning styles, we each have a different "person of God" style. Isn't it great that God adapts to us?
- How are you most alive? By yourself on a hike in the woods? Or in the company of family and loved ones? If you think about it, we are social animals. As much as we appreciate and enjoy some "alone time", we routinely seek out others just the same. If we look at the peak experiences of our lives, I would bet that 99 percent were in the company of others. Why does that matter? If we're wired to love and respond to love in a group, is it so hard to imagine that God is the same? Three persons, one God. God is a *relationship* first and foremost.
- Are you afraid of God? The early Hebrews certainly were! Their whole way of life was atonement and sacrifice to keep God from smiting them. The Jewish Law was designed to keep you in right relationship with God – to be as pure as possible. It doesn't work very well since we're flawed human beings. In fact, as St. Paul came to realize, the Law is actually counter-productive. It leads to death. This is why Jesus came among us, to show us through his teaching, healing, and ultimate sacrifice that God is not a vengeful accountant, but a patient parent, a loving encourager, a compassionate embrace. Last week we

celebrated Pentecost, the coming of the Holy Spirit. Think of Jesus and the Holy Spirit as the arms of God, reaching out to us in embrace – doesn't that feel right?

Finally, realize that as much as we don't understand love, we know love. God, who is love, is just as mysterious and knowable, all at the same time. Don't stop seeking. Don't stop seeking understanding – but don't let that challenging journey blind you to what you *already know*!

Chapter 4 – Seeking Jesus

The study of the person of Jesus has a fancy theological title, *Christology*. From the point of his ascension into heaven to the present day, millions of people have struggled to understand exactly who Jesus was. Was he a great man? Or was he the all-knowing, all-powerful son of God? It took the early Church over 300 years to come to the conclusion that he was *both*, and even then, it was not a unanimous verdict. What is true, however, as much then as now, is that Jesus loves it when we seek him out, however misunderstood our concept of him is. He would love to have that conversation with you. Give it a shot. As that famous poster of the Magi reads, "Wise men still seek him."

Who is Jesus?

Scripture Referenced: Philippians 2:6-11

> Have in you the same attitude that is also in Christ Jesus, who, though he was in the form of God, did not regard equality with God something to be grasped. Rather, he emptied himself, taking the form of a slave, coming in human likeness; and found human in appearance, he humbled himself, becoming obedient to the point of death, even death on a cross.

In the earliest years of the Church's existence, the question "Who is Jesus?" was of paramount importance. Think about this for a moment. Suppose you were to strike up a conversation with a stranger and find out that he had never heard of Jesus. This seems hard for us to believe, but in the early Church, this was a very common occurrence. How do you answer that question? Who is Jesus? If you're like me, you'd probably stumble about for a moment, trying to organize your thoughts, descriptions, and arguments. It's not an easy question to answer. Where to start? The miracles? The resurrection? Some of the best parables? The God-man thing? How does the cross fit in? Yikes, pretty soon, you're over your head and decide to Google Jesus.

Or, you can open your Bible to Paul's letter to the Philippians, Chapter 2, verses 6-11 and there you have it in a theological nutshell. Yes, our second reading today is the absolute starting point for anyone who wants to know who Jesus is. If you take a course on Christology, you'll be all over this reading. We've heard it many times, but I wonder if you've really *heard* it. There are five distinct messages being tossed out here. Listen carefully.

Christ Jesus, who, though he was in the form of God, did not regard equality with God something to be grasped. So, point number one. Christ Jesus was in the form of God. He was divine, from the beginning. This is Paul's starting point and his end point, as we'll see. But then there's that strange statement – Jesus did not regard equality with God something to be grasped. What does that mean? Well, who *did* regard equality with God something to be grasped? Think back to the Garden

– why did Adam and Eve eat the apple? So they could be like God. Adam and Eve are stand-ins for us, of course, so that makes the point even more strongly. Unlike the rest of us human beings, who are always struggling to be little gods, Jesus didn't go down that path. Ever. Let's read on.

Rather, he emptied himself, taking the form of a slave, coming in human likeness; and found human in appearance...Point number two. Jesus was humble enough to become a human being. There's a marvelous painting in the Prado in Madrid of Jesus and God the Father sitting around a big globe, having a conversation. By the gestures, it's clear that they're planning where Jesus is to enter the universe of human beings, the finger of God pointing to Israel. Jesus' mission is under discussion. Jesus was choosing to become human, and that's a pretty scary, if not outright daring choice. What happens next?

He humbled himself, becoming obedient...This third point is subtle, yet important. Jesus "became obedient", that is, he learned about who he was the same way we do, through prayer and awareness. Jesus didn't enter the world with full understanding and knowledge; if so, he wouldn't have been a human being. There's a heresy in the early church called Docetism that took the view that Jesus simply assumed the appearance of a human being; he was not truly human. The Church refuted this heresy strongly and stated emphatically that Jesus is both fully human and fully divine – yes, a paradox wrapped in a mystery. Jesus needed time to figure out who he was and why he was here. Why did this take 33 years? Read the rest of the sentence.

He humbled himself, becoming obedient *to the point of death, even death on a cross.* Jesus's obedience to God, his openness and utter acceptance, led him to a horrible death for our sake. The acceptance of this mission must have been an incredibly painful moment, and we certainly get a taste of that as he second guesses himself and God in the Garden of Gethsemane the night of his arrest. He rehashes the same fears with God, and comes once again to the decision point – I will be obedient, I trust in you, Father, I will suffer all. Your will be done. The fourth point. And now for the finale.

Because of this, God greatly exalted him and bestowed on him the name which is above every name, that at the name of Jesus every knee should bend, of those in heaven and on earth and under the earth, and every tongue confess that Jesus Christ is Lord, to the glory of God the Father.

Because of this. This what? This full trust in God, this full acceptance, this willingness to suffer and die. God exalted him and now allows us to call Jesus *Lord*, the same title reserved for God the Father. Understand, brothers and sisters, how daring this statement was when it was written. In Roman occupied lands, there is only one lord, and his name is Caesar, not some upstart rabbi in Palestine. Calling someone else "lord" was treasonous – it was an invitation to martyrdom. Calling Jesus Christ Lord is not only an act of faith, it is an act of political rebellion against earthly power. I wonder if we really grasp that reality today? When you say that Jesus Christ is Lord, you mean that he comes before *everything* else. Our country, our political system, our money, our jobs, our families, our very lives. Do you really mean it? It's hard – don't minimize the effort. It's a recommitment every day, and I often fail at it. Is Jesus Christ the Lord for you?

If you're not sure of the answer, the gospel passage today shows you how to examine your life honestly. There are two sons. The first one says, yes, Lord, I will work in your vineyard today and.... *doesn't*. The second son says, no, Lord, I will *not* work in your vineyard today, and then changes his mind and...*does*. Both sons are kind of unsatisfactory, aren't they? Yeah, kind of like we are, huh? But of the two, the second one is preferred. Why? Because actions speak louder than words. So, if you're wondering if Jesus Christ is Lord for you, look at the actions in your life. If your actions are all about you and this world, you're the first son. You talk a good game, but it ends there. But if you struggle with the words because they're hard to say, and yet act in the spirit of Jesus, then welcome to the kingdom! In other words, add up what you do, not what you say.

Now you know who Jesus is – I saved you from reading 642 million hits on Google. But as I'm sure you've heard before, knowing *about* Jesus is not the same as *knowing* Jesus. Jesus is real, a person like you and me, but unlike you and me, is available to you 24x7, in fact, would prefer to simply be a part of you. That's a real pleasure, and it can start today. The Eucharist, the physical body of Christ, is available at Communion. The priest acts in the person of Christ leading our prayer.

The people around you are the many parts of the mystical body of Christ. And the scriptures we've just heard are the Word of God, which John's gospel equates with Jesus the Christ. You're surrounded! Invite him in and let him guide your actions. Jesus Christ is Lord!

Knowing Jesus

Scripture Referenced: Matthew 7:21-27

> Not everyone who says to me, 'Lord, Lord,' will enter the kingdom of heaven, but only the one who does the will of my Father in heaven.

Sometimes when I'm in the jail leading a session, an inmate distinguishes himself from the rest of the men by his deep knowledge of the Bible. Any question I ask he is quick to blurt out an answer -- and it is usually correct. Inevitably in circumstances like this, I wonder to myself, "How did this guy end up in here?" At other times, these Bible expert inmates use their superior knowledge to show up all of the other guys, quoting verses here and there, talking fast and furious, as if he is trying to impress God. To him, knowledge of the Bible is like a club, and he swings it every chance he can. Do they remind you of today's gospel? They know the words, can recite them by heart, can say "Lord, Lord, look how much I know, look how I can quote you!" But it's all air, all smoke, or as they say in Texas, all hat and no cattle. They know all about Jesus, but they don't *know* Jesus. Do you know people like that?

On the other end of the spectrum are those people who we think *should* know Jesus, have been through 8 or 10 years of Catholic education, but they don't celebrate Mass, can't say a rosary, and don't seem to know basic truths of our religion. Yes, that's right, our kids! I must get the question once a week, "How do I get my kids to come back to Church? I did everything right as a parent. Why didn't it work?" The answer is simple – you're too impatient. The journey for our kids is still underway and as you've already figured out, their journey is not the same as ours was. And, although you may not realize it, your kids have been given something that will always stick with them, a rock, a foundation that can't be broken. It's up to them whether they use it to build a house.

We're all on a spiritual journey, we're all spiritual beings at our core, and the reason we teach our kids fundamental truths like the ten commandments and morality and treating people as we'd like to be treated is to provide that base, that place to stand at the early portion of our journey. But here's a key point. *You can't stay there*. You have to move, you have to test it, to see if the base holds up in the face of the world. If the adolescent doesn't move, but simply surrounds himself with religion and words and rules, he risks becoming like one of those inmates, spouting "Lord, Lord" and rebelling in so many other ways that his hypocrisy does more damage to himself and ironically, his religion, than any evil doer could. God save us from the person who has all of the answers!

I've lived this journey – I'll bet many of you have too. I spurned religion once, I examined every Church teaching with such a skeptical eye that my belief system began to resemble Swiss cheese. Thomas Jefferson, our brilliant third president, took a pair of scissors to the Bible, and cut out everything that he felt was overly supernatural or unnecessary fluff as an attempt to reach the essence of Jesus' teaching. I could relate. I was building myself a nice little house, but only using about 10 percent of my foundation. When the storm blew, my feeble house collapsed without a trace and I found myself wondering what happened as I clung to a couple of foundation stones. This part of my journey didn't happen overnight – it was probably 17 years after high school before it struck me that I was missing something, that the hole in my heart wasn't being filled by money and career and stuff. My life was full of stress. I was sleeping poorly, drinking more than I should, worrying about everything. Then God stepped in.

It's not that God wasn't there before. He certainly was, but I think God was just waiting, looking for an opportunity to invite me to a relationship when I was ready. In 1990, my wife and I were invited to join a small church community at St. James. I wouldn't have said yes the year before, but for some reason, at the age of 35, something inside nudged me to go along. I found I enjoyed the evenings, liked the camaraderie, the discussions, the occasional deep realization, and I also noticed something else. After an evening sharing God's word with my small church community, I slept like a baby. Something peaceful was settling in my soul.

I started exploring my foundation more and more. I began to read great authors, listen to inspiring preachers, bathe myself in spiritual music, re-learn my faith and relish the wisdom. I slowly rebuilt my house, but this time right on top of the foundation I was given so many years ago. It now feels like it's on the rock. Storms still come, and I lose a shutter or a shingle now and then, but the house stands.

So, parents and grandparents, you hand-wringers worried about your kids and grandkids, here's my advice. Stay connected to your wandering sheep, stay in touch, and most importantly, keep on inviting them, especially when the storms come and rattle their lives. Be creative, ask for the guidance of the Holy Spirit, don't push – be patient. Their foundation awaits – they just don't realize what they have. So let's make a deal. I'll pray for your kids if you'll pray for mine. Can we do that together?

Now, what about all of us out here today? How's the house sitting? Strong and firm on the foundation? Or does it need some shoring up? Well, you're in luck. This Wednesday we begin the season of Lent. Rather than giving something up for Lent, how about *adding* something to your life? As Jesus says, *listen* to my words and *act* on them! Listen and act. Some suggestions:

- Go out to Amazon.com and search on "Catholic Inspirational Books". You'll get 6,698 results. Scroll down until you find one that catches your eye and buy the book. Read it during Lent – promise to finish it by Holy Thursday.
- Explore your faith foundation. Attend a class at the diocesan institute – you can find all of the classes on the Diocese of San Diego web site. Take a class!
- Go the St. James Thrift Store and ask Tim or Madeline if you can volunteer some time to help them during Lent. See what happens to those items you donate. You might get a surprise.
- After Mass each Sunday, we hear lots of announcements – maybe too many – but there's a reason and a purpose. These are opportunities to build on your foundation. Why not attend one or two of these events and see what happens?

Above all, remember that the key issue in the mind of Jesus is that we all get to *know* him. Knowing Jesus is not about spouting facts and rules. Don't box Jesus in by only allowing him to thrive in a church building or a Bible. Jesus is much more accessible in our relationship with the little ones – the ones who aren't on top of society but on the bottom. Head for the margins of our world and ironically, you'll find your heart and soul, the God-core in us all. The rock to build on.

Seek and You Will Find

Scripture Referenced: Luke 2:22-40

> Now there was a man in Jerusalem whose name was Simeon. This man was righteous and devout, awaiting the consolation of Israel, and the Holy Spirit was upon him. It had been revealed to him by the Holy Spirit that he should not see death before he had seen the Messiah of the Lord. He came in the Spirit into the temple; and when the parents brought in the child Jesus to perform the custom of the law in regard to him, he took him into his arms and blessed God…

Today's feast seems a little out of place, doesn't it? We were comfortably back in Ordinary Time, beginning to look forward to Lent, when suddenly we're back in Luke's gospel with the infant Jesus and his parents. It's as if the Christmas season found one more present in the back of the closet. Hello! What's this? If you do the arithmetic, you'll notice that we're exactly 40 days since Christmas Eve, which should tell us something. Yes, we are linked back to Christmas in a special way, and if you look at old Church calendars, this feast was the original end of the Christmas season. In many ways, this feast of the Presentation shares a lot of similarity to the Epiphany, but with a subtle difference. The Epiphany represents Jesus manifesting himself to the Gentiles (the Magi), while this feast is Jesus' manifestation to the Jewish people, as represented by Simeon and Anna.

There's a very key point that often gets overlooked in both of these feasts, however. Even though the Epiphany and the Presentation of the Lord both have Jesus as the focal point, the reality is that Jesus is not doing anything other than being a baby. It's not about Jesus so much as it is about the seekers. It's not about Mary and Joseph, who have nothing to say in either feast at all. They're just being proud parents. It's about the Magi, about Simeon, and about Anna. Don't you find it interesting that in today's reading, as Mary and Joseph bring Jesus into the temple, a simple threesome among hundreds, perhaps thousands of people, both Simeon and Anna zero in on the infant Savior with unerring accuracy, much to the astonishment of the parents? And no, it's not because Jesus had a halo!

The simple truth is that they were looking for Jesus. And if you seek Jesus, you will find him.

About 4 weeks ago, not so ironically on Epiphany Sunday, a bus full of parishioners, plus several car loads of other folks who drove on their own, headed East to follow a star and seek out Jesus. The star is called the Sun, and like the Magi, we were bearing gifts. No, not gold, frankincense, and myrrh, but more practical items like shoes, socks, blankets, and food. On a clear, dusty day, we traveled for three hours over the high desert, out Interstate 10, stopping only once to stretch our legs, invading an Indian casino to use their very nice bathrooms. And if that sounds a bit jarring, remember that the Magi made a stop at Herod's palace, so it all lines up after all!

Our final destination was a village just to the Northwest of the Salton Sea, a little town called --sorry, not Bethlehem, but Mecca. (Ironies never cease!) Just before we pulled into the Galilee Center, I was asked if I wanted to dress up as one of the three kings, robe, headdress, and all. I readily agreed to be Balthazar, and as the bus stopped, we three kings exited first and greeted over 1500 people lined up -- to be Jesus for us. The local Center volunteers created a manger scene on a large platform that they carried before us in procession, and we walked along the long line greeting the people and the kids. We placed the manger on a table in the parking lot that served as a distribution point, paid homage to Jesus, and then turned to serve the first family in line, a spot they had come at dawn to reserve, 4 hours earlier. These families are migrant workers who winter in the high desert, waiting for the growing season to cycle around again to the Central Valley, patiently living in tiny trailers and rented houses, often crammed with extended family members. The average family income is $10,000 per year, and the Galilee Center is the thin rope that holds their existence together.

Our volunteers scattered to their tasks – some manning the shoe tables, others the blanket station, still others acting as family guides, taking the arm of whatever family came up next in line, and helping the kids get the right sized shoes. It was chaotic, but organized, buzzing with activity and movement. Every family got shoes for the kids, a blanket for each member of the family, a box of groceries, and a smile. One little 3 year-old girl came with her Papa and he picked out a nice pair of white sneakers and gave them to her. She shook her head no and pointed. There among the shoes was a sparkling, spangled pair of slippers that glittered in the sunlight. Totally impractical. But I defy you to find a daddy alive who can say no to his 3 year old daughter. She got the sparkly shoes.

Since I was one of the kings, I got to work the crowd like a baseball team mascot. My Spanish is pretty pathetic, but the little kids had no problem understanding me. I walked through the line waving at the boys and girls, most of whom were quite willing to give me a high five. But one little girl took one look at me in my robes, headdress, and sunglasses, and immediately hid behind Mom. I crouched down to her level, and gave her a wave. She peeked out, decided I wasn't so scary after all, and suddenly came barreling out with arms extended to give me a big hug. I wasn't expecting it, and in that moment of surprise, I saw in her delighted eyes another presence, and I knew that I had found Jesus.

It's not all that surprising, really. Many people, saints and seekers, have found Jesus in the poor and broken living in the borderlands. It's a great place to look for Him. There are other places too. You can find Jesus in the hospital, in the prisons, in the old folks' home, in the hospice center, in the food kitchen, and in the day care centers. Yes, you can also find Jesus in Church and among our families and workplaces, but it's often harder. Why? Too many veils, too many layers, too much armor, too much distraction. Sick people, imprisoned people, old people, dying people, poor people, and little children all share a common trait. They aren't bound up in stuff. They simply exist in order to exist some more. When people are exposed to their core, to the soul, we see them as Jesus does, and Jesus looks out from within. It's simple. It's absolutely true, and I can tell you that if you seek Jesus in these situations, you will find him. And it will change you.

After about 3 hours, the last of the people came through the line, and the pickings were slim. Despite our best hopes, we ran out of girls' shoes, and the last of 1500 blankets were passed out. The hot sun had cooked a few people, except for those of us with fancy headdresses!

The volunteers at the Center had lunch for us, and we all enjoyed street tacos and baked goods. Then it was back on the bus for the ride home, with each of us pondering the meaning of the day, and why this feels so right.

You see, we worship a God who is incarnational, that is, who has taken on flesh. The physical presence of Jesus was an historical reality that happened in a place and a time. But the gift of Jesus did not stop with his ascension. Jesus became the *Christ*, the universal reality of God's active presence, no longer constrained to a specific human body, but now available to all of us who follow Him. The irony is that those of us who seek Jesus not only find Him, but in finding Him, we become Jesus as well. The Body of Christ is one. There's no more joyful place to be than the Body of Christ. It's what we were made for, it's the culmination of our existence, it's what we look forward to when we die, and the amazing thing is that we don't have to wait for death to experience it!

There's been a lot of buzz lately about the so-called *New Evangelization.* This sounds rather dramatic and a bit frightening to all of us, because it seems to imply that we have to start knocking on our neighbors' doors. Nothing can be further from the truth. The New Evangelization is about *witness*, about what and how God has worked with you. It can be said with words, but it's better said with actions. Ask anyone who was on that trip to Coachella last month and you'll get evangelized. Better yet, come to our next Mission Circle event and become an evangelizer. You'll see Jesus. But more importantly, come and see the Body of Christ in action and don't be shocked to realize it's *you.*

Recognizing the Voice of Jesus

Scripture Referenced: John 10:1-10

> Whoever enters through the gate is the shepherd of the sheep. The gatekeeper opens it for him, and the sheep hear his voice, as the shepherd calls his own sheep by name and leads them out. When he has driven out all his own, he walks ahead of them, and the sheep follow him, because they recognize his voice.

How do you recognize the voice of Jesus? This reading from John's gospel comes right after the cure of the man born blind, so you can imagine the disciples questioning Jesus – how did this blind man know you were the Son of God? Jesus' answer? The sheep hear the voice of their good shepherd and follow him. It's a striking metaphor, because it's quite true, both for the sheep and for us. You see, in that time, all of the shepherds co-mingled their sheep at the end of the day in a large village corral. Each morning, one by one, each shepherd would open the gate, call out, and only his sheep would come out to follow him to pasture. So the question is simple. How do *you* recognize the voice of Jesus when he calls?

Of course, implicit in this question is the assumption that Jesus is actually, indeed, calling you. Many people stumble right there. Why would God deign to call me, let alone notice that I even exist? This is the number one reaction of every person God calls in the Bible. Moses, Jeremiah, Isaiah, Ezekiel, Daniel, Hosea – after the shock of understanding that God was indeed calling them, their first words are some variation of "who me?" Followed quickly by a variation on "I'm not worthy, try Father Lawrence instead!" God persists, however, and so this is our first indicator of who God seeks. God seeks people who are ordinary, everyday folks, who are not worthy, and quite frankly seem poorly qualified to change the world. Hey, that's us! Drat!

Okay, let's admit that Jesus may be calling. How do you recognize his voice? What does it sound like? How do you distinguish between Jesus and the thieves and robbers? I got a chance to look at this issue pretty closely just recently. On Easter Sunday, I was invited to assist

Bishop Brom as he said Mass at the State Prison. A perfect laboratory for our question – Jesus, thieves, robbers, not to mention gang bangers, murderers, and a few other interesting characters. So I met the Bishop at 8 in the morning Easter Sunday at the gates, and we were escorted into the maximum security yard at the prison. I looked around pretty closely, but I didn't see any Easter Eggs hidden in the bushes, or chocolate bunnies. It's a grim place. Once we got to the chapel, the inmates began to arrive, and soon we had nearly 70 men packed into "chapel", which is simply a large multi-purpose room. We greeted the men warmly and they took their chairs. The Bishop then put on his alb and stole, walked out front and announced that he would hear confessions for any of the men who desired the sacrament. I had told my wife that I'd be home by lunch time, but suddenly that seemed a little unlikely! It was an hour and a half before we started Mass.

Now, I'm not one to just sit in the back and twiddle my thumbs, and quite frankly, as an outsider, I was immediately a magnet for many of the men to come and talk. Several asked me, "Did you hear that Bishop Brom was here on Holy Thursday?" I prompted each one to tell me more and invariably, in awestruck voices, they told me that the Bishop had washed the feet of 12 inmates, *both* feet, and get this – as he toweled off each foot, he *kissed* their feet! Can you believe that? You see, brothers and sisters, in prison, most inmates are very germ phobic. Tight quarters, hundreds of guys, communal showers, difficult conditions. To get a sense of their reality, when you go home today, go into your guest bathroom and imagine replacing the bathtub with a bunk bed. Invite another person in, shut the door, and you have a prison cell. What the Bishop did amazed them.

Mass finally begins, and this multi-purpose room, as bland as can be, transforms into a cathedral. The Easter readings are proclaimed, and Christ becomes present in the men, the Eucharist, and the presider. The Bishop did four baptisms and nine confirmations. Our baptismal font was a plastic wash basin, with a coffee cup to pour the water over each tattooed head. I was on towel duty, gently drying them off, and more than one used the towel to wipe their eyes as well – as tears fell freely. The confirmations followed, the aroma of sacred chrism filling the room. Eucharist, restricted by prison rules to the bread only, was given to every man, and since we had no tabernacle, we had to consume all of the hosts, so some of the guys got seconds and thirds. As part of the final blessing, the Bishop offered to bless any religious articles the men had with them and oh, such an assortment! Home-made rosaries, crosses, scapulars, artwork, you name it, the men held them high for the Bishop's blessing. The Mass ended, it was time to go. But wait, one more thing…!

One of the inmates came forward with a large garbage bag, filled with an assortment of smaller bags. He explained that the inmates had taken up a collection. There isn't any cash in the prison, so what was collected was goodies, mostly food. You can buy sweets, condiments, spices, snacks, cookies, and other such items at the prison store. The men donated these items and then the lead inmate called off names of people who were sick or injured or in the hole, and their cellmates came forward to collect these little offering bags to take back. It's as if we took our Sunday collection and at the end of Mass, asked who needed a little extra today, and handed out some cash. It was simple and touching and real.

Now back to my original question. How do you recognize the voice of Jesus? Did you notice what I noticed?

- The voice of Jesus is rarely expressed as a *voice*. It's usually an act of service, and the more humble the giver, the louder the action.
- The voice of Jesus is loudest when the surroundings are simple, when the symbols are allowed to do some talking too. Water is water, oil is oil, bread is bread – we sometimes miss their significance when we encase them in gold and silver. When we see them unadorned, we're forced to ask why? What is happening here?
- The voice of Jesus strikes a population of believers like a virus, or a wild fire. It catches a big net of fish. It feeds the five thousand, it feeds the sick inmates. It's catching…
- The voice of Jesus is heard the loudest in the worst places. It often draws us to the edge, to the underside of life, to places that seem to embrace death. Jesus never feared death, and he conquers it over and over again, as we celebrate each Mass. We don't need to fear death either.

I finally got home in the early afternoon, having grabbed an Easter cheeseburger at Wendy's on the way. The following Wednesday I received a letter in the mail. It was from the Bishop. He thanked me for serving with him, apologized for how long confessions took, and remarked that despite the challenges, he felt that the guys were pleased with the day. A simple thank you note. I had never received a thank you note from a bishop before. That he would take the time to do so was more impressive than the words themselves.

The voice of Jesus: acts of humble service, in simple, often bad surroundings, catching the attention of lots of people. Not much talking. As *America* magazine editor Fr. Matt Malone says, "…the goal of Christian living is not to be right, but to be holy. The goal is not to *possess* the truth but to be possessed by the one who *is* truth, the one who is the way, the truth, and the life." Listen, look, love. Hear the voice of Jesus and smile. He's calling *you*.

Drawn to Jesus

Scripture Referenced: John 6:41-51

> No one can come to me unless the Father who sent me draw him, and I will raise him on the last day.

Have you ever had a deep sense of frustration, anger, and depression in your life? All at the same time? Perhaps it was the loss of a job, or a loved one. Perhaps it was a grand project that you really believed in, that you hoped for and strived for and came up short? The Olympic Games we are now watching in all of their tape-delayed glory show us athletes who fall into this category, and their tears and angst at losing strikes us with a poignancy that makes the Games such compelling theater. We smile with the victor and weep with the loser.

Our friend Elijah the prophet is one very depressed man as we read in today's first offering from the book of Kings. Some context is important here. Elijah is on the run, fearing for his life. Prior to today's episode, he has just vanquished the false prophets of Baal in an unlikely duel of my God is better than your god. You may remember the story. Both sides sacrifice a bull and the contest is simple. Whoever gets their god to send down fire from heaven on to the sacrificial offering wins. The 450 prophets of Baal dance and scream and jump up and down and nothing happens. Elijah, supremely confident, first soaks his bull with water and adds gallons more to a moat around the altar. With a simple appeal to God, lightning strikes the altar from on high, turning the bull and water into beef stew. As was customary in those times, the losers pay the ultimate price – all 450 prophets of Baal are slain immediately. But the king's wife, Jezebel, is infuriated at these actions and calls for Elijah's arrest. He heads for the desert, fed up with the impossible situation. What should have been a glorious victory has turned into an ignominious retreat. His words say it all: "This is enough, O Lord! Take my life…"

Does God oblige Elijah by zapping him? Nope. God does the exact opposite. Through the ministration of an angel, God provides food and water for the journey. The journey to where? Did you catch the destination? Yes, to the mountain of God in Horeb; that is, the very mountain where Moses received the covenant. God has provided food for Elijah's long journey to Himself – is that beginning to resonate with you a little bit?

Each of us is on this journey, aren't we? We begin our lives as young adults, full of optimism and energy, hopes and expectations. Some of us go into work right away, others to college and beyond. Still others enter the armed forces or travel the world for a time, seeking our path. I took the education route myself, and I distinctly recall that when I finally left graduate school, I felt that I was way behind my peers in the all-important goals of prestige, power, and possessions. I didn't think of it specifically in that way, I'm sure, but in essence, I bought into the big lie that happiness lies in what you own, who you own, and how much you own.

As these apparent roads to happiness prove false, a journey that may take many years to uncover, especially if you're "successful", it is not uncommon to begin wondering what is going on, why is happiness so elusive, why is stress my most common life companion? If you're in that place now, I want to tell you that you are very fortunate – because you're starting to wake up. If you've already made that discovery, you're nodding your head and smiling, because you know I'm speaking the truth. If you're not there yet, you've already tuned me out.

So, let me speak to you who are in this place of discernment, this desert, much like our heroic, yet misguided friend, Elijah. Jesus says in the gospel today that no one can come to me unless the Father *draws* him. The word "draws" here seems a bit too weak to me. I think God pulls us, yanks us, bumps us, shoves us, and hounds us. But like Elijah, we don't want to hear it. Why not? Lots of reasons – here are a few:

- We look for miracles and when they don't come as expected, we are disappointed that we still have a mess on our hands
- Since we don't look for God in our everyday lives, He seems invisible
- We have our plan and we want God to work within our plan
- We are afraid of what might happen if we really let God into our lives

It's time to let go. It's time to take some food for the journey, offered every day of the week and four times on Sunday, and head for the mountain of God. What does that journey look like? Well, your mileage my vary, but typically, people who embrace this journey are characterized as follows (and I'd like to thank Fr. Anthony Gittins for inspiring this list):

- People on this journey go looking for trouble, for troubled people, just like Jesus did
- They pray for awareness, to be *disturbed*, so that they hear the cries of the poor and see the structures of sin that permeate our society
- They ignore false borders of country, religion, race, gender, and privilege
- They know that God is relying on them as much as they rely on God
- And oh yes, lest I forget, they live exciting and worthwhile lives!

Listen again to the words of Jesus:

- It is written in the prophets: they shall be taught by God
- Everyone who listens to my Father and learns from Him comes to me
- Whoever believes (note present tense) has eternal life
- Whoever eats this bread (this living bread) will likewise live forever

Now lest we get too Pollyannaish (is that a word?), understand that Elijah still had to walk 40 days through the desert to reach the mountain of God. That couldn't have been much fun. People who embrace the journey to God are not guaranteed lives of peace. But there is a big difference just the same. People who hand over their lives to Christ have a resilience, an assured quality that is quite remarkable. They accept life's challenges with an equanimity and confidence that is startling at times. Let me give you an example. A friend of mine was told in early June that he would be losing his job at the end of the month. I commiserated with him, of course, and he said (as I knew he would) that it was fine because like everything else, God was in this situation as well. Then he really surprised me. He told me that he was boosting the amount of money he was giving to the Church because he knew that the next job would be even better than this one. I heard from him last week. He was unemployed for exactly two weeks and his new job? He's making more money. He's not only on the road – he's approaching the mountain of God.

Will I See Jesus Today?

Scripture Referenced: Matthew 2:1-12

> And behold, the star that they had seen at its rising preceded them, until it came and stopped over the place where the child was. They were overjoyed at seeing the star, and on entering the house they saw the child with Mary his mother. They prostrated themselves and did him homage.

A few years ago, I and about 45 other people boarded a bus to go to the Coachella Valley and minister to a large community of very poor migrant workers. This area a little south and east of Palm Springs is their winter headquarters as they wait for the crops to mature up north in the San Joaquin valley. It's a very hard life, and most of these families may make $10,000 per year if they're lucky. As we prepared to head out that morning, I remember thinking, "I wonder if I'll see Jesus today?" It's really not that crazy a question. I know that Jesus is particularly present in the poor and downtrodden of our world, and I have certainly met Jesus in other situations, notably our prison system. So that thought entered my head and teased me a bit as we boarded the bus. I wonder if I'll see Jesus today.

The Magi we read about in today's Gospel must have had a similar thought. They didn't know about Jesus, of course, but they were aware from their astrological studies that the appearance of a new star in the heavens predicted the birth of a king. So their thought was probably, "I wonder if we'll find this king?"

In seeking a metaphor for the spiritual life, many of our great mystics and authors use the term "journey" or "pilgrimage" to describe the movement from spiritual darkness to dawning light. Did you ever notice how many popular works of fiction feature a quest? Our imaginations are continually fired up by people who achieve a lofty goal, whether it's climbing a mountain or overcoming a physical malady or getting that college degree at an advanced age. This restless yearning and struggle to better ourselves and our families is from the same root, the desire to beat down anxiety, push back evil, and find a measure of peace in our lives. This feast of the Epiphany, so often misunderstood, is the feast that celebrates the quest, the journey to enlightenment.

The Magi begin their journey. They consult their libraries and come to the proposition that Judea is the source of this new king who is heralded by the star. They act, they move, they take some chances, they risk ridicule, and they obey the yearning in their heart. On reaching Jerusalem, they realize that they are close and unlike most men, they stop and ask for directions! In doing so, they clearly upset King Herod and all Jerusalem by extension. Understand that Herod is near the end of his 40 year reign and has become an increasingly fearful and vengeful king. If a powerful and paranoid king is threatened, we are not at all surprised that the people are quaking in their sandals. Herod calls in his priests and scribes and hears the prophecy repeated. In his fear, in his grasping, Herod hatches a plot to discover this new king and destroy him.

When we reached the Coachella Valley and stopped our bus in a large vacant lot, we were astonished to see over 400 people queued up, patiently awaiting whatever we could provide them. We scrambled out, quickly unloaded the bus, and then each of us accompanied a family through and around the tables loaded with clothes, blankets, food, and toiletries that we had brought. It was a simple, heartwarming activity, the moms grateful, the little kids excitedly picking out a new pair of sneakers, no one pushing or shoving. As the day wore on, more people showed up, and the line seemed to go on endlessly. But everyone got something. Somehow, there was enough.

Back in Jerusalem, oddly enough it seems, the Magi get good information from the scribes and move on to Bethlehem, finally arriving at the place where Jesus, Mary, and Joseph are camped. We're not told exactly how, but somehow they recognize Christ the King in this little baby. How remarkable! These learned men, so well educated, so honored, so upper class, have discovered through the grace of God that the prince of peace is a baby lying in a feeding trough, a manger. Recognizing the gift given to them, the Magi, we are told, lay down on the muddy ground in a gesture of utter humility, and give of *their* treasure.

As the line in Coachella finally wound itself down, a man walked up. He was dressed in the typical migrant worker outfit – jeans, boots, a warm coat, a straw cowboy hat. His face was brown and lined from many hours in the sun, and he looked tired. I know a very few words of Spanish, so when he came up to us, I put out my hand, and said, "Como estas? Me llamo Pedro." He broke into a huge grin, shook my hand warmly and said, "Muy bueno! Me llamo Jesus." Now, I know as well as you do that the name Jesus is fairly common in the Hispanic culture, but I was still a bit startled. So we got Jesus a blanket and some food, and off he went. I could have sworn I heard God chuckling…

So what's it all about? The journey to enlightenment is a wide open road – all we need to do is to embark on the journey. What will you find? Well, just like the Magi:

- Look for the unexpected, look for the invitation, look for the interruption --maybe you'll hear it or see it today
- Seek the truth wherever it may take you
- You may meet hostility, indifference, and evil along the way
- Listen for truth even amongst those who seem to have a very different agenda
- Bring your gifts to the search
- When you find truth, be not surprised by its simplicity and profound depth
- When you find truth, you will be compelled to share your gifts to spread the truth

If you read the lives of many of our saints, you will see this journey lived out in vivid detail. Read the life of St. Augustine, read the life of St. Francis, read the life of St. Ignatius, read the life of Mother Teresa. Even though they are saints, their journey is our journey. We honor them for their humility and honesty.

What you will discover is that the revelation that they arrive at is each uniquely their own, tailored to their lives and circumstances. You will see this as well. Your understanding of the truth is ultimately part of who you are, the inner being that God knows and cherishes.

Would you like to know the one common denominator, the key element among those who find revelation, both then and now? The path is always through Christ Jesus. Always.

Chapter 5 – Faith

I think you'd all agree that faith is somehow important to the spiritual journey, right? But what is faith? Yes, it's a virtue, like hope and charity. Is that all? Many good Catholics equate faith with the teachings of the Church; after all, it is called the *Catholic faith.* But Jesus seems to have a very different idea in mind. Jesus makes a firm connection between one's faith and the ability to be healed. Over and over again, he completes a requested healing with the cryptic statement, "Your faith has saved you."

Maybe faith has little to do with what you believe, and a lot to do with what you hope for, what you expect, despite contrary evidence. In fact, I think faith is so tightly wound up in the other virtues of hope and charity that it is sometimes hard to see one for the other. Faith is important, absolutely, and worth diving into the mystery.

Stop, Look, Listen

Scripture Referenced: Matthew 1:18-24

> All this took place to fulfill what the Lord had said through the prophet: Behold, the virgin shall conceive and bear a son, and they shall call him Emmanuel, which means "God is with us." When Joseph awoke, he did as the angel of the Lord had commanded him and took his wife into his home.

When we hear the story of the birth of Jesus, we usually hear the version from St. Luke's gospel. The long journey to Bethlehem, no room at the inn, a baby in a manger, angels singing, and shepherds gawking, are all from Luke. As befits most of Luke's gospel, a woman takes center stage, a woman named Mary, who is remarkably receptive to these amazing events. In Matthew's gospel, however, in keeping with what his Jewish audience expects, we get the male perspective. In addition, as we will see throughout Matthew's gospel, a specific connection is made to an Old Testament prophet. One of Matthew's agenda items is to prove to this Jewish audience that Jesus is the foretold messiah. So here we go, right from the start.

The Old Testament prophet that Matthew uses for this first link is, no surprise, *Isaiah*. Isaiah is actually three different people, writing over a span of 200 plus years, from roughly 740 BC to 500 BC. The reading we hear today is from "first Isaiah", and takes place in Jerusalem. King Ahaz is in a pickle, trying to figure out how to keep his kingdom from being overrun by the Assyrians. Ahaz turns to his prophet, Isaiah, for advice, and Isaiah gives him a simple answer – ask God for a sign. But Ahaz lacks faith and refuses to turn to the Lord, afraid to ask, afraid of what the answer might be, afraid of losing his authority. You know that expression, "be careful what you ask for." That's Ahaz. Completely exasperated, Isaiah gives him the sign anyway: the virgin shall conceive, and bear a son, and shall name him Emmanuel.

Did the prophecy come true? Yes, as a matter of fact, it did. Ahaz's new wife, who was of course a virgin when she married Ahaz, became pregnant, bore a son, named him Emmanuel, and he grew up to become the next king of Israel. The Assyrians were thwarted from overrunning Jerusalem, and everything worked out as Isaiah said it would. (pause) But, wait a minute. Wasn't Isaiah referring to Jesus? Well, no – not in a literal sense. Isaiah's intent was not to foretell the coming of Jesus. But from *Matthew's* point of view, Isaiah's prophecy was clearly pointing to Jesus. Matthew, with the knowledge and understanding of Jesus the Messiah, had no problem looking back into this wealth of God-knowledge called the Jewish scripture, and identifying the evidence of Jesus coming, over 700 years earlier. It's as if he had a giant search beacon in his hands, and turned it back to the past to see what glistened in the muddy road behind him. And he saw gold nuggets! Keep an eye out for these gold nuggets as we walk with Matthew this year. There's many to be found.

But let's go back to Joseph. Here he is, a righteous Jewish man of the times, well-respected in his community, and betrothed to a woman of the village named Mary. Now understand that this was probably an arranged marriage, and some traditions suggest that Joseph was a widower. Although the Bible does not confirm this, it would make sense on a practical level. If Joseph had children from a first marriage, he would naturally seek a new wife to help out. It would also explain the reference to Jesus' brothers and sisters, and further account for the apparent fact that Joseph died well before Mary did, indicating that he may have been many years older. This is all speculation, but it also helps to explain how Joseph handled the shocking news that his fiancée was pregnant. I suspect that a younger man might have been a little less calm about the whole thing! Joseph, however, ponders the situation carefully, and because he is a compassionate man, decides to divorce her quietly and allow her to leave the village and have the baby in another town that doesn't know the story. After all, Joseph was well aware of the penalty for adultery. Death by stoning.

But now something amazing happens. Joseph hears an angel in his dreams, an angel that gives him some very startling explanations, and asks him to do the exact opposite of what he intended. Not only does Joseph listen, he takes the message to heart, and changes his plan. In doing so, Joseph demonstrates two of the key characteristics of the spiritual masters. First of all, he had a well-tuned awareness of God's voice. He could discern truth from lies, clarity from confusion, and light from darkness. Secondly, Joseph understood implicitly that awareness does not equate to comfortable outcomes. His culture, his religion, is very manhood demanded that he abandon this girl to her fate. No one would have blamed him. Instead, he bet it all on the words of an angel in a dream. Compare Joseph to King Ahaz from the first reading. Awareness vs. fog. Confidence vs. fear. Action vs. inaction. Joseph the carpenter vs. Ahaz the king. Which one do we revere to this day?

How can we develop the awareness and faith of Joseph? Let me give you a simple memory aid that has helped me over the years. When you approach a railroad crossing, there's often present there a simple sign in the shape of an "X" with three words on it. Can you see those three words? *Stop. Look. Listen.* They're meant to keep you from getting clobbered by the Chattanooga Choo-Choo. But they're also the keys to developing a practice of spiritual awareness!

Stop! You need to find time every day where you consciously cease the buzzing activity and simply be at rest. And no, bedtime does not count. The monks in the abbey get together five times a day to stop and pray. The prayer is rarely longer than 15 minutes, but it is predictable and devoted to God. Stop.

Look! As one theologian put it, God comes to us disguised as our life. Fortunately, God is lousy at hiding. He is there in the beauty of the sunrise, the ethereal mist of a foggy field at dusk, the smile of a child, the caress of a lover, the sound of a bird or a Beethoven concerto. God is present in everything. Look.

Listen! The voice of God is speaking at all times in our hearts. If we're living a life of dissipation, as the Prodigal Son did, that voice urges us to change, to turn around, often annoying our little egos. If we're living a life of discernment, that voice will insistently call us to our best selves. If we're living a life of spiritual awareness, that voice is consoling and challenging at the same time, acknowledging God's love for us and asking us to share the news with this person and that person who walk in darkness. Listen.

Advent ends in 5 days. These next five days may be some of the busiest of the year for us. Don't succumb to the madness. Take a bit of each day and stop, look, and listen. Truly look at your surroundings. Listen to the small, still whisper as Elijah did in the mountains. And in the spirit of St. Joseph, I offer one last piece of advice. Pay attention to your dreams.

Don't You Care?

Scripture Referenced: Mark 4:35-41

> A violent squall came up and waves were breaking over the boat, so that is was already filling up. Jesus was in the stern, asleep on a cushion. They woke him and said to him, "Teacher, do you not care that we are perishing?"

When I was about 12 years old, my father surprised us one day with the announcement that he had bought a sailboat. Now don't get the wrong idea. We lived on a lake in upstate New York, and although there were some nice sailboats, most were small, not much more than 14-18 feet long. Well, the sailboat my Dad bought was a little 6-foot dinghy, with one sail, a rudder and a centerboard. It was as basic as you could get, and although utterly unimpressive, I was smitten. None of us knew a thing about sailing, and the first time we set off, just my Dad and me, the wind promptly pushed us backward down the lake, the sail flapping madly, as the whole family raced along the shore shouting unhelpful advice. A mile later, we pulled out the oars and rowed the boat all the way back to the beach, a bit embarrassed, but determined to figure it out. Which we did, sort of.

A few weeks later, I took the boat out on the lake by myself, feeling quite confident in my ability to master the elements. I was doing quite well, especially as the wind grew stronger in the late afternoon, and then I headed back toward the shore. What I didn't realize is that the wind had shifted - it was now blowing directly from the shore out to the lake. As most of you know, I'm sure, you can't sail a boat directly into the wind. The best you can do is to sail at a 45 degree angle, tacking back and forth as you make your way. I was too inexperienced to fully understand this technique, and as you can guess, in a very short while, I was quite frustrated and a little scared. I could see the family on shore, eating dinner, occasionally waving at me to come in, me waving back. But it was a good hour before someone on the shore finally figured out that I was in trouble.

I always think of that incident when I read today's Gospel. Almost every commentator will focus on Jesus calming the sea and rebuking the wind, showing his divine mastery over the elements of nature. But to me, the key line in the reading is the plaintive question the apostles ask Jesus. *Teacher, do you not care that we are perishing?* This is a nice translation. I'll bet the question was a bit more pointed and panicky than that, something like, "Hey, I thought you loved us. This is a serious mess we're in! Don't you care?!" Do you hear the rebuke in that statement? It's one of the most authentic and honest questions the apostles ask Jesus. And let's face it, I'll bet every one of us has had those same words come out of our mouth at some time in our life. If not, you will, believe me. Hey, God, it's me. I'm in a real jam and I see no solution. Don't you care?

As I drifted a half mile off the shore, my sail flapping ineffectively, a man set out from shore in his own little sailboat and headed in my direction. As he was sailing with the wind, it took him only a few minutes to reach me. At this point, tired, hungry and wet, I was ready to abandon ship and hop in his boat, but something held me back. He looked at me across the water, smiled, and said, "Follow me." He set his sail, waited for me to mimic him, and off we went, not directly toward the shore, but at an angle. We zig-zagged in, getting closer with each tack, until finally we reached calm water and the shore. I was never happier to get off that boat and accept a welcoming hot dog.

Note what Jesus says to the apostles after he calms the storm. Why? Why are you afraid? Where's your faith? These are embarrassing questions. Grace is like this. You can always tell when God gives us some unexpected grace – it usually hits us right in our ego. Have you ever pre-judged someone and thought, wow, there's a real loser. Then, before you know it, someone else introduces you to that same person, and lo and behold, they're actually pretty nice, and you have that sense of shame and dismay? That's grace in action. People are deeper and more complex than we realize, and Jesus speaks through them to us over and over. It is typically through people that God tosses us that life line.

But let's face it. Sometimes life does throw us for a loop. A careful plan, poof. A job we felt secure in – gone. A loved parent or grandparent – heart attack. A child, sick. The worst of it is when something we've grown to rely on, something we take for granted, is suddenly taken away or is put in serious jeopardy. We're bewildered and feel alone, and God seems miles away. Someone says something about God's presence in our pain and we react angrily. Sure, where is God? I've been told he loves us, and yet, here I am in this big mess. He doesn't really care. If he did, he'd fix this.

A man is walking along the edge of a cliff and the ground breaks away. Flailing his arms as he slips off the cliff, he somehow is able to grab a tree root and hang on for dear life. He cries for help and no one answers. Finally, in desperation, his arms weakening, he cries out, "God, if you're up there, save me!" To his amazement, a voice comes down from the heavens. "It's okay! Just let go! I'll save you!" The man looks down, looks around, looks up, and calls out, "Is there anyone else up there?"

The point, of course, is that help comes from unexpected directions and often pushes us into uncomfortable solutions, solutions that are so uncomfortable that we'd rather not follow through. So we complain some more. Just as my only path to the shore was by a zigzag route, which I simply couldn't see how to do, maybe your solution is just as counterintuitive. Just as I needed someone to come out and say *follow me*, perhaps someone is saying that exact same thing to you right now. The only question is, do you have the faith?

The story of Job is a story of faith. Our first reading is taken from the end of that disturbing story. Job has experienced one crisis after another, each one more devastating than the last, until finally he is reduced to a shell of a human being, sitting on a heap of trash, insisting to his friends that he is not giving up on God. But even Job has his limits and he finally confronts God with words of anger and despair. And God gives it right back, as we read today, basically telling Job, "Who do you think I am? Do you control the universe? Were you there when it was all made?" You can hear the words of Jesus being echoed, "Where is your faith?" Having made his point, God immediately restores to Job his life and happiness, with more abundance than before.

This is the point of faith. God is always looking to better our life, not worsen it. But "better" is from God's perspective, not ours. Faith is simply the trust that whatever this path, even if it appears to be crazy or impossible, will actually better our lives in a measurable way. Try saying yes next time. Even if our gut is crying out, "Is there anyone else up there?" Just say yes.

With a Little Help From My Friends

Scripture Referenced: Mark 2:1-12

> They came bringing to him a paralytic carried by four men. Unable to get near Jesus because of the crowd, they opened up the roof above him. After they had broken through, they let down the mat on which the paralytic was lying. When Jesus saw their faith, he said to the paralytic, "Child, your sins are forgiven."

Every time I read this gospel, I think of the Beatles' song, "With a Little Help From My Friends". Jesus is preaching the Word to the crowds in the house, and to everyone's surprise, the roof tiles are suddenly being removed, and here comes a pallet lowered from the roof with a paralyzed man on board. It must have caused quite a ruckus. The gospel carefully notes Jesus' reaction: he "saw *their* faith". So here's a key question for this reading: who is displaying faith here? Is it the paralytic? Or his friends? I think it's his friends, don't you? Because Jesus quickly tells the paralytic that his sins are forgiven. That's a very odd statement unless the paralytic needed to be forgiven. What sin could a paralytic commit? Oh, here's a few: anger, despair, cynicism, bitterness, hardness of heart. This guy needed forgiveness, needed healing in his heart, and Jesus saw that instantly, saw that *sin* was killing this man, not his paralysis. Jesus knows that the heart is what rules the man, not the body. However, Jesus almost casually tosses in the physical healing as well, to make a point to the crowd that He is Lord of the heart *and* the body, make no mistake.

But let's return to the man's friends. What was their motivation in all of this? What prompted them to perform such an action, very close to heroic? All of us are moved to perform acts of generosity, but it's a safe bet to say that in deciding whether or not to give of our time, talent, and treasure, we go through a mental calculus to assess just how much we should give. Some of the most important factors: proximity, importance, and impact.

1. Proximity – is the need local? The closer the issue is to my home town, the more likely I am to respond. Seeing the need firsthand is a powerful influence on our propensity to give. Fr. John will tell you that people respond to a specific need with amazing speed. People want to be able to say, "I fixed that, right there!"
2. Is the need serious? Are people in really big trouble? Especially people I can identify with? This is why everyone rallies around when a huge natural disaster occurs somewhere in the world, especially a tsunami or an earthquake. Living where we do, we can relate to the danger of both types of disaster.
3. Will my generous act make a difference? Especially a difference I can see? This is why people who volunteer of their time and talent are generally much happier with their generous action than someone who simply gives money. Diving into a problem area often provides immediate feedback. There's nothing like the smile of a grateful receiver to reward a giving individual.

There are two causes that I'm bringing before you today that force us to consider these exact calculations in our minds. The first is the Annual Catholic Appeal, and the second is Operation Rice Bowl. These two causes represent very different points on the spectrum of giving, so let's see how we might look at each of them.

So, the first screen we use – is the need local? Clearly, the Annual Catholic Appeal is local – all monies go directly to our local Diocese for a number of ongoing programs:

- Catholic Charities, our primary diocesan social service agency
- Priestly and Religious Vocations - ongoing prayer and financial support in promoting vocations to the priesthood and religious life and in the formation of candidates.
- Parishes and Schools in Need- Some of our parishes and parochial schools struggle financially and need our assistance to provide basic facilities and programs.
- Marriage and Family Life - assisting parishes in providing good programs of preparation for marriage and family enrichment.

- Youth and Young Adults - attempting to offset the negative influences that bombard our youth and young adults today by offering programs that will promote their human and spiritual growth and development.
- Religious Education - to offer culturally sensitive evangelization and systematic catechesis to all Catholics, whether children, youth or adults, and to reach out to those interested in becoming Catholics.

In the scheme of things, we have an extremely well-run diocese. It is fiscally conservative, with well-qualified individuals serving at salaries often far below market levels. Over the past 20 years, I've gotten to know many diocesan staff members, and I can tell you that these people care a lot about how their actions affect the people of San Diego.

Operation Rice Bowl, on the other hand, is not local at all. ORB money goes to overseas needs under the auspices of Catholic Relief Services. Like many of you, I worry about funds going overseas. We hear horror stories of corruption and bribery, with visions of some dictator using our money for a water bed rather than a water well. So we need to dig a little deeper (if you'll excuse the ongoing analogy). CRS is really an amazing organization, one of the Catholic Church's best kept secrets. One program that CRS operates that has proven remarkably effective is micro loans. For what to us is an amazingly low sum of money, CRS helps very poor people (70% of whom are women) to launch and sustain a livelihood. For example, a $50 loan allows a woman to buy a sewing machine that she uses to make colorful blouses for the local market. She pays back the loan pennies at a time, but meanwhile she's in charge of her fate. Did you know that nearly 98% of micro loans are paid back?

Closer to home, CRS helped a Mexican family purchase apple tree seedlings to start an orchard on their land. The apples provide a second crop that supplements the meager corn crop that the family lived on and most importantly, allowed them to stay on their land. The alternative was to sell the land and seek employment elsewhere – and we all know what that often means.

Operation Rice Bowl is clearly a more focused charity, and one that I also support, but in a different way from the Annual Catholic Appeal. It's no accident that Rice Bowl is a Lenten program. The point is to remind us of the needs of our brothers and sisters throughout the world as we embark on our personal tasks of prayer, fasting, and almsgiving. A simple way to view Rice Bowl is to give up something of our excess, something to share. Put the little box in a prominent place in your house, and throw in a coin or two each day. It's a great kids activity as well, but keep an eye on it. Last year, when the boxes were turned in, we were amused to find all sorts of things in those little boxes – buttons, pins, sticks of chewing gum, pesos, and of course, guilty $20 bills! All were put to good use!

There's little doubt that these two charities are important – many people are affected in direct ways and the impact can be enormous. I personally stand before you, grateful that parishioners across the diocese gave generously to the Annual Catholic Appeal during the years from 2001 to 2006. Those were my diaconate formation years, and I couldn't have become a deacon without that help. In a similar way, a poor village in Africa can have a well dug for mere hundreds of dollars – CRS uses money very, very efficiently.

It's easy to get discouraged or cynical about the constant requests for money. I only ask that you think about today's gospel. Jesus was impressed by the persistent and innovative friends of the paralytic. Did they really think that Jesus would come through in such a spectacular fashion? Whether they did or not, they at least *tried.* We need to keep trying too! Thanks for whatever you can give. You sure as heck always impress me!

Faith Needs Hope

Scripture Referenced: Mark 10:46-52

> So they called the blind man, saying to him, "Take courage; get up, Jesus is calling you." He threw aside his cloak, sprang up, and came to Jesus. Jesus said to him in reply, "What do you want me to do for you?" The blind man replied to him, "Master, I want to see." Jesus told him, "Go your way; your faith has saved you." Immediately he received his sight and followed him on the way.

As our year of Mark draws to a close, we hear the simple story of Jesus and the blind beggar. Many times in the Gospel we hear of Jesus healing people, but rarely are they named. In today's Gospel, we know precisely who the blind beggar is – that guy, right there, Bartimaeus. You know him, he's the son of Timaeus. What moved Bartimaeus to call out to Jesus on that spring day in Jericho? Who knows? But call out he does, and he's annoying about it. People keep telling him to pipe down, but he keeps at it: "Son of David, have pity on me!" Finally, from amid the sizable crowd, Jesus hears him and stops. "Bring him over." Now the crowd decides to help out (illustrating how fickle the world is) and they tell Bartimaeus to hop to it, Jesus is calling. He comes to Jesus and what does Jesus say? "What do you want me to do for you?" Really? Jesus, isn't it obvious?

I was in the prison a few weeks ago for our Bible study session. We had 18 guys, about typical, and during the course of the evening, one of the guys, Michael, mentioned that his health had taken a bad turn. He was getting some medical attention, which is good, but we could tell that he was a little worried. Then another guy, John, told us that he too was having some health issues, but it was okay, he was coping just fine. Now it's not unusual for the guys in prison to suffer from a variety of ailments. Many of them had some serious drug addictions before entry, and prison is not exactly the best place to recuperate. In addition, with the poor diet and minimal care, fairly routine medical issues can blossom into full-blown problems. It happens. Anyway, at the end of the evening, I asked the two guys who had the medical complaints if they would like to be prayed over. Michael says yes enthusiastically. But the other guy, John, says *no*.

Our friend Bartimaeus doesn't hesitate in answering Jesus, does he? *Master, I want to see.* And Jesus heals him immediately. But note how Jesus heals him. He doesn't spit on the ground and make paste, nor does he lay hands on Bartimaeus, nor does he groan out loud to His Father in heaven. His words are almost dismissive. *Go your way; your faith has saved you.* Apparently, Bartimaeus has so much faith that Jesus' actions are minimal! All Jesus needs to do is initial the memo, enter the password, provide a thumb print – it's done. Bartimaeus can see!

Back at the prison, we all gather around Michael and lay hands on him. We pray for his healing, calling upon the power of the Holy Spirit, and he's visibly moved. He sheds a tear, thanks us, and goes on his way. I turn to another inmate, Barry, and ask him why John didn't want to be prayed over. Barry smiles ruefully. "Oh, that's easy," he says. "If you pray over John, you'll give him hope. And hope is a very dangerous thing to have here in prison. Hope can kill you." Barry went on to explain that the most dangerous time for an inmate is when he is up for parole. Despite his efforts, he can't help but hope for release, and more often than not, parole is not granted. Why not? Because the parole board contacts the crime victims and asks for their opinion. Not surprisingly, many victims cannot forgive that long ago crime, no matter what. It's understandable, yes sad, but understandable. May you never be put in such a position. But the reality is that inmate suicides spike after negative parole hearings. Hope can kill you.

I used to think that faith and hope were totally different virtues. I'm not so sure anymore. We've been reading from the letter to the Hebrews these past few weeks, and there's a wonderful phrase at the beginning of Chapter 11. *Faith is the realization of what is hoped for and evidence of things not seen.* Note the tight relationship between faith and hope. You could almost retranslate this to say that faith is the *expectation* of your highest hopes. Bartimaeus' highest hope was to see. And his expectation was so strong that he was willing to make a fool out of himself and scream Jesus' name out loud again and again, despite the shushing of the crowd. Jesus is practically a bystander to the resultant healing. Faith is hope on steroids.

What are *you* hoping for? Healing from a long illness? A new job? A reconciled relationship? A baby? Perhaps you want to be married. Perhaps you'd like to retire soon but are worried about money. Perhaps you'd like your children to come back to the Church. Perhaps you simply want to get through the school year. How do these hopes become faith?

1. Pray to God about your hopes. Are these hopes reasonable? Better yet, are they good for you and others in an objective way?
2. Do you feel like you're fighting God to see these hopes realized? God might indeed have a better plan in mind. Can you accept that?
3. Is your hope being met in small ways already? Are there little indications that God is already on the job?
4. And don't forget love. As St. Paul tells us, in the end, faith, hope and love will remain, but the greatest of these is *love*. If your hope is expressed through the lens of love, I can think of no better recipe for great faith, for love never fails.

Here's an example. You're hoping that your child finds God in their life. So is this hope good for you and for your child? I think it qualifies, yes! Do you feel like you're fighting God to see this hope realized? Maybe you're insisting that your child come to God the same way you did. Can you let God do the hard work here and not try to force it? Are you beginning to see signs that your child is recognizing God in their life? It may be very subtle, like a plant poking up through the soil, but there it is. And finally, are you loving your child through it all? Through the bad choices and missteps and face plants? This is how expectations grow and that little hope becomes more and more confident until you can say, "I believe that my child will know God!"

Last week, I was back in the prison and I ran across Barry. He had a grin on his face. I said, "Barry, what's up? You seem quite chipper." He said, "I was given a parole hearing date today." "But I thought you were a lifer," I said. He smiled sardonically and said, "I'm 68 years old. They don't want to take care of me anymore. I'm getting expensive." "Well, Barry," I said, "I'll certainly pray for you." He nodded. "Yeah," he said, "please do. I'm starting to hope."

Never. Lose. Hope.

One Yes at a Time

Scripture Referenced: Luke 5:1-11

> When Simon Peter saw this, he fell at the knees of Jesus and said, "Depart from me, Lord, for I am a sinful man." Jesus said to Simon, "Do not be afraid; from now on you will be catching men." When they brought their boats to the shore, they left everything and followed him.

Whom shall I send? Who will go for us? These two brief questions, nine words in all, rank high on the list of life-changers – full of potential, full of risk, full of dread. Note that they are different questions. Whom shall *I* send – God is looking for a volunteer that will have God's full backing – yikes! Who will go for us? This person is not simply doing this for God, he's doing this for everyone! God wants a hero, it seems. Are you feeling heroic today?

We took up the theme of "the call" last week with Jeremiah's account of his dawning awareness of being chosen as God's prophet. Today we hear about Isaiah's call, a vision of great power and dramatic scenes that call to mind the book of Revelation. On a parallel track, we have the Gospel readings for the past 3 weeks featuring the early days of Jesus' ministry, starting with his awareness that he is destined to bring glad tidings to the poor, liberty to captives, and sight to the blind. The people of Nazareth reject Jesus so he moves on to Capernaum and begins his ministry of healing and teaching, culminating with the call of Simon and his companions. Jesus moves from being called to doing the calling.

Have you ever been called by God? Don't answer too quickly. It rarely comes as a dramatic vision such as our friend Isaiah experienced. It usually comes as a request. The first one that I remember happened over 30 years ago. I was living in Massachusetts and one Sunday after Mass (I was the lector – my first and favorite ministry), I was chatting with the pastor in the sacristy. The director of religious education came in and told the pastor that he was short two teachers for the upcoming year. He particularly needed a 7th grade teacher. Without missing a beat, the pastor turned to me and said, "How about you, Peter?"

If we look at the stories of Jeremiah, Isaiah, and Simon, we note some striking similarities. When each of them becomes aware that God is calling them, what is their first reaction? Do they leap for joy? High fives all around? Send out a few tweets? Not exactly. Jeremiah complains "I'm too young!" Isaiah moans, "I'm doomed!" Simon falls to his knees and says, "Depart from me, Lord, for I am a sinful man." Do you want to know what I said? I said, "Father, I'm not ready to do that!"

Do you think God gets exasperated? I know that pastors, religious ed directors, music ministers, homeless shelter directors, and virtually every other volunteer coordinator does. But God never seems to mind our reluctance. He simply keeps on coming. One of God's best follow-up lines is "Don't be afraid!" My translation is a little bit different – "Don't be such a chicken!" After all, God knows your weakness, knows that you are a sinful creature, knows that you are risk averse, knows that you are utterly unqualified. For some strange reason, God doesn't seem to want any credentials. He just wants a little cooperation. And God can be pretty persuasive.

God to Jeremiah: "Before I formed you in the womb, I knew you, before you were born, I dedicated you, a prophet to the nations I appointed you." "…I am with you to deliver you…"
God to Isaiah: "…your wickedness is removed, your sin purged."
Jesus to Simon: "Do not be afraid; from now on you will be catching men."
And what did the pastor say to me when I complained, "Father, I'm not ready to do that!"? He looked me hard in the eye and asked, "And when *will* you be ready?"

Jeremiah took up the challenge of being a prophet – a particularly difficult ministry because almost every one of Jeremiah's prophecies was bad news. He was not exactly a popular guy. Isaiah had an easier time of it, mostly because he was called to be a comfort to the Hebrew people as they suffered exile and slavery. And Simon? Well, you know his story pretty well, don't you? He became the foundation rock of our Christian faith, a flawed rock for sure, but God seems to prefer imperfect instruments to play his tune to the world. And what did I do? I went home from church and pondered the pastor's words, looking at who I was and what I claimed to be. I called the religious ed director that evening and volunteered to teach 7th grade CCD.

I don't know about you, but I'm always jarred by the last line of today's gospel: "When they brought their boats to the shore, *they left everything and followed him.*" These were hard working men with property and families – did that really happen? What does it take today for someone to make such a decision? I'll answer that question – it's rarely, if ever, that dramatic. Changing one's life direction is a series of decisions. You kind of get on a roll and the journey becomes a new life. Richard Rohr says it well. You don't *think* yourself into a new way of living, you *live* yourself into a new way of thinking! Action in the name of Christ inevitably leads to seeing the world as Christ sees it.

Did I become the greatest 7th grade CCD teacher in the history of that parish? Nope! I wasn't very good at it. I struggled for two years before I finally said to the pastor, "This is not for me." But here's the key. Sometimes a "wrong" ministry is just as important as a "right" ministry. Learning what your gifts are takes some experimentation. I learned that teaching pre-adolescents wasn't my gift, but I did discover that I enjoyed teaching, and I next volunteered to teach adults in RCIA. God simply nudged me in the next best direction, and that path was much more joyful. From RCIA, I went to prison work. From prison work, I went into the diaconate. To manage my desire to minister, I needed to cut down the hours on my job in the secular world. To leave everything and follow Jesus is an somewhat dramatic way of simply saying yes, one yes at a time.

We enter the season of Lent this week. I'm going to level a challenge on you. Rather than giving something up for Lent, I'd like you to say yes to an invitation from God. Be on the lookout – the invitation can come in many different ways. An email, an article in the newspaper, a call from a friend, an invitation to come and see, a bulletin announcement, a suggestion that will feel like swimming into deep water. God is subtle and persistent, and doesn't care a fig about your qualifications. He just wants a little help. No heroics necessary. Just a yes.

Chapter 6 – Christmas and Easter

The seasons of Advent, Christmas, Lent, and Easter make up a significant portion of our liturgical calendar. Plumbing the depth of meaning these seasons offer is always an exercise in listening, hoping, praying, and discernment. The fact that many readings are repeated every year makes for a particular challenge in finding new insight. Fortunately we are different each year and this is often the starting point for reflection. How do my present circumstances steer me to some new fruit on the same tree? Let's see…

Nefarious Characters

Scripture Referenced: Luke 3:1-6

> In the fifteenth year of the reign of Tiberias Caesar, when Pontius Pilate was governor of Judea, and Herod was tetrarch of Galilee, and his brother Philip tetrarch of the region of Ituraea and Trachonitis, and Lysanias was tetrarch of Abilene, during the high priesthood of Annas and Caiaphas, the word of God came to John the son of Zechariah in the desert.

As you are probably aware, we've moved from a focus on Mark's gospel to the gospel of Luke, long a favorite of mine and many others. Luke's account is beautifully written, with an emphasis on Jesus as a healer, a forgiver, a rule-breaker (in the best sense), a person who has no trouble associating with many of the marginalized groups of the time – lepers, prostitutes, tax collectors, and all kinds of broken people. However, before we get to Jesus, Luke feels compelled to do a little name dropping.

We're told that John the Baptist arrived on the scene "in the fifteenth year of the reign of Tiberias Caesar," which calculates to 29 AD. Tiberias was a great general in the Roman army and helped conquer much of northern Europe. He ruled from 14 AD until 37 AD, when upon his death at the age of 79, his great nephew Caligula took over. Tiberias was known as a dark, gloomy, reclusive individual and, to my surprise, he and I share the same birthday. Still getting my head around that one…

Now we move to the next person of significance in Luke's account, as he gets a bit more local, the Roman governor of Judea, the well-known Pontius Pilate. He served as governor, or prefect, from 26 to 36 AD. As governor of Judea, despite the grand title, Pilate did not have a lot of power. He was mostly responsible for collecting taxes and maintaining the Roman peace, especially in Jerusalem. He reported up to the legate of Syria, who had a substantial force of Roman soldiers at his command. Pilate comes across as a cowardly figure in the gospels, a man who would rather placate the crowds than set free an innocent person. But also understand that Pilate's first concern is his reputation, and the best reputation in Roman eyes is a quiet province. Executing an innocent man for the sake of peace is not a big leap for him.

Now we come to Herod, the tetrarch of Galilee (and Perea). During the period from 74 BC to 100 AD, there can be found evidence of seven King Herods throughout the region. The most famous was Herod the Great, who was responsible for building the great temple in Jerusalem. It is this Herod who, according to Matthew's gospel, slaughtered the innocent baby boys in Bethlehem. We're told that Joseph escaped with his family into Egypt and did not return until Herod had died shortly thereafter. The Herod mentioned here in Luke's gospel is the son of Herod the Great, born about 20 BC and died in 39 AD. His nickname was Antipas, and his title was "tetrarch" which means "ruler of a quarter".

The other three "quarters" were held by his brother Philip (also mentioned by Luke), as well as Salome, Herod the Great's sister, and Archelaus (tetrarch of Samaria, Judea, and Idumea). You can see that Jesus may have been under the influence of two Herods in his time, Antipas and Archelaus, but the gospels are clearly pointing at Antipas, probably because he ruled Galilee, where Jesus performed most of his ministry.

To round out the Roman appointed rulers, Luke mentions Lysanias, the tetrarch of Abilene, which believe me, is not the one in Texas. Abilene is thought to be a small region north of Palestine, about 20 miles from Damascus, Syria. It's unclear why Luke felt that he had to mention Lysanias, who has no role in Jesus' life, but remember what Luke is trying to do. At the time of his writing, perhaps 60-80 AD, Lysanias was a known historical figure, perhaps due to the writings of the Roman historian, Josephus. So Luke grabbed the reference as further validation of the historical reality of Jesus.

Finally, Luke gets down to the last two VIPs in the Palestine of 29 AD, the high priests Annas and Caiaphas. A high priest was appointed by the local prefect and had a very important, solemn role. On Yom Kippur, he alone entered the Holy of Holies to make atonement for his sins and all of the sins of the people. As there can only be one high priest at a time, understand that Annas came first. He was high priest from 6 to 15 AD. After a couple of years, the Roman governor appointed

Caiaphas, the son-in-law of Annas, who was high priest for the next 18 years, and played a pivotal role in the trial of Jesus. Caiaphas comes off very poorly in all of the gospels, and Dante depicts him in the sixth realm of the 8th circle of Hell, where hypocrites are eternally punished. Not a nice ending…

So, you're probably wondering, here I came for a homily and it looks like the History Channel broke out! What's going on? Recall the audience Luke is writing to – primarily Gentiles, very much a part of the Roman Empire, and likely a bit confused about the roots of this movement called "the way". Luke is making two points. As I mentioned previously, Luke uses these figures to establish the reality, the historicity of Jesus. These people are in public records – you can look it up. Caesar existed in a time and a place. So did Pilate and Herod and Annas and Caiaphas. Even if you've never heard of Jesus, you've probably heard of one these guys. Luke anchors Jesus in the world of first century Palestine.

Fr. John made the second point very nicely last weekend. Advent anticipates two events, the historical birth of Jesus into this world two thousand years ago and the hoped for arrival of Jesus at the end of the age. In the context of eternity, where time is meaningless, these two events are then, now, and in our future all at the same time. Luke is proclaiming a simple, profound message. In the caldron of history, in the midst of the overlapping rule of power-hungry, ruthless, cynical individuals, Jesus enters the world. His herald, John the Baptist, quotes the poetry of Isaiah: "*Prepare the way of the Lord, make straight his paths. Every valley shall be filled and every mountain and hill shall be made low. The winding roads shall be made straight, and the rough ways made smooth, and all flesh shall see the salvation of God.*"

Note the striking contrast. On the one hand, we have these powerful political leaders who maintain control over the known world of the time. On the other hand, we have John the Baptist, a weird looking guy from the desert quoting a long dead wise man. Who are you inclined to listen to? If there's one thing that God seems to love to do, it is to hide in the realm of the small and insignificant. This point is made by Luke over and over again, and nowhere more so than his infancy narratives. The stars of his story are wild men, ragged shepherds, a very poor but feisty young girl from a backwater town, and a baby born in a barn. You can't get much more unimportant. Who are you going to listen to?

The story of Jesus as told by Luke happened a long time ago, but the question is just the same today. Who are you going to listen to? We have plenty of politicians who are screeching to be heard. We have movie stars, sports heroes, musicians, and bloggers who measure their influence by how many Twitter followers they have. You can check out their "tweet level score". So many people clamoring to be heard. If you're paying attention to Luke's gospel, you'll know that God is NOT speaking through these folks, no more now than back then. Furthermore, ponder on the fact that to a great extent, each public figure cited by Luke is either an enemy of Jesus from birth, or is soon to become one. So where is God speaking today?

I'll tell you where. Syrian refugees, the unborn, men locked away and forgotten, migrant children with undocumented parents, AIDS patients, cold and wet homeless people, drug addicts, and the hungry, thirsty, naked, sick people among us. Are we listening to these insignificant people? Are we hearing the voice of God through them? Or are we caught in the big lie that power is important?

I don't mean to sound overly downbeat. Advent is actually a hopeful season. Just as Jesus came among us in a particular place and time under the rule of some nefarious characters, the reality is that we'll always have nefarious characters in power. It's unavoidable. Jesus still comes. Remember that. Jesus still comes. Put that in your tweet!

True Peace

Scripture Referenced: Luke 2:1-14

> The angel said to them, "Do not be afraid; for behold, I proclaim to you good news of great joy that will be for all the people. For today in the city of David a savior has been born for you who is Christ and Lord. And this will be a sign for you: you will find an infant wrapped in swaddling clothes and lying in a manger."

Last week, my family and I were in Hawaii taking some end-of-the-year rest and relaxation. So, before you start throwing fruit cakes at me, let me assure you that this was a bit unusual, and it certainly turned our Christmas traditions completely upside down. For those of you who have spent any time in a tropical climate in December, you know how jarring it is to see Christmas trees and ornaments while lounging on the beach, not to mention hearing Silver Bells over the hidden pool speakers. It forces us to take our pre-conceived notions of what Christmas should be, those cultural images of snow and cold and horse-drawn sleighs, and consider the holiday in a different light. It brought me to ponder what other unspoken assumptions I've gathered over the years that affect the meaning of Christmas for me personally, and whether these are good to hold onto.

With all of the emphasis on shopping and decorating and cards and party times, we sometimes slip into a sort of Christmas automatic pilot. The days count down, the tension rises, and suddenly, pow! It's Christmas Eve. Here we are, surrounded by greenery, the crèche on display, the familiar readings. It's all comforting, it's always the same, yet, aren't *we* different from last year? Each year layers on another ring of life, sometimes literally as our waist size attests, but more to the point, is the meaning of Christmas evolving with us? Or does it come from a dusty attic box ready to be put away again in less than a week? What assumptions do we blindly carry forth year over year? Let's look at a couple…

One assumption that we blindly accept is that Mary and Joseph gave birth to Jesus in a barn or a cave in awful conditions. Cultural historians have some doubts about this interpretation, and if you have ever visited the holy land, you can appreciate what the probable reality was. Most first century families lived in simple two story huts that were designed to maximize protection and shelter in the simplest possible way. The ground floor was dirt, probably covered with straw, and for all practical purposes, acted as a barn. The family's animals, sheep, goats, and donkeys, were brought into this room at night to protect the animals and provide warmth to the upper floor. A simple ladder provided access to the upper floor where the family slept and it was typical for the ladder to be hauled up at night when it was time for bed. This had the added benefit of an effective deterrent against robbers or thieves, sort of like raising the drawbridge.

If Mary and Joseph were gathering in Bethlehem, they most certainly would be looking to stay with relatives of "the house of David" when they arrived. If the house was full, an inn was a viable option, but lacking that, the family would have had Mary and Joseph bunk down with the animals on the first floor, an inconvenient, but natural accommodation. A woman in labor would have had a very difficult time going up a ladder as well, so in many ways, this was not necessarily a sign of rejection, but a simple solution. There was no room at the inn, so bunk down in the barn where it's warm and probably a bit more spacious. I'm not mentioning this to dash your assumptions about where Jesus was born, but to point out a different interpretation of the event.

Jesus was born to ordinary parents in ordinary circumstances. It appears that the Christ child would enter our reality not in kingly splendor, but in simple terms. This reality persists to today. We don't find the Christ in world leadership or political might, or in royal families. In fact, to the extent that we attempt to dictate the message of Christ through political and legal and financial centers of power, the more that message is tainted and discredited. The saddest chapters in our Church's history are the centuries when Christianity was a theo-political system. Ask yourself, when does Christianity catch the world's attention? When does the message resonate and sink in? When does the beacon of Christ seem to shine the brightest? There's a couple of guys named Francis that come to mind. The common thread? When the Church tosses off the trappings of power and wealth, when the Church stops asking what its members can do for it, when the Church starts with the poor and disenfranchised, then the world takes notice. The bottom line is this. When the Church enters into the ordinary lives of ordinary people with a message of hope and love, the Kingdom comes. Why do we get this wrong so often?

A second, most obvious assumption, perhaps, is the focus on the Christ child, with all of the maternal and paternal triggers that engenders. Is this feast really about a baby? Well, there's one sitting in the manger back here, so yes, I suppose it is. But let's go a bit deeper. The amazing truth about Christmas is not the baby, but the baby's Father, our almighty God. The subtitle of Christmas is quote "The Incarnation of The Lord" and that is a very amazing reality. Christianity is the only religion that teaches that God would deign to become fully human as a sign of solidarity and love. Other religions have gods coming down to earth, but the gods typically have mischief in mind, not salvation, and none of these gods give up their divine power on arrival. That we have a God that loves us that much is a profound truth of this day, for as John the Evangelist so aptly put it, "God so loved the world that he gave his only Son..."

God became powerless to reach out to us. In turn, through the powerlessness of God, can you see the path back to God? We need to stop the need to control, stop the need to dictate terms, stop the ego-centric focus on driving our own destiny. Can you begin to recognize that our only choice, our only path to ultimate happiness is to fall into the hands of the living God? This is what Jesus did over and over again. And never so much as at the moment of his greatest agony - into your hands I commend my spirit! Perhaps this is the prayer for Christmas this year - mimic the powerlessness of God, and just let it happen. How can we do this?

Take some time in the next couple of days to get some quiet moments with the Lord. Guys, peel yourselves away from the football games. Women, especially you Moms, hand yourself a gift from the kids and the cooking. Here's a radical thought – coordinate with your spouse so that no one feels taken advantage of. Take a walk around the block and just be with the Lord. No praying allowed! Just listen and let your heart do the talking. Let your disposition be one of obedience, which comes from the Latin word *obediere*, which means "to be open". A particular thought or idea may enter your consciousness after a while. I suggest that you ponder that idea over the course of the next few days and see where it leads you. If you realize that it will take you closer to the simple, everyday Jesus of this feast, then you're on an interesting track. If the idea scares you a bit, that's OK. Mary was certainly scared; Joseph was certainly scared, Jesus was so scared he sweated blood. God will work with you wherever you are right now. Be assured of that.

One of the paradoxical realities of the spiritual path is that *true peace* only comes our way when we give up the *apparent* freedom of self-reliance. Submitting to God allows the best of us to shine through, mostly because we remove the strain and tension of having to be God! That can be such a relief. God became human to show us what it is like to have this relationship – see how Jesus and the Father work together. It is truly a match made in heaven. You can have the same relationship. That's what Christmas introduces us into.

So, rather than Merry Christmas, I'm going to say, Mele Kalikimaka! That's Hawaiian for Merry Christmas. Either that or a volcano is about to erupt nearby. And don't forget, we have a gift for every family here tonight – make sure you grab one on the way out after Mass is ended. It may give you some ideas of what it means to live in the cooperative spirit of Christ this year.

Peace on earth, good will to all!

A Light Still Shining

Scripture Referenced: Luke 2:1-14

> And suddenly there was a multitude of the heavenly host with the angel, praising God and saying: "Glory to God in the highest and on earth peace to those on whom his favor rests."

Over two thousand years ago something interesting happened. It was simultaneously an act of simplicity – the birth of a child to a poor family in Palestine – and an act of profound importance, so important that the Western world reset its calendar to mark the event as a new beginning of time. We celebrate this event tonight, the birth of Jesus, and as is true of all God moments, there are many layers of depth to the meaning of this day.

The gospel account from Luke we just heard illustrates many of the subtleties of this feast, little details that can easily be missed. For example, note that Luke begins his story by referencing the emperor of the known world, Caesar Augustus, who unwittingly sets the wheels in motion to force Joseph and Mary to travel to Bethlehem, where the messiah was prophesied to be born. Luke's point? God holds all of the cards – even Caesar contributes to the fulfillment of God's plan.

Second key point – despite the overly romanticized spin we put on the cozy manger scene, with docile animals and clean sterilized straw, the stark reality is that Mary and Joseph are very poor. They are literally homeless this night – and if you travel to Bethlehem and see where the shepherds actually lived, you realize that Jesus was very likely born in a cave on a hillside. Luke makes it clear that God has a special affinity for the poor – that somehow poverty, whether intentional or accidental, has the capacity to open a door to the divine. This should disturb us a bit. Has the wealth and comfort we seek so relentlessly cost us access to the most important relationship of all?

Third point – note carefully what the angel says to the shepherds. Don't be afraid. This is great news, joyful news! Everyone benefits, all the people – even the rich ones. A savior is born – and he's just like you and me. A human being. God is not simply with us in a creator/created being kind of way. No, God has literally become a human being. This is absolutely unprecedented. No other religion makes such a claim. No other religion has a god that would humble himself so profoundly so as to become a measly human being. Theologians have a word for this amazing event. It's called the *Incarnation*, the taking on of flesh.

When I was a kid growing up, one of our standard questions to argue about was our favorite holiday. There aren't really that many that resonate with kids, so you can probably figure out what the top four were: Halloween, Christmas, Easter, and the 4th of July. The leading vote getter was always Christmas, although the nuns at our school would disagree, telling us that Easter is far more important. Without the Resurrection event, they would say, there would be no basis to our Christian faith. Yes, I retorted, but without Christmas, there would be no Jesus in the first place. That didn't go over well…

But now, from the perspective of a more mature outlook, how would we answer that question? Is Christmas as important as Easter? Or not? Well, with a little thought, you come to realize that the question is actually a false dichotomy, truly an insignificant point. It's like asking what is more important, the source of the river or the delta? The river is not one or the other, it is both at the same time. So too with Jesus – the Redemption of us all, the ultimate point of Jesus' life on earth, is completely present in the very act of Incarnation. The Savior is the Savior no matter what part of his historical presence we consider. The Savior saved us 2000 years ago, and he continues to save us now. We celebrate a past event and a present reality.

Here's another way to look at it. When we see the stars at night, we experience a present reality – light shining on us, light shining from all of these stars in the sky. But astronomers tell us that the light from these stars actually flamed forth years ago – the closest about 4 years ago, the farthest literally millions of years ago. And yes, just like Jesus, some of these stars produced their original light 2000 years ago, and just like Jesus, they light our path today.

Why is this important? It's so easy to get wrapped up in the little petty things of this world, isn't it? Our worries about money, the kids, the grandkids, the price of gas, the neighbor's dog, whatever pushes our button today. In all of this petty anxiety, we can miss the most incredibly important reality of our lives. God loves you. God loves us! God loves us so much that he decided to become a human being. Despite all of the pain of our lives, God's outrageous claim is that it is *good* to be human. In the face of all of the little problems of our life, God encourages us to stop a moment and take a look at the big picture. Widen your gaze, take off the blinders, open your eyes!

Living a life completely immersed in our American culture is an exercise in anxiety. Once we get past the fulfillment of our basic human needs – food, clothing, and shelter – and begin to buy into the lie that having more stuff is a ticket to happiness, we're walking in darkness. I challenge you to tell me three things you got for Christmas last year, and if you succeed, give me simply two things you got the year before that. It's a struggle, isn't it? But, if I were to challenge you to think of the warmest Christmas memory you have, I'll bet that the memory had to do with people – people you love, people you surrounded yourself with, people that warmed your heart. That's the big picture of Christmas. Love.

Why do we celebrate this day? We celebrate this day because God, who is love, decided to love us so completely that he became a human lover. Loving that deeply is profoundly impactful. The poor, the sick, the outcast are particularly benefited, and the ones who live at the top of society, who have the most to lose, get very worried indeed. They don't see a savior, they see a threat. The story of Jesus we hear throughout the church year is a story of Jesus journeying among the poor and the powerful, and how each react to him. Jesus the Christ continues the journey today, not in the flesh as he did 2000-plus years ago, but in the minds and hearts of those who are aware, who open their eyes to see him. The poor, the outcast, the sick still benefit, and the rich and the powerful are still threatened.

We hear from Isaiah that "The people who walked in darkness have seen a great light." Whether you consider yourself rich or consider yourself poor, the warm light is shining. That light burst forth over 2000 years ago, and it burns even more brightly today. How do you respond to that light? The Christian message, at its most basic, suggest how to respond. Appreciate that God loves you, and act out of that knowledge, act to make a difference. Every positive action you take makes the light shine a little brighter, and the darkness recedes. May the light and the happiness of Christmas shine throughout your year. Peace on earth and good will to you all!

The Beginning of Salvation

Scripture Referenced: Isaiah 60:1-6

> Rise up in splendor, Jerusalem! Your light has come, the glory of the Lord shines upon you. See, darkness covers the earth, and thick clouds cover the peoples; but upon you the Lord shines, and over you appears his glory. Nations shall walk by your light, and kings by your shining radiance.

You realize of course that we've been talking about Christmas for a while now. It started in late November, with the taste of Thanksgiving turkey still in our mouth. Advent marched us, candle by candle, into the arms of Christmas day itself, when we all met a lot of new friends at Church. Advent themes were about waiting, supposedly with patience, and if you asked most kids what they were waiting for, they would say Santa. Now we're a whole 10 days removed from Christmas, and I suspect that most of you have already started taking down the decorations. It's a bit jarring to see the Church in the same condition it was on Christmas Day, continuing to sing hymns and carols. But, if you're not careful, you'll miss the answer, the answer we've all been looking for since that first Advent candle was lit, the answer to the question of the meaning of Christmas. Today, the feast of the Epiphany, gives us that answer. Or, to put it more accurately, *answers*.

Each of the readings shed light, each from a different perspective. The first reading from Isaiah bursts with hope and joy, almost absurdly so given that the Hebrew people were in exile when this was written. It's hard to imagine nations walking by the shining radiance of Israel as the people toil in Babylon. But the reality was that the Hebrews were only a few years from release at this point, and indeed, the time for hope was at hand. This is the first meaning of Christmas, one that is often unremarked, but evident just the same. God sent Jesus to the Hebrew people, to a Jewish mother, living in a poor Hebrew town, subjected to Roman rule. Jesus is a Jewish man, and he most certainly saw his mission as saving the Hebrew people first and foremost. Even after his death and resurrection, his disciples, notably Peter, saw their mission as the reformation of Judaism through the application of Jesus' teaching. Peter wasn't interested in starting a new religion, nor was this of much interest to another early convert, Paul.

We all know the story of Paul, how he initially reacted to the early followers of the Way, how he was converted on the road to Damascus, how he began to preach the gospel. Following his instincts and his heart, he began by preaching to the Jews wherever he went. He certainly understood the first meaning of Christmas, and he was bound and determined to see a new flowering of Judaism as expressed through the spirit of Jesus. We also know, by reading the Acts of the Apostles, that Paul's efforts were not met with awestruck joy. So, he decided to broaden his reach. Our second reading, from Ephesians, expresses beautifully the realization that Paul came to, namely, that Jews and Gentiles are all a part of the same body, that God's grace extends to everyone. This is the second meaning of Christmas, that Jesus has come to save the Gentiles, not simply a loose confederation of tribes in Palestine.

The gospel reading, in the well-known tale of the Magi, hammers this point home. We miss the shocking bits because we've heard it so often. Note that the so-called "three kings" are not Hebrew, nor are they Roman, nor Greek. In fact, they're not even from the Mediterranean region, the center of the "known" world. They're from the East, perhaps from Babylon itself, the source of the dreadful exile the Hebrews were subjected to some 400 years earlier. So, they're not simply foreigners. They're this close to being enemies! Put yourself at the feet of Matthew the evangelist as he tells this story. His audience would undoubtedly be rocked by this – not only are the Magi seekers after God, but God leads them right to Jesus. What?! Adding further insult is the clear contrast Matthew draws to Herod, who is supposed to be the king of the Jews. It's an indictment of the religious power hierarchy in place, a far cry from Isaiah's vision of a community "proclaiming the praises of the Lord." Apparently, God has a plan in mind, and he intends to accomplish it with whoever is willing to cooperate. As Jesus says, "You're either with me or against me."

How many of you have been in a Lutheran church? How about a Jewish synagogue? A mosque? How about a Buddhist temple? Okay, a more interesting question. If you've been in any of these houses of worship, did you see evidence of Jesus? It's a pretty easy "yes" for the

Lutheran church, right? The Jewish synagogue doesn't reference Jesus directly, but the rites, the book, the feasts all resonate with us Christians at a root level. In fact, most of our Catholic rites are based in Jewish ritual. These are our ancestors in faith. But what about a mosque? The Koran reveres Jesus as a prophet, although we would see no artistic images of Jesus in the mosque. But he's most certainly present. A Buddhist temple? A bit more challenging, perhaps, but if you read the Buddhist mystics and analyze their observations on the presence and action of God, you'll see substantial alignment with Christian mysticism.

The point of all of this is simple. God acts in human history, through human hearts, enticing us in many ways, pulling us gently and firmly into His embrace. The meaning of Christmas, reinforced by today's feast of the Epiphany, is that Jesus is born to save *the world.* Not just the Jews, not just the Catholics, not just our Christian family, but everyone. Shinto, Shiite, Hindu, Sikh, Mormon, agnostic, Wiccan, and yes, even the atheists. Regardless of where you were born, and how you were raised, and what religion your parents profess, God is out to capture you, and the ultimate response is up to each one of us.

Now wait, you may be thinking. Don't we have a leg up, being Catholic Christians? Don't we have an advantage since we have access to the fuller truth of God's embrace through the teachings of Jesus? Yes! We do. But what difference does that make if we take it home and stuff it under the mattress? Remember that what God wants is cooperation in the business of saving the world. Our fuller understanding of God's plan should put us first in line to help. From those who are given much, much is expected! But also understand, God will continue to draw everyone to him, however He can. So how do we help? How do we cooperate fully?

Live your Christian life as if it makes a difference. If it's important to you, show it. Do people know that you're a Catholic Christian? How long would it take a stranger to discover this about you? 30 seconds or 30 days? Little things make a difference. A cross in your office. Christian music on your radio. Peace-making in your life. Service to others. Prayer in response to challenge, especially praying the Mass. In short, are you a light in the darkness?

The meaning of Christmas? It's the *beginning* of the salvation of the world. The weeks ahead show how Jesus lights the fire, first in his immediate followers, and then in the people around him who seek God, sometimes desperately. Jesus never asks for any religious ID card, he simply teaches, heals, listens, heals, challenges, and heals some more. Not a bad recipe for cooperation with God. This is how it's done. Join in the mission! And the best part? You'll find that deep-seated joy that Christmas promises, the meaning of your life.

An Audacious Claim

Scripture Referenced: Luke 24:1-12

> They found the stone rolled away from the tomb; but when they entered, they did not find the body of the Lord Jesus. While they were puzzling over this, behold, two men in dazzling garments appeared to them. They were terrified and bowed their faces to the ground. They said to them, "Why do you seek the living one among the dead? He is not here, but he has been raised."

Ahh, the empty tomb. All four evangelists tell the story of the empty tomb. The details are slightly different in each version. Was the messenger from God one man dressed in white? Or is it two? Or were they angels? It really doesn't matter – the key factual element remains a simple observable reality – the tomb where Jesus was laid is quite empty. What has happened here? What are the women to think? Imagine reading this passage the first time, as if at the end of a fascinating short story. We as readers are invited into the same questioning attitude – what just happened?

Why do you seek the living one among the dead? Why do you seek the living one among the dead?

The question resounds to this day. Who do you think this Jesus is? If he's simply an historical figure, then yes, you can read a large number of books, whole sections of libraries, about this Jesus. But then again, you can read a large number of books about Abraham Lincoln too. Do you think about them in the same way? As pretty important, very influential, very famous, beloved in their time, but in the end, two dead men?

Or perhaps we study the words of Jesus, the philosophy and ethics of this great teacher, a shining example of how to live a life to the fullest. We ponder his teachings, wonder at his parables, consider the meaning of forgiveness and mercy, and admire him from the sidelines. Much as we might do with Buddha, or Mohammed, or L. Ron Hubbard, or any other figure who claims to have a handle on the truth. Is Jesus simply another great preacher and teacher, who, alas, is as dead as the others?

The audacious claim of Christianity is that Jesus is not dead! He is a living presence, a person to get to know, a companion we can count on in every circumstance. I can't emphasize this enough – if Jesus isn't real to you, then all of this religion stuff is nonsense. Or as St. Paul puts it – pathetic. Many of us who have this experience of Jesus as a living presence in our lives wonder why it isn't obvious to everyone else. Why did we receive this gift and others not? It doesn't seem fair, and we worry about our kids and siblings and friends and others who live lives of quiet desperation. Is there anything we can do? How can we help them see the empty tomb and come to the aha moment that of course it's empty! You don't seek the living in a cemetery…

Of course, many people have pondered this question over the ages and written great theological treatises on the process of awakening and conversion. Some are quite fascinating, others need to stay on the shelf. I'd like to reflect on one aspect of this process that seems to be a prerequisite for experiencing Jesus as a real presence, a person. I consider this a starting point, a necessary frame of mind if you will, in order to open the door. This starting point is sometimes called the *beginner's mind*, and it simply means an openness to the possibility that the world is not completely understandable, that there is something beyond the tactile reality of earth and air and fire and water. In the ages leading up to the so-called Enlightenment, you might have described the world as an enchanted place. Is it any wonder that religion was so critical to the people of that time? So much of the world was mysterious, with seemingly random events that were as often frightening as reassuring.

So yes, science has been a huge boon to our understanding of the world. So much of the natural world is explainable and more to the point, controllable, that the need for religion seems quaint and odd. Why do you need this belief system when the world is completely explainable? There's a pill for everything that ails you. Obviously, with all of these great answers, everyone is as happy as can be. Right?

Adopting the beginner's mind is simply recognizing that maybe science doesn't have all of the answers, that maybe happiness is not simply about physical well-being, that there is a third way, an *enchanting* way, used in the best sense of that word. It's exactly the attitude of a teenage girl who can't wait to fall in love. It's exactly the attitude of a young man who wants to explore the world. It's a sense of adventure and willingness to be surprised, and hopefully, delighted. You see, my friends, we can't manufacture meaning. We must seek it out. This is the starting point in the spiritual journey, this is the openness needed to meet Jesus, this is where He can gently enter and show us a thing or two.

How do we encourage our loved ones who don't know Jesus to adopt this beginner's mindset? It can be difficult. The prevailing culture is heavily dominated by the ethos of self-reliance, independence, and personality cults. We're encouraged to work hard so that we can play hard so that we can – what exactly? Repeat the cycle until we die? And if that distresses us, just take this pill or drink this bottle or puff on this joint until we don't need to ask these embarrassing questions anymore. This is why it often takes a personal crisis for a person to begin asking the hard questions, to begin to recognize that the world is not fully explainable, and they cry for help.

This is where we come in. Can you share the peace that is the presence of Jesus in your lives? Can you offer a new path? Be careful, though, not to bring them to where you are in your journey too quickly. It won't make sense. That's why bringing a troubled person to Church rarely helps. It helps *you*, but that's only because you already know Jesus. You've got to start where they are – and that means an invitation to a life of enchantment. Seeing nature not as an explainable problem, but a source of wonderment. Introducing them to people who are grounded in meaning and truth, and just hearing the melody of a life in tune.

I invite you to meditate on the last words of tonight's gospel. "Peter got up and ran to the tomb, bent down, and saw the burial cloths alone; then he went home amazed at what had happened." That's the beginner's mind in a nutshell – the capacity to be *amazed*. Jesus can work with that mindset! But, before the person can ask *who*, they have to ask *why*. If you have a chance to evangelize a loved one at Easter dinner, you might try this question: "Do you think the world is an enchanted place?" Or perhaps this one: "When was the last time you were amazed?"

Why Are We Here?

Scripture Referenced: 1 John 2:1-5

> The way we may be sure that we know him is to keep his commandments. Those who say, "I know him," but do not keep his commandments are liars, and the truth is not in them. But whoever keeps his word, the love of God is truly perfected in him.

Here we are, three Sundays into the Easter Season, continuing to focus on the resurrection of Jesus, the cornerstone event of our faith. It happened at a particular point in time, forever changing the nature of man's relationship with God. Jesus, through his resurrection, has become the *Christ*, the anointed one foretold in Scripture, who is unconstrained by time and place. He is who *was*, who *is*, and who is *to come* again. The whole business is enough to make your head spin, just as the apostles exhibit in today's Gospel, moving from startled to terrified to joyous to amazed. So here's the question, the one we need to grapple with today, the ultimate *so what?* What does the resurrection mean to our everyday, often mundane lives?

I find it interesting that many people prefer Lent to the Easter season. It makes sense, actually. Lent is very down to earth. We fast, we give alms, we pray fervently, we walk the walk with Jesus as he heads to his doom on Calvary. At a heart level, we get it. Death is stalking Jesus just as death stalks us. We are simpatico with the Lord. Even the treachery of Judas and the cowardice of the apostles rings true. It only takes a scan of the front page news to see that treachery and cowardice still inhabit the world. We nod our heads as if to say, "Yes, I've seen this too…"

But Easter is kind of jarring, isn't it? If Lent is down to earth, Easter seems just the opposite. The veil of the sanctuary has been torn in two – God has violated the laws of his own universe to make a startling statement. What we think we know about life and death is quite simply – wrong! No wonder the apostles are startled. It's as if God has given us some new eyes to peer through. If we bother to look, what would we see?

At the heart, you would see that life is only partially about what happens here. Yes, we are born, grow up, learn a little about the world we live in, and strive to become independent and successful. This drives our early existence, until at some moment, when we least expect it, we're suddenly confronted by the question, "Why am I here?" The cornerstone of our faith, the resurrection of Jesus, gives us five reasons why we're here.

1. Notice how Jesus interacts with God. Jesus treats God like his Daddy. This is the core relationship of Jesus' life on earth. He loves the Father and the Father loves Jesus. It's simple and we are invited to do the same. Our prayer, our worship here at Mass, our eyes to heaven, all of this in honor of the first and most important relationship of our lives – God loves, we love back. Get that right first. I'm not saying that it is a perfect relationship – God doesn't expect praise and adulation all day long. He wants you to get to know Him, and he'll be happy to give you some good advice, just he like he did for Jesus. So, number one reason we're here – love God back.
2. God apparently likes people in general, not just us specifically. I know that's disappointing to many, but now is a good time to get used to this concept. Heaven has a lot of people in it, and some who get there will surprise you. We can act like the Father in the story of the prodigal son and enjoy the big party, or we can sulk outside like the older brother in the story, who is annoyed that his little brat brother is getting all of the attention. Here's the bottom line – God has formed us for his family, and our existence here on earth is a laboratory for eternal life. Number two reason we're here – get to know the family of God, and how to live with all of the fruits and nuts in the big salad. If you hate everyone here, why do you think you'll enjoy heaven?
3. Jesus was the perfect human. What made him this way? He was *whole*. He was perfectly integrated physically and spiritually. All of us who make it to the age of 16 are physically mature, but spiritual maturity is rarely achieved at this age. Sorry, kids, but it's true. Spiritual maturity is a life-long journey, but one that we must take if we wish to achieve any sort of integrity in life. God wants spiritual character, and the good news is that He will grant us that gift if we seek it with a humble heart. The third reason we're here – to grow up *spiritually*.

4. The fourth reason we're here is to cooperate with God. We are shaped to serve others. Jesus' message, his teachings to the people, resonate in large part because he not only preached, he healed. The purpose of the miracles was not to make the headlines. When Jesus performed a miracle, he didn't pull out a cape and say "Watch this!" His miracles were almost always personal – an interaction with a person in pain, usually performed with a simple gesture or phrase. The simple lesson is that God specializes in extracting good from bad. Thank goodness for that – God will use both the good and bad in us to serve others, if we let Him! Fourth reason – to cooperate with God.
5. The fifth reason is a direct outgrowth of the fourth. When we start cooperating with God, we gradually but surely find that our life is most joyful when we find that confluence of our gift and cooperation with God. Using our gifts, our talents, in cooperation with God is the definition of *mission*. You are made for a mission – your life is not about you, it is about your mission. Do you know what your mission in life is? Most people don't, so don't feel bad. But that's not an excuse for not trying to figure it out! Gift, cooperation, together.

Here it is in a nutshell. The resurrection, the key to our faith, the reason for the Easter season, the seven weeks of pondering the mystery. What is God asking of us? Love Him back. Understand you're part of a big human family. Grow up spiritually. Cooperate with God. Find your mission in life. If you do these things, you will find joy, peace, and an abiding confidence in God's loving action. I'm not saying that you will avoid pain – oh no. Remember that Jesus, the perfect embodiment of a human being, was confronted constantly. But Jesus, because of his relationship to the Father, because of his spiritual integrity, because of his love for others, was able to endure the pain the world dealt him. It led him to the cross, but it also led him three short days later to the resurrection. That's the promise for us too. That's where faith comes in. That's what Easter is all about – a glimpse of the promise. A glimpse of the reason that we're here. Are you up to the task? Ask that question as we continue our prayer today – ponder where you are on the spiritual walk and let's help each other all get to heaven.

Peace.

Chapter 7 – Sacraments

Sacraments are special moments, moments of focused attention on God's presence. In return for our focus, God offers his grace. To the extent that we are aware of God, so too is grace's impact felt in return. A conversation is considerably more interesting when both parties are engaged, correct? Sacramental moments are an exquisite mix of symbol, elements, and intention that are designed to facilitate the God/person dialogue. We can take them for granted, alas, so every so often, we need a gentle reminder. Hey, look! God is here!

Enter the Water

Scripture Referenced: Matthew 3:13-17

> Jesus came from Galilee to John at the Jordan to be baptized by him. John tried to prevent him, saying, "I need to be baptized by you, and yet you are coming to me?" Jesus said to him in reply, "Allow it now, for thus it is fitting for us to fulfill all righteousness." Then he allowed him.

A number of years ago, I had the privilege of visiting the Jordan River in the land of Palestine, the site of today's reading. The Jordan is not a wide river like the Mississippi – you can't take boats on it. It's perhaps better described as a stream or a creek, maybe 50 feet wide at most. For a river with so much Biblical history, it's surprisingly simple and unassuming. The locals have built several Baptismal centers on the river to accommodate the pilgrims who come to be immersed in the waters just as Jesus was over two thousand years ago. You can buy little vials of Jordan river water to take home and use for whatever purpose you choose. It seems an oddly appropriate blend of the secular and sacred – as is much of the Holy Land today.

It's easy to imagine the scene of today's Gospel. The people sitting on the banks of the river, the slow moving line of pilgrims coming to John as he stands knee-deep in the shallows. We can imagine him saying something to each person, perhaps a word of encouragement or a shared prayer. And then, to his surprise, the next person in line is his second cousin, Jesus.

If there is one question that arises almost every time this reading comes up in the liturgical cycle, it is this: why? Why did Jesus allow himself to be baptized by John? Even John is uncomfortable with the idea, saying "I need to be baptized by you, and yet you are coming to me?" Jesus insists that John proceed, with the somewhat cryptic statement, "..it is fitting for us to fulfill all righteousness." What's going on here? Why is this simple action so important, if not momentous?

It's all about symbolism. It's all about getting beyond the obvious. It's all about recognizing that God works with all of the elements, past, present, and future:

- Why the Jordan? The Jordan River is the historical boundary between the desert exile and the Promised Land. Moses was not allowed to cross the Jordan River. When Joshua was given the mandate to lead the people into the Promised Land, he didn't just wade into the river. No, he had the Ark of the Covenant carried into the water first, and in a precise re-enactment of the Red Sea crossing, the river literally stopped flowing to allow the people to pass. The Jordan River is a symbol of transition – a movement into something new, into something of great promise. Jesus was entering the Promised Land.
- Why else the Jordan? The Jordan River flows from the Sea of Galilee in the North to the Dead Sea in the South. You need to go to the Dead Sea to appreciate why it's called that. Nothing lives on either shore. There is no outlet to the Dead Sea. The river water flows in, and that's it – it eventually evaporates. The River Jordan, in a very real sense, connects life and death. Jesus enters the Jordan to demonstrate his complete immersion into the journey we all take – from life to death. He is part of this, he is part of us. It is right and fitting that he do so.
- Why be baptized at all? Consider this. The last time God used water in the Bible was to flood the earth in order to "restart" the human race with Noah's family and a new covenant. Water was a frightening reality for first century people. Storms, sea monsters, floods – these were all part of the local legends. To many Biblical scholars, Jesus entering the Jordan is a sign that God is re-consecrating the waters of the world – is reconciling the purpose of water. Jesus is not simply baptized in the Jordan, he is in turn blessing the water by his presence, and in doing so, making it the premier symbol of Christianity. You can't claim Christianity unless you too enter the water and submit to it's cold reality.
- Then there's the dove. It's unclear in the reading who actually sees the dove and hears God's voice. It seems to be only Jesus in Mark and Luke's versions, but here in Matthew's version, God seems to be proclaiming the Son-ship of Jesus to everyone. Regardless, this is clearly a moment of amazing validation for Jesus, that he is on the right track, that his ministry is beginning.

It made such a huge impression on Jesus that immediately afterwards, he heads into the desert to fast and pray and discern what to do next. Jesus takes on a mission.

One of the joys of being a Deacon is performing baptisms. It is especially delightful when the family having the baby baptized really understands the meaning of the sacrament and enters into the ceremony with awe and reverence. Of course, we get families who treat baptism as a sort of magic "stay out of limbo" act, or worse yet, as a family naming ritual, with no meaning other than a cultural tradition and a big photo opportunity. We try to prepare the parents and godparents, of course, but it's hard to give someone a present when they aren't present to the gift. Which leads to the next question, "Why baptize infants?" Simple answer really – the Holy Spirit. Let me explain.

A child under the age of seven is an amazing creation. There is a wonderment to life, a reaching and trying and tasting and yes, falling and crying that reflects the innate curiosity of the human being and the slow formation of what it takes to learn the ways of the world. Hopefully, the child finds many more positives than negatives and comes to trust the goodness of creation. It is this very openness that makes Baptism particularly effective. A child has no barriers to the Holy Spirit, no suspicions, no gritty armor. The child is an open door. Yes, I would also prefer that the parents and godparents be just as open as the child is to the Spirit, but even if they aren't, I know that the child is. And just as the Spirit of God cannot be channeled or tamed, so too is that little squirming bundle of joy. Baptisms are delightfully unpredictable, just as God is.

I assume that most of us here are baptized. How many were baptized as infants? Adults? It's interesting that most of us here were not intellectually aware, or conscious, of our own Baptism. This is surely one of the perceived drawbacks of our practice of infant baptism. But that doesn't mean that the Holy Spirit wasn't present or hasn't been active since that long ago day. The Holy Spirit hangs on long after the water dries off. It's incumbent on us to consider the following. How has the Holy Spirit been active in your life since your baptism? Can you identify times and events where you were inexplicably guided to a good choice, or avoided a truly disastrous situation? How would your life had been different if you weren't baptized? Obviously, this is pure speculation, but if the opportunity is there, I would suggest that you talk to people who were present at your baptism. What were they thinking? What was their prayer for you that day? Has it come true?

And there are other possibilities as well. Whether you remember your baptism or not, you are frequently given the opportunity to *renew* your baptismal vows. This happens at every baptism you attend. Although it appears to be a simple shorthand for the Creed, I invite you to take it a bit deeper. It is meant to be a reaffirmation of something you perhaps were not able to say when you were originally baptized, but can say it now. Your "I do" in response to each question is a thank you to God, to your godparents, to your parents, to whoever took the time to make this a priority, on your behalf. What a generous gift! And as you know, the best response to a gift given is to give a gift in return. Not to God (he doesn't really need gifts), but to other people on God's behalf, and that is the best thank you of all. Generosity begets generosity.

Simply put, the act of giving yourself to another on God's behalf is the definition of what it means to be a Christian. That's why the generous action of inviting someone into the Church family is the gift that keeps on giving, the very nature of the Church's mission. Now do you see why Jesus got baptized? It truly was a momentous event.

Spiritual Hunger

Scripture Referenced: John 6:51-58

> Whoever eats my flesh and drinks my blood remains in me and I in him. Just as the living Father sent me and I have life because of the Father, so also the one who feeds on me will have life because of me. This is the bread that came down from heaven. Unlike your ancestors who ate and still died, whoever eats this bread will live forever.

For the last four weeks we've been reading from the 6th chapter of John's gospel, the so- called Bread of Life discourses. It all began with Jesus feeding the five thousand people, multiplying a few barley loaves and a couple of fish into a feast. Intrigued by this miracle, the people following Jesus grow in number, chasing him now with reckless abandon, because let's face it, there's nothing like a guaranteed free meal. When you're poor and hungry most days, who can resist being fed? Jesus is growing in power and influence, and to the apostles, this must seem like the exact outcome they're looking for. Power, prestige, and influence – it's all coming together.

But Jesus, in his increasingly typical fashion, doesn't play the power and prestige game. He turns the tables on the crowd by linking bread to his very self, implying without any irony or subtlety that if the people want eternal food then they need to chew on Jesus himself! In today's gospel he's asked to clarify what he means, and far from backtracking, he emphasizes his point. "For my flesh is true food, and my blood is true drink," he exclaims. And as we hear next week, the damage is done. The crowds drift away, shaking their heads in puzzlement, and the five thousand becomes a measly twelve apostles once again.

I was in Ireland for the second and third weeks of this 5-week bread of life discussion. One of the critical historical events in Ireland's stormy history is the great potato blight of 1845. Potatoes were the absolute staple crop of the poor farmworkers, providing 80-90% of their nutritional needs. When the potatoes were ruined by a fungus, nearly 4 million people were suddenly in grave danger. You see, all of the other crops grown, the barley in particular, was being exported by the British landlords. There is no doubt that famine would be averted if the exports were simply stopped and diverted to the people, but that did not happen. A million people died of starvation over the course of the next 4 years.

A million more boarded famine ships and emigrated to America, or tried to - many thousands died well before reaching Ellis Island. This critical failure of compassion was the seminal event in driving Ireland's break from British rule, and that country, as well as ours, was never the same again.

There's no famine in Ireland anymore, at least, not in any obvious way. People seem well fed, as they appear to be here in the U.S. But another type of famine walks the land. It's not a physical hunger, but it is a *spiritual* hunger. As is true in most of Western Europe, Catholic church attendance in Ireland has dropped precipitously. Once the most Catholic of all the Catholic nations, now it is Catholic in name and culture, and that's about it. When we asked on Saturday what time Masses were being held in the village, no one in the hotel we were staying in had a clue. And the sad fact remains that spiritual hunger will kill you just as dead as physical hunger, and like carbon monoxide poisoning, you won't notice you're dying. Point of fact, alcoholism rates in Western Europe are nearly double that of the United States. People have simply replaced Church with the local pub, substituting the bread of life for the distilled drink of death. Don't get me wrong – I enjoy a drink as much as anyone. But I'll stop after one, or on occasion, two. The average quantity consumed at a single sitting in Ireland? At least five drinks.

Spiritual hunger is a part of all of our lives. It seems wired into our beings, as if God set us free on this earth with a God magnet pulling us back to Him. Our battle is between our stubborn pride and willfulness and that God magnet, as if God was a person to avoid. We try everything we can to prove to God that we can go it alone, and every path we take fails. The Eucharist is the one food that satisfies – it's no wonder that this sacrament is the keystone of our Catholic religious life.

There's a lot of debate going on right now on the topic of individual worthiness and the Eucharist. The two sides are simple enough to describe. On the one hand, you have classic Church teaching that states that those receiving the Eucharist should be baptized Catholics in a state of grace, that is, without grave sin. The idea is that the Eucharist is a privilege, a sign of communion with fellow Catholics, an integral part of the worship experience. This teaching has held sway for many, many years, and is the basis for the prohibition from receiving the Eucharist for those Catholics who have divorced and remarried without having their prior marriages annulled. In the strictest sense, these persons are living in sin. On the other hand, you have a growing opinion in the Church that the Eucharist is as much about healing and growth in holiness as it is about worship. Those in this camp would lower barriers to receiving the Eucharist, under the assumption that denying Jesus to a person in need is cruel and counterproductive. The Synod on the Family that was recently called by Pope Francis is addressing this very debate as we speak. Expect some breathless headlines in the next few weeks.

In the end, it all comes down to why you receive the Eucharist - is it habit? A reason to stretch your legs? Or something more? God, through Jesus, is offering us nourishment that lasts forever. But we have a role too. We need to be engaged in the mystery. I know that sounds a bit new-agey, but if we don't engage, we're no better than those followers of Jesus who just wanted a free meal. What does it mean to engage? It means to heighten your awareness, to pay attention to what's happening. God wants to transform us into images of Jesus. He offers us the opportunity to change, we in turn consume the change agent, the Eucharist. If we're unwilling to change, nothing will happen! If we're open to change, something *will* happen. That something will vary from person to person, but there is a common element. Our appetites, those often addictive qualities of the world we live in, will be diminished. In a very real sense, our hunger will be satisfied.

How do you know if change has happened to you? You'll go from a person who is looking to be fed to a person doing the feeding. For just as in the feeding of the five thousand, there was plenty of leftovers, so it is with spiritual food. The more we receive the Eucharist, the less spiritually hungry we are and the more we see the world through Jesus' eyes. And that world, my friends, is hungry for meaning, fulfillment and happiness. Share your food with a starving person – that's the meaning of the Eucharist. Hunger, food, nourishment, awareness, feeding others. Full circle – and Jesus smiles.

Active Presence in the Present

Scripture Referenced: Hebrews 9:11-15

> When Christ came as high priest of the good things that have come to be, passing through the greater and more perfect tabernacle not made by hands, that is, not belonging to this creation, he entered once for all into the sanctuary, not with the blood of goats and calves but with his own blood, thus obtaining eternal redemption.

I'm sure you've noticed that the last four Sundays, today included, have each been feast days, what I call *pay attention* days. The Church, in her wisdom, has placed these feasts at this point in the calendar year for a very specific reason. Let's review. It all started 3 weeks ago with Ascension Sunday, then we had Pentecost, the official end of the Easter Season. Ordinary time begins. But almost as if we couldn't let go of the celebration, we were invited to ponder the glorious mystery of the Trinity last Sunday, and today, we embrace the final mystery, the body and blood of Christ. Another way to look at the sequence is to take it from two points of view. First, that of Christ. Ascension – Jesus leaves us in body, but with a promise to send the Spirit so that the apostles would be able to fulfill the mission. Pentecost celebrates that reality, the ignition point of Christianity. Now the second point of view – that of the Church. Imbued with the wisdom of the Spirit, the Church defines how God, though one, is really three persons. And finally, today, we ponder the meaning of the scandalous claim of Jesus that eternal life is only possible if we literally "gnaw on Christ". As we face the long hot summer of Ordinary Time, we have plenty to think about, and we need to struggle a bit with these mysteries. It's a *pay attention* day.

Ten days ago my wife and I were in the Boston area visiting family and friends for a wedding/reunion. It's interesting isn't it? If your family is like ours, geographically dispersed, the excuses for a reunion are either weddings or funerals, right? Fortunately, we're still in the wedding –slash- reunion phase, but there's no illusions that the funeral –slash- reunion phase is around the corner.

Today, in this feast of the Most Holy Body and Blood of Christ, we're also celebrating a reunion of sorts. Do you see the connections? First of all, we're gathering for an event, friends and families together, old and young, connected and disconnected. Some have travelled far, some not so far. But wait, shouldn't there be a wedding or a funeral? Yup. We got both. Christ is the groom, the Church is the bride. Just as in a wedding ceremony, we celebrate the two individuals becoming one flesh, so too do we celebrate Christ's flesh becoming one with each of us through the Eucharist. It's a wedding feast at many profound levels. But what about a funeral? Who died? Oh yeah, we do commemorate the death of Jesus, don't we? It's unlike other funerals, however, in that there's very little sorrow expressed. This was a death followed immediately by new life and the promise that new life is available for us too.

Now, regardless of the occasion that is the focus of a reunion, there is one topic that predominates in the conversation, especially among us seasoned folks. Remembering! It starts with the simple question – do you remember when? In Boston, we had lots of "remember when" moments.

We had funny memories – like the time long ago when I stepped on a bee while barefoot and could hardly walk up the aisle for my brother's wedding. We had sad moments – when we took a family picture and all of us realized that my younger brother was missing – he's been dead for nearly 13 years now and we still feel the loss. We shared memories of vacations, usually spiced with arguments (well, discussions) of exactly where we went in 1963, and what disasters befell us. Why are the disasters always the key memories? We discussed relationships that we had, friends from the past, neighbors that we liked or avoided, and all of the other flotsam and jetsam that began to float to the surface as we reminisced. It was enjoyable to us, but boring as all get out to the in-laws, of course. But it all evens out when we go to their family reunions, doesn't it? We laugh because if we didn't, we'd simply cry. Life is like that – and wisdom is the ability to laugh at ourselves in all our ego-driven folly and hubris.

Moses said to the people: "Remember how for forty years now the Lord, your God, has directed all your journeying in the desert…"? Later on, we hear Moses again saying: "Do not forget the Lord, your God, who brought you out of the land of Egypt, that place of slavery…"

Reunions are about remembering, and today we celebrate the memory of God working in the lives of our ancestors in faith. These memories are collected in the Scriptures and one of the truly amazing things about our Scriptures is their honesty. It's not simply about great victories and celebrations of one great king after another. No, just as our lives are not one triumph after another, the Bible has been aptly described as a "text in travail", two steps forward, one step back. For every two smiles, there's a sigh. Remember when. Every Eucharist we "remember when".

And if we're truly wise, these "do you remember" times are also times to forgive and seek forgiveness. In this past reunion in Boston, I can think of at least 3 relationships that were restored. An old axe was buried, an old injustice forgiven, a long-ago hurt exposed as just so much misplaced pride. We see the other person not as an enemy or a rival, but as a co-journeyer with scars and wounds just like us, and our heart moves enough to say, "Can we talk?" Matthew 5:23: If you have a grievance against your brother or sister, go first and be reconciled with them, and then come and offer your gift.

The other reality of reunions, of course, is that we age. Everyone is older than the last time, and if you're a child, so much the better. If you're the acned teenaged girl that has somehow become a beautiful bride, so much the better. If you're the scowling teenaged boy with the hat pulled low that has somehow morphed into a beaming groom, so much the better. Other than that, well, it's rarely a physical change for the better. And here, thankfully, our analogy of reunion and Eucharist breaks down, because the Eucharist never gets old. Christ is the same yesterday, today, and tomorrow. He is always in the present, and we are invited to abide in that place. Today, when you receive the Eucharist, do your best to forget yesterday, forget tomorrow, and simply be with Christ NOW. Just be. Active presence in the present. That's the mystery of the body and blood of Christ. Active presence in the present.

Today's feast is a celebration of reunion. We gather together, we remember the past, we seek forgiveness, we acknowledge a wrongful and untimely death, we celebrate a resurrection to new life, we attend a wedding feast, we partake of the flesh and blood of Christ that never gets old. And today, in a special way after the 11:30 Mass, we're going to take a walk with Jesus. We will process with the Body of Christ from the Church here down to the St. Leo mission. We'll have the Knights accompany us, we'll have folks praying aloud, and we'll probably stop traffic a few times. Some of you may wonder at the wisdom of carrying the body of Christ out in public in such a way, but I assure you, the symbolism is beautiful. We need Christ out there just as badly as we need Christ in here. If you can join us, please do.

You Do the Feeding

Scripture Referenced: Luke 9:11-17

> Jesus spoke to the crowds about the kingdom of God, and he healed those who needed to be cured. As the day was drawing to a close, the Twelve approached him and said, "Dismiss the crowd so that they can go to the surrounding villages and farms and find lodging and provisions; for we are in a deserted place here." He said to them, "Give them some food yourselves."

Today's feast of Corpus Christi, Latin for the Body of Christ, has a long and inspired history. A nun from the early 13th century, Juliana of Liege, was inspired by a series of visions to advocate for a special feast to celebrate the Eucharist. The local bishop at that time instituted the feast in an area of Europe that is now part of Belgium, and it became popular in other parts of Europe soon after. St. Thomas Aquinas, who was living in Orvieto at the time, was so taken with this feast that he composed the prayers for the Mass of Corpus Christi, and also wrote a hymn that has lasted through the ages as *Tantum Ergo*, sung at Benedictions and during the Holy Thursday procession. The feast is officially celebrated on the Thursday after Trinity Sunday in most parts of the world, but here in the US we move it to Sunday to give it that much more prominence in our calendar.

The readings offered by the Church today are quite interesting. The reading from Genesis is the first mention of bread and wine in the Bible as a sacrificial offering, with the mysterious Melchizedek of Salem presiding. Melchizedek is actually two words, Melchi, meaning king, and Tzedek, meaning righteousness. It is no surprise that the early Church connected bread, wine, and the "king of righteousness" to Jesus. The Letter to the Hebrews specifically names Jesus as a priest forever in the order of Melchizedek. Our second reading from Paul's letter to the Corinthians is the source of the Eucharistic prayer recited over the bread and wine by the priest at the institution of the Eucharist at each Mass. We've heard it so many times that we could probably recite it by heart. It is the high point of our liturgy, a moment of profound depth, when each of us is invited to gaze on the elevated bread, the elevated cup, and ask what it means and more to the point, what it calls us to do.

Our faith teaches us that at the moment of consecration, the bread and the wine are transformed into the true presence of Christ. Our western scientific minds scream for an explanation of *how* this happens, as if it were some kind of chemical reaction verifiable by objective measurement. The fact that we *can't* explain how it happens leaves us uneasy and mildly disturbed, which is ironically a good place to be. Good religion should leave us uneasy and mildly disturbed, because one of the key purposes of a journey into faith is to make it clear that we do not have all of the answers, that our lives are not simply about us, and that God's purpose is intentionally beyond our ability to process and understand. To many people, God is just a very smart invisible being who holds all of the cards. It is very hard to love such a being in the abstract, and that cognitive dissonance is enough to send these people running from the Church. What part is missing from their understanding?

Now we get to the heart of the Gospel. It is clear from reading the Old Testament that the Hebrew people had a worship/ignorant/fear/awe relationship with God. Despite God's continued assurance that He would not abandon them, the people continued to act in their own blockheaded way, with all of the resulting damage and destruction in their lives, which they immediately blamed God for causing. All of these bad things just happened, so I guess God is punishing us. There's no self-awareness in such statements, no understanding that God is not dictating events, but is allowing us to drive our lives down any road we choose, despite clear instruction that the road to happiness is often in a different direction. So God in God's wisdom and perfect timing, sent His son Jesus to the earth to show us how it's done, to show us how God really views things, how God invites our cooperation in making the world a kingdom, a place where all are cared for. How does that happen?

The gospel today, the feeding of the five thousand, shows us how that happens. After a day of preaching and teaching, the disciples in their practicality note the coming of evening and a serious problem. They're in the middle of nowhere with no food anywhere to be seen, and here is a big crowd of people who are certainly getting hungry just as they are getting hungry. Let's send them on their way, back to the dog eat dog world, so that we can go rustle up some grub ourselves. You can almost hear the frustration in Jesus' voice. Haven't you been hearing what I've been saying all day? This isn't a bunch of theology lessons, these are life lessons. Feed them yourselves! God wants to help, but you need to show them how it's done.

So Jesus sets the table. Everyone is seated in groups, the cloths are set down. Bread and fish are shown to the crowd. Jesus says grace, breaks the food into pieces, and passes it around. Note what the gospel says. They all ate and were satisfied. So what actually happened? Did the bread and fish suddenly multiply? Maybe. Or did the people simply start sharing what they had in their packs to begin with? Maybe. Does it matter *how*? No. What matters is that all were fed. Jesus knew it was going to be just fine, because God always provides in five thousand different ways, not just one.

A couple of weeks ago, the parish was offered the opportunity to purchase a used yet high quality piano for the Church. It cost $10,000. Obviously, we can't afford that. We've been counting pennies carefully for months. So Fr. John announced our opportunity at this Mass and the 7:30 Mass that Sunday. He didn't talk about it at the 9 or the 11:30 or the 6. Why? Because we had the money in hand by 8:30 in the morning. Did it magically appear? Nope. Did God provide? Yes. Several people came forward with portions of what we needed. We actually were pledged with more than $10,000. Some baskets of fragments left over. You folks who pledged know who you are. Thank you!

You see, when we come to Communion as a community of believers and take the real presence of Christ into our bodies, we absorb the reality of Christ. That reality expresses itself as God acting in the world. God acts as Jesus demonstrated, by taking our lives, blessing them, and then breaking and giving. If we get caught up in how God makes this happen, we miss the punch line, the movement into the world, the instruction to go and make disciples of all nations. We do this by taking the gifts that each of us represents, accepting the blessing of Christ, and through the power of the Eucharist, distributing our essence to the world who needs to hear the good news that our God loves us and always will.

You are the body of Christ. You are his blood poured out. You are Corpus Christi.

Forming Families

Scripture Referenced: Luke 2:41-52

> He went down with them and came to Nazareth, and was obedient to them; and his mother kept all these things in her heart. And Jesus advanced in wisdom and age and favor before God and man.

On this, the feast of the Holy Family, it's a good opportunity to look at the state of our families, on both a broad scale as well as a personal scale. It comes as no surprise to anyone that what we mean by "family" has changed in quite a dramatic way in the past 30 years. What was once considered typical, a Mom, a Dad, 2.3 kids – is now much less so. I just finished reading a fascinating study of the state of marriage in America today called *The State of our Unions*, published by the National Marriage Project out of the University of Virginia. As a one-time sociologist, I am a very critical reader of such studies that might seem to have an agenda, but this study was quite well-done and referenced very credible source material. You can find it on-line and it's free of charge. Feel free to read it and form your own opinion!

What I found out is rather shocking. Virtually every study done in the past 50 years would agree that marriage is good for the husband, good for the wife, and particularly good for the kids. Over 80% of young women and 72% of young men want to get married, and hold marriage as an ideal. Yet in 2008, among women with less than a college degree, 54%, over half, who had children were unmarried. What was once considered a scandal is now commonplace! It's not that these women don't want to get married, they simply choose not to. What's going on? Well, many of these women are simply living together with the father. It's not that the couple don't love each other, but the sense of a commitment, a choice for the relationship, is clearly not happening.

One study asked high school seniors if they agreed that living together before marriage was a good idea because the couple would get to know each other better before making the commitment. Over 60% agreed. The reality is that couples who cohabit before marriage are more likely to divorce than those who don't. Furthermore, children born to an unmarried couple who are living together generally lead less happy lives as measured by several indicators. Again, why, in the face of all the evidence that marriage is good for all, is the marriage rate dropping?

Some blame it on easy divorce. Some blame it on Hollywood values. Some blame it on easy, no fault birth control. Some blame it on pure and simple immorality. Some blame it on poverty. And some, of course, blame it on our government's policies, or lack of them. Certainly all of these factors contribute to the sorry state of our American families today. So, who is getting married? What parts of our society still buy into marriage? The reality is that those who are college educated, go to Church, have a good income, come from an intact family, and postpone childbearing until at least 25 not only get married, but stay married. Folks who have these characteristics have a divorce rate of only 6 percent. They get married and they stay married. If any of these characteristics are lacking, the divorce rate creeps up. Once again – college degree, Church-going, good job, come from an intact family, postpone having kids until mid-20's. If those characteristics describe you, you're likely in good shape. But the majority of people do not fall into these categories. Is a happily married life simply unattainable for most people?

I think all of us cringe at such a generalization. But the numbers are alarming and we need to look at what we're doing as a society and as individuals to help families form, flourish, stay together, and pass on values to the next generation. What can we do? Let's take some cues from today's gospel reading, which is surprisingly relevant to our discussion.

Notice in the very first sentence that Jesus' parents were taking Jesus to Jerusalem for the feast of Passover, as was their custom. So, clearly, a very important family tradition is being played out. The family is gathering for a religious event, celebrated with many others, and it is not a simple get-together. They travel a substantial distance with others, a large contingent of relatives and friends. So, what is the lesson for us? Family traditions, especially of a religious nature, are very important! Christmas, Easter, weddings, funerals, Mass on Sunday, the rituals of religious life – these feed families in unique ways. Moreover, the fact that it is a challenge to get together on these events –costly, perhaps very inconvenient, is not a negative, but actually a very positive factor. The more we invest in these events as a family, the more value we get, even if we don't see it at the time. A recent study of young people asked what memories of Christmas past stuck with them, and not a single person mentioned presents. What they talk about is making cookies with Mom, traveling for hours in a storm to get to Grandma's, talking and arguing about current events around the table, and attending midnight Mass. Memories are based on people, not stuff. Spend more time, less money.

Later in the Gospel reading, Jesus is lost for three days, a horrible ordeal for Mary and Joseph as they search the city. On finding Jesus, who is baffled by their anxiety, Mary and Joseph are challenged to see Jesus as more than simply a son. Even at the tender age of 12, Jesus is exhibiting a sense of who he sees himself to be, and it is clearly more than a carpenter's son. Again, there is a profound lessons for us here. Families are the incubators, the formative sculptors, of our children – for a period of time, somewhat arbitrarily set at 18 years. Those 18 years go by very slowly for the kids, yet in a surprising blur for the parents. Parents set educational expectations, model work ethics, solve challenging ethical problems, deal with other family members, all in the spotlight gaze of their children who take it all in. When Jesus realizes the pain he has caused his parents, he returns to their loving embrace, and is obedient to them. He advances, the Gospel tells us, in wisdom and age and favor before God and man. What parent wouldn't want the same for their children? The message for us? Good families beget good families! If your marriage is challenged, if your daily life is racked by conflict, get some counseling, get some help from the many sources that are out there to help. Do if for your sake, do it for the kids, do it to keep the garden of life growing. People who come from intact families tend to form intact families for the long haul.

As I look out on the congregation today, I see a lot of couples who have been married for a long time. If you think your marriage has been a success by whatever measure you want to use, please share your happiness with others, especially young people who can't seem to make that commitment. Talk up the value of marriage in your lives, the value of that commitment. I work in an office with 14 other individuals. Of that 14, 2 are married, 3 are divorced, 4 are living together with another person, and the other 5 are unattached singles. I make a point of talking up marriage every chance I get. At lunch, in casual conversation, whenever. I always ask the women in the office for ideas on what to get my wife for Christmas or her birthday. That little conversation opens up lots of interesting threads. I occasionally ask embarrassing questions to the living together crowd, like "So, when are you two getting married?" I always ask in a very matter-of-fact way, as if it's a foregone conclusion, and I simply must get the date in my calendar. It's a great door opener to why marriage, why it works, why it works for me, why it can work for you.

Obviously, there's a lot more that we can do to embrace marriage, family life, and the values that set the path to happiness for our kids and grandkids. I'd love to hear your thoughts and ideas too. Please feel free to share an email with me and I'll gather ideas for a future homily on the topic. Keep your family together and holy. Please. That's a good place to start!

Dependent and Independent

Scripture Referenced: Mark 10:2-16

> The Pharisees approached Jesus and asked, "Is it lawful for a husband to divorce his wife?" They were testing him. He said to them in reply, "What did Moses command you?" They replied, "Moses permitted a husband to write a bill of divorce and dismiss her." But Jesus told them, "Because of the hardness of your hearts he wrote you this commandment."

There's a point in everyone's life when they consciously recognize that they are not children anymore, but adults. I remember my moment of recognition. I was 17 years old, and away from home at Santa Clara University as a freshman, living in the dorms. After the predictable first couple of weeks of homesickness, I began to get into the rhythm of campus life, made some new friends, and suddenly one evening, as I was walking to my dorm, I had this wonderful sense of well-being. The homesickness was gone. I was, in my own mind of course, an independent adult man, and that was pretty cool. So what did I do with this new-found independence? Two radical things – I let my hair grow long, and I stopped going to Mass on Sunday. When I went home for Thanksgiving, my hair was bushy black and stuck out in all directions. I looked like a walking Q-Tip. And when it was time to go to Mass on Sunday, I looked my Mom straight in the eye and said, "Sure, let's go!" I was an independent adult male coward, apparently.

Now what does this have to do with marriage and divorce, the obvious theme of today's Scripture readings? Hang on, we're getting there. I'm working backward from the end of today's gospel when Jesus says, "…whoever does not accept the kingdom of God like a child will not enter it." Note that word "accept". The reality is that children (and in this case, I'm not talking about babies, but self-aware children, perhaps 7 or older) have a distinct sense of their place in the scheme of the universe. They know that they are not adults, and they furthermore know that they are utterly dependent on their parents and other folks in authority. It is painfully clear to an 8 year old that bucking the child dependency system is a recipe for hunger, cold, fear, and disarray in life. When Jesus invites us to accept the kingdom of God like a child, he invites us to this same sense of dependency on God. In the end, he is saying, "Trust God the same way you trusted your mother, your father, or whoever played the role of a loving parent in your life." That is the way of happiness and peace.

Why didn't God just leave us with the minds of children, open and dependent on Him, for now and for eternity? Apparently, God wants us to take the round trip from child to adult to child again, for that journey is worth the effort. That journey is the journey of discipleship and spiritual maturity, and that's who God wants – people who have the intelligence of mature adults and the humble mindset of a child. God seems to treasure the humble heart above all, the one who knows that God is God and we are not. And that is not only okay, but preferred.

So there I was, eating Thanksgiving turkey, bushy-haired and fearful of my mother's discovery of my new found agnosticism. I couldn't wait to get back to school and start being an adult again. So off I went back to school and did more manly things, like growing a beard. You know those caveman ads on television? Yeah, that was me. I persisted in avoiding Mass, because I was an independent man, you see. And then I met this girl. She was pretty and smart and full of life, and wouldn't you know it, she went to Mass on Sunday. To her, it wasn't a question, it was a way of life. So I went to Mass with her, discovering a new appreciation of the liturgy as an independent adult male who happened to be in love.

My mother always told me to marry the woman who would help me get to heaven, so four years later, I did. And to this day, she remains bone of my bones and flesh of my flesh, a most "suitable" partner, to quote Genesis. When a marriage works, there is a mutual interdependence, a dance within life and through life, an awareness of one's individual role and a celebration of the partnership. We respect and enhance each other's journey, dependent and independent at the same time. That childlike acceptance of the reality of being dependent plays in marriage as well, and in this understanding, we taste the kingdom of God.

Why do marriages break up? There are many root causes, but in the last several years of working with couples who are divorced, I find that there is always a tipping point, a moment when one of the partners decides he or she would rather be independent of the other than dependent, and the bond is broken. I also see that marriages do not typically break apart overnight. It is a series of cuts, a series of decisions that exclude the other, an erosion of trust and a building of walls. If you sense this happening in your own marriage, I implore you to waste no time in getting counseling. The slide to divorce can be stopped. Two-thirds of divorced people in the United States say that they wish they had tried harder to save their marriages. Two-thirds!

There is some good news too. Divorce rates have been dropping steadily after peaking in the 1980's. You've all heard that often repeated statistic that 50% of marriages end in divorce? Not true today – the number is trending downward, largely because people are waiting longer to get married – divorce rates drop significantly if a person marries over the age of 25. But divorce still happens and always will happen. We're not naïve. The Church has struggled over the years to accommodate this reality without disobeying Jesus. If a marriage is meant to be forever, and it fails for a very good reason, the Church allows the marriage to be annulled. Annulment is a process, and to be honest, it is not an easy process for a couple who has married following all of the Catholic practices. Don't get me wrong, it can be a very healing process, but many are loathe to undertake the journey because of the need to relive the reality of their loss. The pain runs deep, and my heart breaks for them.

You may be aware that the Pope has recently made some significant changes to the Church's annulment process, to be implemented on December 8th of this year. Although we don't have the official procedures from our Diocese yet, we can expect that an uncontested annulment process will be greatly simplified, bringing the timeframe down from the current 9+ months to a matter of weeks. I certainly don't want to promise anything specific, but I am greatly encouraged by the Church's direction here. If the Church is to be a field hospital to the world, this is a great place to apply intensive care.

Perhaps it goes without saying, but if the Church is to be a field hospital to the world, what does that make our Parish? A MASH unit? Yes, indeed. We are the front line to the pain of the world. If you are hurting, please make yourself known to us. If you know someone who is hurting, please reach out. If you are not specifically qualified to help them, please ask one of us on staff. We'll do the best we can to get help. As Jesus said, "…do not prevent them, for the kingdom of God belongs to such as these."

The Whole Church

Scripture Referenced: Mark 6:30-34

> When he disembarked and saw the vast crowd, his heart was moved with pity for them, for they were like sheep without a shepherd; and he began to teach them many things.

Just recently, I, as a deacon, had the pleasure of playing golf with a bishop, a priest, and a layman. Yes, all four of the church's ecclesial ranks were present at one time in one place, and I was bemused by the entire experience. None of us were especially good golfers, but there's something about the outdoors, sunshine, and a common frustrating task to bring people together. We had a marvelous time. Not wanting to waste the opportunity, I asked the bishop a theological question that has been eating at me for some time. "Bishop," I asked, "is there golf in heaven?" Without missing a beat, he declared solemnly and firmly, "No!" So, I said, if I die and find myself on the first tee of the Ever After Golf Course? He shook his head with a smile. "Sorry, you missed the cut." Rats. I guess I'll need to get golf out of my system while I'm here!

I tell this story because I was thinking about how the Church has tried to follow Jesus' example of the good shepherd over the centuries. From the beginning of the Church, it became clear that the remaining 11 apostles, despite their enthusiasm, could not do everything for everybody. Early in the Acts of the Apostles, we are told that people started to complain – the widows were not getting what they needed, and others were likewise neglected. The apostles got together and decide to appoint deacons to help with serving tables and the community at large, leaving the apostles the role of praying and ministry. So literally within weeks of the Resurrection, we have the followers of Christ attempting some kind of organizational structure. This loose arrangement of "bishops" and deacons was the norm for the next hundred years.

As the faith spread, once again it became clear that the needs of the people exceeded the capacity of the bishops and deacons to help. The most logical area of demarcation was liturgical, so priests were appointed whose purpose was to celebrate the sacraments, particularly the Eucharist, within the area controlled by each bishop. This decision further focused the role of the bishop to one of administration and teaching, although it is interesting that the bishop reserved the role of ordination and confirmation to themselves. As the role of priest became more and more important, the role of deacon diminished, almost to the point of disappearance. Gradually the diaconate was seen as simply a step to priesthood. This was remedied at Vatican II, when the permanent diaconate was re-established, and the role of each Holy Order was clarified as this:

- Bishops: administration and teaching, the guardians of the deposit of faith
- Priests: liturgical and sacramental, leading the people in prayer
- Deacons: servants of the Church, encouraging the people to serve the world by example

Notice that Cardinals are not a specified Holy Order. They are ordained Bishops appointed to a role in the Church. In a similar way, the Pope is an elected role, usually chosen from among the Cardinals, but not necessarily, nor even historically. In fact, in the history of the Papacy, 34 deacons have been elected Pope, including Pope St. Gregory the Great. However, since the Pope is also the Bishop of Rome, St. Gregory, along with those other 33 deacons, each had to be ordained a priest and then a bishop shortly after election!

In the end, the simple image of the good shepherd Jesus provides us is perfectly realized in the Church's hierarchy. Teaching, praying, and serving – bishop, priest, deacon. Now lest you get the wrong idea, it's not as if I'm not allowed to pray or teach, any more than a priest is restricted to simply leading prayer. The roles are icons primarily, illuminating dimensions of Christ's ministry for the good of the Church.

Of course, people being people, or better stated, men being men, the Church's hierarchical structure has often caused more harm than good. Hierarchies look like mountains on paper, and when it comes to men, there's something about a mountain. Ego, power, prestige, control – it takes a man with incredible humility to resist these siren songs, and to be honest, many could not, and many cannot. The Church has been damaged by such men over the centuries, and we still struggle to strike the right balance between necessary structure and a humble, prayerful stance. It's a bit ironic that one who does so like Pope Francis stands out as such an exception!

But let's face it, the Church is not equivalent to the hierarchy, while you folks in the pews are spiritual spectators. The Church is the entire people of God, and, as emphasized at Vatican II, the hierarchical structure of the Church exists to serve the whole People of God, not to dominate or control it. This follows Jesus' example in today's Gospel perfectly. From the depths of compassion, Jesus teaches, serves, and as we'll hear next week, feeds the people. The part that is often underplayed, however, is the expectation that having been taught, served, and fed, the People of God will go and do likewise. This has been slow in coming, and even after 50 years, there still exists a solid minority in the Church who believe that nothing is worth doing if it's not led by an ordained person, preferably a priest.

Many people are concerned about the future of the Church, and I hear a lot of these worries. You may be one of them. But ask yourself this question. What is it that you're worried about specifically? Is the concern the slowly decreasing number of priests and religious? Or the slowly decreasing number of Church-goers? Are you worried that other religions, particularly Islam, seem to be gaining numbers? Do you hunger for the days when the hierarchy was quick to condemn bad behavior by Christians and non-Christians alike? Are you sad that many in your family have stopped going to Church? These are all concerns I've heard in the past year – there may be others.

To paraphrase Jesus after the storm at sea, "Where is your faith?" Please don't take that as a scolding comment. Search yourself. Does your faith come from the Bible? Does your faith come from identification with the Catholic Church? Does your faith come from within, from a certainty of the presence of God in your life? Is your faith subject to the latest scandal? The latest Gallup poll? These are important questions because they speak to what your faith is built upon, sand or rock. If you want your faith to be rock solid, it needs to start with how deep you let God into your heart. This is the unique power that St. Paul acquired after his conversion. He spoke of being "in Christ", a profound meshing of his life with Christ, to the point that there was no distinction. This gave him the ability to tell St. Peter that the Gentiles were just as faith-worthy as the Jews, and to act in that vein.

It's deceptively simple, brothers and sisters. The future of the Church is in your hands. It's in the hierarchy's hands too, yes, but it's in all of our hands, since we're all the People of God. Teach, pray, serve – it's Christ's mandate and the heart of what it means to follow him. It's what a shepherd does, and you've all been graduated from sheep to shepherd. Congratulations! Now let's go out there and save some souls, shall we?

Chapter 8 – Fear vs. Happiness

What's the opposite of happiness? The quick answer may be sadness, but I think that the opposite of happiness is fear. Does that ring true to you? When people are truly unhappy, it almost always boils down to fear of loss, whether it is a loss of love, a job, a family member, or one's health. But here's the good news. Practically the first thing out of God's mouth when he addresses one of us is, "Don't' be afraid!" God is the calmer of all fears, if we simply ask him to help. The second bit of good news? Happiness is not just the opposite of fear, it is a truly attainable state of being that goes way beyond the absence of fear. It can be attained with the help of Jesus. Let's explore that some more, shall we?

The 4 AM Wake-Up Call

Scripture Referenced: Matthew 14:22-33

> During the fourth watch of the night, he came toward them walking on the sea. When the disciples saw him walking on the sea they were terrified. "It is a ghost," they said, and they cried out in fear. At once Jesus spoke to them, "Take courage, it is I; do not be afraid."

In the gospels, Jesus performs various signs and miracles. Many have to do with healing people. But there's a subset of miracles that for lack of a better term, I'd call nature miracles. Jesus calming the sea, Jesus inducing a big catch of fish, and this one, my favorite nature miracle. It is by far the most incredible of them all. In every other nature miracle, one could plausibly offer an explanation that allows the laws of nature to remain intact. Calming the sea might be simply good timing and the big catch suggests stupid fish. But not this one! Walking on water? Mark, Matthew, and John all follow up the feeding of the thousands with this event, and all tweak the story to some degree. And, do you realize that this miracle is *not* in Luke's gospel? Why not?

If I were to further ask you about the theme of today's gospel, I wonder what you'd say. On the face of it, we have a rather amazing miraculous event, Jesus walking on the water. We have a storm, we have impetuous Peter, we have the apostles worshipping Jesus in the end. It's a pretty astonishing story all around. That Jesus is a pretty cool dude. Is that it? But what's the point *for us*?

There's a wonderful book by spiritual author Megan McKenna called *The Hour of the Tiger*. Have any of you read it? The subtitle of the book is *Facing Our Fears*. Ms. McKenna explains the origin of the title in the first chapter. The hour of the tiger is specifically 4 AM. For most people, 4 AM is the time when we're quite sound asleep. But, not always. Due to the cyclic rhythms of our sleeping patterns, 4 AM is actually a time when most of us cycle up toward consciousness, even if we don't wake. But, if something is on our mind, whether a worry or a concern, it is very easy to break through to wakefulness and we find ourselves staring at the clock with a mixture of dread and unhappiness and fear. Adding to the uneasiness is our body's chemical balance, which is at low levels at this time of night. More people die at the 4 AM hour than any other time of day. It is the hour when tigers are on the hunt, and their prey are stupid with sleep. This is the hour that tigers feed.

Note the odd opening line in today's gospel. "After he had fed the people, Jesus *made* the disciples get into a boat and precede him to the other side…" Other translations are stronger – "Jesus *compelled* the disciples to get into a boat…" This is important. Jesus has commanded them to leave, on their own, together, in a boat. Remember the last words of Jesus before the Ascension? Go and make disciples… Go! So they go. And in another interesting turn of phrase, we are told that the wind is against them. They aren't doing so well. It's a bit worrisome, maybe scary. Then comes the fourth watch of the night, the hours between 3 and 6 AM, the hours when our body's chemical balance is out of whack, the hours when most people die, the hour of facing your fears. The hour of the tiger.

So what are you afraid of? What wakes you up at 4 AM? The fears are usually around a finite number of issues. There's physical issues like suffering, pain, or death. There's fear of isolation, loneliness, and despair. There is the fear of losing money or possessions. And one of my favorites, there is worry about family members, especially our children. If only they'd listen to me, then I could get some sleep! And now, the first lesson of our gospel today. When we're lying in our beds, tossing and turning, do you catch sight of Jesus? He's right there, on the edge of the dream perhaps, on the outside of our boat, looking on, walking toward us. Do you see him? Do you call to him?

I remember a few years ago dealing with a very difficult work situation. I had a customer who was completely unreasonable, at least in my eyes. Due to many factors, some on our side, some on theirs, we were behind schedule on a large software project. Usually when this happens, you and the customer accept the reality and work to a mutually beneficial outcome. But this particular customer apparently felt that the right way to fix the problem was by yelling at us angrily. Whatever suggestion we would make was met with stony silence followed by an escalating rant that was truly breathtaking. Needless to say, the tiger visited every night at about 4:30 AM (he was a lazy tiger). I could have sweated it out, tossing and turning, but my solution was simple. I reached to my bedside and pulled out my rosary, because to me, at 4:30 in the morning, I needed *both* Jesus and Mary.

The Gospel tells us that at the fourth watch, Jesus came to the disciples in the boat. They were terrified. There's two kinds of fear seen here and each has a lesson for us. Most of the apostles simply cowered in the boat at the sight of the ghostly Jesus. But Peter, who is certainly just as afraid, faces his fear head on. "Lord, *if* it is you, command me to come to you on the water." At Jesus' word, he leaves the boat and begins to walk. But facing one's fear takes practice, and Peter is new at this game. His resolve falters and fear wins over yet again, and he sinks. But his instinct is sound, and he asks Jesus for help. *Immediately*, the text reads, Jesus catches Peter.

Think back on the times when you said, "Lord, save me!" Maybe not in those words exactly, but similar enough? What happened next? Did something dramatic happen? Generally, that's not the case, even though we wish it would. Our first reading about Elijah tells the truth of it. Was the Lord in the strong and heavy wind, crushing rocks? No. Was the Lord in the earthquake? No. Was the Lord in the fire? No. How did God come to Elijah? A tiny whispering sound, the true presence of God.

After my rosary that long ago early morning, I lay in bed with my mind whirling and my stomach churning, dreading the dawn. I really wanted God to smote that customer, that was for sure. I felt sorry for myself. I felt trapped. I felt alone. And then I felt something else. It was a voice. Now I know, you really can't "feel" a voice, but in actuality, I did feel it. It came from deep inside and the words were simple and commanding. The words that came to me were "Enough is enough!" The words were comforting and a little scolding, just as Jesus spoke to Peter. In a flash, I realized that the problem here was my own ego. I could not accept the fact that I was not able to fix this customer problem single-handed. And Jesus was telling me to stop this silliness and think of a new solution that just might be a little humbling for me. It came quickly. I apologized to the senior management, took responsibility, and brought in a new team to fix the problems. It cost me some good will and the company some money, but in the end, no one second-guessed me. It was the right thing to do, and it was Jesus' idea.

Earlier I asked why this miracle is not in Luke's gospel. He clearly knew about it, since it is in Mark's gospel, one of his sources, but Luke saw no need to include it in his account. Why? Understand the audience. Both Mark and Matthew were writing to persecuted communities. And for them, this story is strikingly appropriate. Jesus sends the apostles out in the boat – he's left them. They're on their own, seemingly. They get into trouble, and the comforting message is right there in front of them. Jesus is always, always, by your side, and usually when you don't expect him. But especially when you're the most afraid, in the fourth watch, the hour of the ??

Let's change that, shall we? How about the hour of the *rosary*? I suggested this once to a young woman who complained, "I don't always have a rosary with me. What do I do then?" Well, you have a head, and a heart, and ten fingers. The head is the Our Father, the fingers are the Hail Mary's, and the heart is the Glory Be. You're a walking rosary! Pray and listen. Listen with an open heart. Listen for the small voice. Jesus is right there!

The Rosary

Scripture Referenced: Matthew 22:1-10

> The king said to his servants, "The feast is ready, but those who were invited were not worthy to come. Go out, therefore, into the main roads and invite to the feast whomever you find."

This last Friday, if you happened to miss it, was the Feast of Our Lady of the Rosary, instituted by Pope Pius V in 1571, some 440 years ago. The Bishop has asked parishioners throughout the Diocese this day to ponder the meaning of this feast, and furthermore asked us who preach this Sunday to take as our topic the Rosary. Outside of the Mass and the Pope, I think the Rosary is the most enduring icon of the Catholic faith, so tightly linked to Mary, the Mother of God, that it is nearly impossible to find a statue of Mary that does not feature a rosary somewhere. Many devout Catholics pray a rosary every day. And, many devout Catholics do not. It's a prayer form that has been associated with miraculous events and, unfortunately, abused by some people who treat the rosary as magic beads to get God to do what they want. On measure, however, there are a lot more positive elements about the rosary to emphasize, so I'll avoid the false dichotomy of giving the positive and negative equal time and focus more on what this remarkable prayer has to offer.

First, a little history. The legend goes that the Blessed Virgin Mary appeared to St. Dominic, the founder of the Order of Preachers, the Dominicans, in the 13th century and handed him the first rosary. It's a nice story, but alas, completely made up. The reality is a bit more down to earth, but fascinating just the same. Well before St. Dominic came along, in the age of the great monasteries, perhaps 800 AD or so, it was the habit of the monks to pray all 150 psalms in Latin each day, often by singing. The peasants working in the fields wanted to pray along, but couldn't read, so the monks strung beads together, 150 of them, and gave them to the people so that they could keep track along with the monks. Variations began to appear, the most common a shortening of the psalter to three 50-psalm segments, necessitating fewer beads – 50 to be exact. Hmmm, sounding familiar?

The people wanted to pray along, however, so the monks suggested that the people pray an Our Father for each bead. This became popularly known as the *Pater Noster* rosary and soon craftsmen were employed in the making of these rosaries across Europe. The Hail Mary, as we know it today, did not exist until the 15th century. But as it became popular, people began to pray it in the same way, and soon the *Ave Maria* rosary caught fire as a devotion. The exercise however, remained the simple recitation of 50 Hail Marys in a row, nothing more. It took Dominic to evolve the rosary to its present form, just not the Dominic you think. This was Dominic of Prussia, a Carthusian monk who lived in the early 15th century. His brainstorm was to associate an event in Christ's life with each rosary bead. This idea, although a good one, was still a bit difficult, since memorizing all 50 events for someone who couldn't read was obviously a challenge. So, over the course of the next 50 years, the number of episodes dropped to 15, as in three sets of five – the glorious, joyful, and sorrowful mysteries. As devout pray-ers of the rosary know, Pope John Paul II added a new set of episodes, the Luminous Mysteries, which focus on Christ's adult ministry. In any event, by the time the feast of Our Lady of the Rosary was pronounced, the current formula of 50 Hail Marys interspersed with 5 Our Fathers, 5 Glory Bes, and the introductory prayers (the Apostle's Creed, an Our Father, 3 Hail Marys, and a Glory Be) was firmly established.

A friend tells me the story of serving in the prison one day when an inmate asked him about this "rosary thing". My friend carefully described the prayer sequence and the man went away counting on his fingers and muttering to himself. A couple of minutes later, he comes back and says, "I don't get it. Why all this fuss over something you can say in two minutes?" My friend looked at him a bit puzzled and asked him what he meant. "Well heck, listen. Our Father. Hail Mary. Hail Mary. Hail Mary. Hail Mary…etc."

But in a funny way, this inmate was hitting on a truth we should all keep in mind. There's no one way to say a rosary! Yes, the traditional approach is well understood. But people add prayers at the beginning, after each decade, and at the end. They change the prayers altogether, as in the Chaplet of Divine Mercy. Heck, you don't even need beads. I remember when my sister and I drove across country in 1981, we drew a picture of a rosary on a piece of scrap paper and used this to count our

Hail Marys each morning as we embarked on the next 400 mile leg of the journey. Fingers work really well too, especially at 3 AM in a lonely place. The mysteries are nice to contemplate, but I find the rosary much more meaningful by assigning each decade to a particular person or set of persons. First decade to those who have recently died, second decade to those who are sick, third decade to family, fourth decade to my own worries or concerns, and the fifth decade to potluck – whatever is in the news that day. It's all good.

Notice that the rosary can be said in community or as part of a private prayer practice. Today, we're saying the rosary either before or after each Mass, in community. There's a certain rhythm to the rosary that quickly becomes apparent when said in unison, almost a chant. I liken it to soldiers marching or a clock ticking or the regular breathing of a sleeping child. The repetition at first seems jarring – our brain rebels at the discipline needed. But that's the point of the prayer form – to engage our conscious brain so that our unconscious brain can surface, can become more aware, can listen without judgment or expectation. This is contemplation 101 – an excellent method, whether public or private. I have to be careful sometimes when I say a rosary in the car. I can contemplate myself right into a guard rail!

A lot of non-Catholics are a bit puzzled by the rosary and it's obvious connection to Mary. Many claim that the rosary is evidence that we worship Mary as some sort of goddess. The irony of this, of course, is that Mary herself would be quite indignant over such an accusation. Mary is always pointing to Jesus – always. In fact, one of the criterion used to determine if a Marian apparition is credible is by what Mary says. If she is calling on us to get closer to her Son, then that's powerful evidence in favor of her presence. What also impresses me is her humility, a lesson all of us, especially those of us in leadership positions, can benefit from emulating. The more humble we are in our prayer and actions, the more Christ can shine through to the darkness.

Just recently, I was alerted to an interesting facet of Michelangelo's painting of the Last Judgment in the Sistine Chapel. I've seen the painting twice, but never noticed it before. In the middle left side of the painting, there is an angel pulling two people up into heaven with a rope. But if you look at the scene closely, you'll suddenly realize that the rope is actually a rosary!

Denying Yourself

Scripture Referenced: Matthew 16:21-27

> Jesus began to show his disciples that he must go to Jerusalem and suffer greatly from the elders, the chief priests, and the scribes, and be killed and on the third day be raised. Then Peter took Jesus aside and began to rebuke him, "God forbid, Lord! No such thing shall ever happen to you." He turned and said to Peter, "Get behind me, Satan! You are an obstacle to me. You are thinking not as God does, but as human beings do."

I don't know about you, but I don't like hospitals. I really really try to avoid them. I have two sisters and a niece who are nurses, and an uncle who is a physician, so you would think that I would be a bit more serene about hospitals. But I'm not. My heart rate jumps, I'm as tense as can be, and my flight mechanism is in full gear. But to be clear, I love doctors and nurses. You guys go into hospitals every day, and I am ever grateful that you do. You have my full, if distant, support!

Jesus said to his disciples, "Whoever wishes to come after me must deny himself, take up his cross, and follow me."

It was a cool evening, the sun setting, a typically beautiful day in Encinitas. I was parked in the lot outside Scripps Memorial Hospital, my hands sweating. I was in my second year of diaconate training, and my task that evening was to go into the hospital and visit with patients. It was a simple job really. Just knock on their door, introduce myself, ask if they needed any prayer, and if so, offer a few words of support. I was not there to draw blood, or perform an MRI, or consult on the merits of a surgical procedure. I was there to offer "spiritual care", whatever that meant. I was expected by the chaplain, and it was time to go in. I sat frozen in the car. How could I offer them any spiritual care when I was a basket case myself?

Note carefully what Jesus says. Whoever wishes to come after me must deny himself, take up his cross, and follow me. The key words

– deny himself. Take up his cross. Note that Jesus isn't referring to people who have suffered setbacks, such as serious diseases or financial disaster. Yes, these are "crosses" without any doubt. But these crosses came into these people's lives, totally unbidden. Jesus wants us to *take up* our cross. That's *intentional*, and that's a big difference. These words came to me in the parking lot that evening, and I realized that if I wanted to follow Jesus, I'd better deny my fears that evening, pick up that cross and enter the hospital. So I did.

Jeremiah, often referred to as the "crying prophet," is clearly unhappy with his calling. He is compelled by God to speak words of warning to the thick-necked people of Judah, and he is not a very popular guy as a result. What he once considered a privilege has become a royal pain, and he feels duped by God, who is too strong for him. It is not inaccurate to say that Jeremiah has been "possessed" by God, at least in his opinion. This feels disturbing to us, for it appears that God has taken away Jeremiah's free will. But there's another explanation that is just as compelling. Once Jeremiah aligned himself with God, once Jeremiah opened himself to the burning justice that is God's middle name, once Jeremiah conformed himself to God (to use Paul's term), there is no going back. Because once you lose your life for the sake of God, you will find it. And what does "it" look like? The person you were meant to be, and you know it right down to your toes.

That evening, I went to the chaplain's office and picked up the list of Catholic patients who were presently in the hospital's care. I was only authorized to visit Catholic patients so there would be no accusations of proselytizing, that is, stealing sheep. I was not told why they were in the hospital – that's privileged information of course – but depending on where they were in the hospital, you can get a sense of how serious their situation was. So, I started out, armed with a little book of prayers, and headed to the second floor. I had a little badge on my shirt that had my picture, my name, and the grand title of "spiritual care volunteer". All the nurses were very busy and no one paid me much attention, and I felt totally lost. I went to one room, peaked in, and the patient was sound asleep. It didn't seem a good idea to wake them up and ask if they wanted a prayer. I can imagine the response! So I moved on. Another room had a bunch of people gathered around the patient and again, it seemed sort of intrusive to barge in and offer to hold hands and sing kumbaya around the bed side. It's amazing how easy it is to talk yourself out of carrying the cross.

I came to another room and there was a young woman sitting up in bed. Okay, this was good. She's alone, awake, and looks pretty healthy. She noticed me at the door, said hello, and I thought "here goes," so I introduced myself and she smiled and said, sure she could use a prayer or two. So I sat by the bedside and with little prompting from me, she told me that she had just been diagnosed with inoperable brain cancer. I was shocked – she couldn't have been more than mid-thirties in age. What could I possibly say to her? My eyes welled up in tears, and she noticed and said with a smile, "I'm not dead yet". She was comforting me. And then, with a burst of noise, two young boys dashed into the room and leapt onto the bed and into her arms yelling, "Hi Mom!". Dad was at the door, with a rueful smile. I quickly got up, introduced myself, and made my excuses to leave. She stopped me and said, "I still need those prayers". It was clear, however, that those boys were not going to sit still for a second, so I asked if I could hold her in prayer in the coming days, and she said, yes, please do. As I was backing out of the room, I glanced at the nameplate beside the door and I realized with a shock that I was visiting the wrong patient. She wasn't on my Catholic list. And the other part of today's reading came to me. "You are thinking not as God does, but as human beings do." Jesus' rebuke of Peter is the real challenge of today's reading.

How often we find ourselves frozen in place by human laws, peoples' opinions, societal norms, and political correctness. How often in our zeal not to make little waves, do we allow a tidal wave to wash over us? How often do we blindly stay the course, assuming that everyone thinks the same way we do, and find to our shock that this simply isn't true? Don't get me wrong. I'm not talking about politics necessarily, even though it is often most glaring here. The question to ask is, "What does God think about this?" Remember that God made everyone, not just Americans. Remember that God doesn't care about borders and money and skin color and who leads the Fortune list of the wealthiest people in the world. What profit is there to gain the whole world and forfeit your life? We are all God's children, and until we see that reality, we are thinking as grasping, competitive, petty human beings. It's not a pretty sight.

The next week, I went back to the hospital. She wasn't there. I don't know what happened to her. I hope she's not dead yet. I continued my rounds of the Catholic patients, just as uneasy as ever. Hospitals are not my thing. Put me in a maximum security prison any day. But two things I did change since that fateful night. After my rounds, I went to the chapel and said a specific prayer for everyone on my list, whether I spoke to them or not. Prayer is a powerful healing tool, don't forget that. I also made a point, whenever I finished with the Catholic patient, to acknowledge the other person in the room and offer a blessing if they wished. I was a little tired of thinking like human beings do. No one ever complained, and many accepted with enthusiasm.

What cross is waiting for you to be picked up? Think about this a bit. What is something that you know you should do, but are avoiding it? It doesn't need to be dramatic. It could be phone call to an estranged family member. It could be an invitation to a parish function on your favorite TV night. It could be Just Faith, a marvelous program this parish offers, one of the few in the diocese. It could be a retreat. It could be a neighbor who just moved in down the street that could use a friendly visit and some of your famous brownies. It could be a major job change, or a move to a non-profit organization. It only requires your yes, your intention, and your choice of cross. Find your life by losing something of yourself. It's hard to start, but once you get going, prepare for a life of amazing compassion. Guaranteed.

Simplicity, Purity, Awareness

Scripture Referenced: Isaiah 49: 3-6

> The Lord said to me: You are my servant, Israel, through whom I show my glory. Now the Lord has spoken who formed me as his servant from the womb, that Jacob may be brought back to him and Israel gathered to him; and I am made glorious in the sight of the Lord, and my God is now my strength!

Today's reading from Isaiah is very special to me. Isaiah, as a prophet, acts as an intermediary between God and the people of Israel. In this passage he hears a command from God that he shares with the people. It's a very challenging call, one fraught with great significance. Did you hear it? Listen again: "The Lord said to me: You are my servant, Israel, through whom I show my glory." When you hear the word *Israel*, understand it to mean the *believers*; that is, all of us! Apparently, we are all called to *servanthood*, and as a deacon, since my very title means *servant* in Greek, I perked up when I read this. What does it mean to be a servant? Could I become a better servant, a better deacon? How? How do we all become such servants?

I suspect that if I asked the kids in the congregation what they wanted to be when they grew up, I doubt I'd hear the response, "I want to be a servant." In the days of Christ, servants were typically slaves, and this didn't change much over the next 2,000 years, even when slavery was largely outlawed. Servants remain low on the social status meter, even when we give them new labels like nanny or chauffeur or maid or housekeeper. So what are we missing here? Why are asked, no, not asked, *commanded* to become servants? What is it about servanthood that is somehow a bridge to the Holy?

Let's dig in a little deeper, shall we? When you are a servant, are you in control of your situation? No, not really. Do you have a lot of money? No, not typically. Do you get to tell other people what to do? No, not usually. So you need to be obedient and you are poor. Hmm, sounding a little familiar? Consider this – in virtually every spiritual tradition in the world, the path to the Holy is marked by a decision to lead an ascetic life, a decision to detach oneself from the typical measures of earthly success and freely choose a life of simplicity, prayer, and perhaps the hardest of all, obedience. Every religious order features these characteristics, elevating them to the level of profound promises that we call vows. Vows of poverty, chastity, and obedience. So what do we do? We always zoom in on chastity and kind of ignore the other two. Well, I chose the married life, so there goes "chastity". So much for the religious life!

Not only does this attitude abuse the notion of what chastity is, it also conveniently dispenses with the other two equally important characteristics of servanthood, poverty and obedience. But let's take these characteristics one by one, talk about what they don't mean, and show them in a clearer light.

Poverty: it doesn't mean that you choose to dress in a potato sack and live under the freeway overpass. Poverty is about living simply, about living in a neutral stance with God's creation. Living simply is about taking from the world what is needed for one to live, and if you've been blessed with abundant advantages, to freely share your excess with others who haven't been so blessed. Poverty, in this context, means intentional simplicity.

Chastity: it means abstaining from sexual activity until you are married, but even then, in the context of married life, to be chaste means to be faithful to one's spouse. We're all called to chastity, regardless of what vocation we choose. There's nothing special or weird about it – it's about purity and faithfulness. When did these stop being important? Why is chastity so celebrated in the Christian tradition? Could it be actually good for you?

Obedience: despite our notion of this word as meaning "to follow orders", it actually has a much more profound meaning in the spiritual walk. Obedience comes from the Latin *obediere*, which means "to listen with the heart". It's a call to deepening awareness, to seeking with an open heart and an open mind. It means never underestimating the wisdom of God.

So how do these ideals, these choices, work together? A choice for poverty is a choice for two important elements of the spiritual walk. First of all, a choice for poverty is a decision to clear one's life of distractions, to clear the sight lines, to clear the impediments away, to refute the lie that material things bring happiness. Material things may bring short-term comfort, but the more one has, the more one grows anxious of losing them, and the more the stuff we *think* we own is found to *own us*. The second benefit of poverty is the choice to walk the path with the *unintentionally* poor, those who have no way of ever being rich. This is the path of compassion, the path to "suffering with", not just cheering from the sideline.

Chastity is likewise beneficial in multiple ways. For the single person, chastity is a pure light in the darkness, a gift waiting to be opened, a gift of exclusivity that profoundly honors the one to which it is given. Likewise, within marriage, chastity is a simplicity of focus, an acknowledgement of the relationship as being more important than a passing desire. Chastity within the religious life is expressed as celibacy, which in its simplest form is a dedication to an exclusive relationship with the whole body of Christ, all of us. Celibacy is a gift to *us* – do you realize that?

And finally, obedience ties them all together by seeking and finding an overall context, a meaning that brings reason and purpose to these intentional choices. Obedience takes our ego out of the picture and allows God's will to be truly done. In an important way, can't you see that as a relief? God's in charge!

We're all called to poverty, chastity, and obedience, the building block of servanthood. But if the words give you trouble, let me rephrase them. We're all called to simplicity, purity, and awareness. Same ideas, just as challenging, but the payoff is immense. Take a look at Isaiah again – note the beautiful image contained in the last sentence. It's not simply about being a servant, it's what will happen when we all become servants of the Lord. Listen: "I will make you a light to the nations, that my salvation may reach to the ends of the earth." Yes, you'll glow in the dark and be seen from a distance! That's the payoff to being a servant. You'll shine!

You know what to do…simplicity, purity, and awareness! The initials are *S,P,A*. The *SPA* treatment!

Levels of Happiness

Scripture Referenced: John 4:5-42

> Jesus said to her, "Everyone who drinks this water will be thirsty again; but whoever drinks the water I shall give will never thirst; the water I shall give will become in him a spring of water welling up to eternal life."

What is happiness? What is happiness? If you think about it, you realize that the answer seems straightforward enough at first, but then it gets a bit elusive. I think it is fair to say that there are levels of happiness. At the basic, sort of animal level, there's nothing like a good meal, right? Your favorite food, well-prepared, set off with some interesting side dishes and a big piece of chocolate cake at the end –who could resist? You push back from the table – quite frankly – happy! But let's face it. In 4 or 5 hours, you're hungry again. Let's call this simple fulfillment of basic human needs Level 1 happiness. Food, drink, favorite TV show, sleep, repeat.

Level 2 happiness involves a bit more effort on our part. Level 2 is called comparative happiness, because, as the name implies, this notion of happiness is all about comparison to others. Am I faster, smarter, prettier, richer, better dressed, nicer, have more friends on Facebook, etc. It's all about the happiness we derive from *winning*. Our identity can get invested in comparison, to the point that our lives are a constant cycle of stress and striving, lest we fall down the ladder a notch or two. Brothers and sisters, most of us are stuck at this level, especially if we're young adults, but not exclusively. Our competitive world loves to cheerlead this game from the sidelines – hurray for the winners! But wait. There's a problem. What if we don't win? If we are fully invested in seeking Level 2 happiness, losing can feel catastrophic. We can feel much like the heroine in today's story, the woman at the well.

Do you think she's happy? In the context of first century Palestine, I don't think so. She's alone, at midday, drawing water. Understand that in that culture, women would conduct any outside-the-home activity in groups. Why? Security in numbers for certain, but also as a social activity. Without TV or radio or iPhones, people crave human interaction. Going down to the well together was an exercise in both Level 1 happiness (need water to live) and Level 2 happiness (who's where on the small town social status ladder). But this Samaritan woman, acting alone, disengaged, was clearly a loser, a social pariah. Jesus sees it clearly and draws her into a discussion on happiness.

The conversation operates on two levels at first, the woman talking about water to drink and Jesus offering so-called "living water". She doesn't buy into it, until Jesus zings her with that pointed observation that she has had five husbands. How's that working out for you? Are you happy? From a Level 2 point of view, no way. She's dropped down to base Level 1, with zero prospect of getting back to Level 2. But here's the heart of Jesus' message. You don't need Level 2 happiness to be happy! There's a Level 3 and a Level 4 that make Level 2 totally irrelevant. Living water! What's that?! Did you ever wonder?

To get the full measure of Levels 3 and 4, I refer you to Fr. Robert Spitzer's book *Healing the Culture*. It's a marvelous book, especially if you have a scientific mind. I'll share a couple of nuggets with you that I think get to the heart of this notion of "living water". First of all, let's discuss Level 3 happiness. If Level 1's objective is to please our so-called "lizard brain", and Level 2's objective is to be better than anyone else, Level 3's objective is to do good beyond ourselves. This happiness is quite different from the other levels because it is long-term. In both Levels 1 and 2, sensory pleasure and winning the most recent contest are short-term happiness events, with the need to repeat these actions frequently, if not compulsively. Doing good for others is a long-range effort, typically made up of actions that seem small at first, but tend to build on each other until you suddenly find yourself engaged in a daily life of charity and justice that has redefined your mission in life. This is the hidden secret of true philanthropic actions. The more you give, the more you get. The more you put others first, the happier you are. And that happiness is enduring, deep, and profound. I can tell you without hesitation that some of the happiest people I know are people who think of others first. It's paradoxical and counter-cultural, isn't it?

And here's the real kicker. If you have Level 3 happiness, you don't need Level 2 happiness. The whole comparison, game-winning mentality, who's richer than who, is quickly seen to be shallow and insignificant. Furthermore, Level 3 happiness even trumps those base instincts at Level 1. A person who seeks Level 3 happiness will fast for 2 weeks on behalf of Syrian children and not blink an eye. No, they're not masochists. They are drinking *living water*.

But wait. If Level 3 seems pretty amazing, what's Level 4? Level 4 happiness is bound up in the transcendent, the ultimate Good, the perfect dialogue, in short, in God alone. As wonderful as Level 3 happiness is, it has a fatal flaw. We are not perfect, nor is the object of our self-giving (other people) perfect. Giving ourselves up to the benefit of the other is bound to be a little bit frustrating. We want things to get better, we want people to thank us, we want our actions to be efficient and life-changing. We want some results! Not always happening… The only object of our desire that matches our desire and fulfills our desire is God alone. This is the true source of enduring happiness, what Jesus calls the "peace beyond all understanding".

How do you get to Level 4 happiness? We get a clue by reading the words of people who have attained this Level. People like John of the Cross, Theresa of Avila, Clare of Assisi, and other mystics. If there's one thing that characterizes their spiritual demeanor it is a self-conscious disengagement of their ego in favor of the will of God. In essence, they replace their flawed and wounded ego with the person of Christ, and suddenly, it no longer matters who gets the credit, or where this all fits in the grand scheme, or why this recipient isn't grateful enough. The person has given it all over to God, and that is supremely enough. Talk about peace. Talk about happiness. It doesn't get any better than this and you all know it to be true deep down. St. Augustine: "Lord, you made us for yourself, and our hearts are restless until they rest in you." And who says that you have to die to have your hearts rest in God? Level 4 happiness is available to you today.

Why doesn't everyone attain Level 4 happiness, or at least strive for it? Why do most people get stuck at Level 2, to their everlasting grief? I think that there are two reasons, two hindrances. One is that the happiness attained in winning, as fleeting as it is, is still very powerful. It is a bit like a drug, and can be very addictive, especially if we're good at achieving things. Studies have been done with birds that have them peck a lever to get some food. As you can imagine, they then peck the lever to get food when they're hungry. But you want to know how to get them pecking that lever all day long? That's right – only give them food at random intervals. Peck, nothing, peck, nothing, peck, food!, peck, nothing. Play, lose, play, lose, play win!, play, lose. The only way to break that pattern is to stop playing that game. It's no wonder that many theologians these days equate sin with addiction. We're kind of wired that way.

The second reason we get stuck in Level 2 striving is that the move to Level 3 does not feel like a step in the "right" direction. We are so ingrained in thinking that the right direction is all about more and more and more for each of us, often at the expense of someone else, that Level 3 seems a step back, or a step down. It's counterintuitive. Giving something of myself away, whether it's through money or time or sharing, feels like a loss at one Level. Our addictive minds fight it – and Jesus is well aware of how hard it is – sort of like a camel going through a needle's eye. But if you take that step, the rewards are stunning. I asked you at the beginning of the homily what happiness is. Here's a different question. Do you *want* to be happy? The formula is right here in front of you. It's all about giving at first – giving of our stuff, our time, our money. That's Level 3. And Level 4 is about giving over our ego. That's a bit harder, and you have to have some time in Level 3 before Level 4 makes any sense at all. But the invitation is right here. Do you *want* it?

Chapter 9 – Grace

Grace is a term we tend to overuse, and as such, it loses meaning and context. Sit for a moment and consider what grace is – a gift from God. But not just any gift, it is a gift of God's *self*, a sharing of the essence of God with us very undeserving creatures. The very fact that we're alive is a grace, but the day-in, day-out play of our existence numbs us to the overwhelming reality of this truth. God wants you alive, well, and in relationship with Him! And he's willing to do *almost* all of the work. You have one key job in this relationship – to humbly say yes. Is that so hard? Apparently it is. What happens when you do say yes?

My Grace is Enough

Scripture Referenced: 2 Corinthians 12:7-10

> [The Lord] said to me, "My grace is sufficient for you, for power is made perfect in weakness." I will rather boast most gladly of my weaknesses, in order that the power of Christ may dwell with me. Therefore, I am content with weaknesses, insults, hardships, persecutions and constraints, for the sake of Christ; for when I am weak, then I am strong.

Whenever I read a phrase or teaching in the Scriptures that seems counter-intuitive or paradoxical, I have a tendency to skip over it. I'll think, "Must be a poor translation". Or I'll think, "the author must mean something else…" Do you ever find yourself doing that? We just move right on past -- but in doing so, we may miss a real nugget of insight, a truth so deep that it can be mined for a considerable benefit if we take some time with it. This brief passage from Paul's letter to the Corinthians is a perfect example.

Paul is sharing a painful reality with us, a so-called thorn in the flesh, that truly bugs him. As we all do, he prays for healing, for release. Now realize that Paul has a pretty amazing relationship with God – he's had direct revelations of Jesus Christ after all – so if anyone should have an inside track, it's Paul. But God does not grant Paul his wish.

Why not? Here's the first paradoxical statement, "my grace is sufficient for you, for power is made perfect in weakness." Hmmm, you call that an answer to a prayer? Must be a poor translation! But let's look more closely. Grace is God's gift of God's self – God's gift of God's power. This we know. Apparently, God is saying that grace enters into us most freely when we're weak, not when we're strong. Somehow weakness opens a door to God, provides an entry where none existed before. Here's the real test of a paradoxical statement – does it ring true?

Like many of you, I start and end my day in prayer using the Church's Liturgy of the Hours. The Liturgy of the Hours consists of psalms, short excerpts from Scripture, petitions, and reflections from the writings of many saints. The Liturgy of the Hours rotates through a basic 4-week cycle as we go through the Church year. So, you're going to read many of the same psalms over and over again. When things are going especially well in my life, I just breeze through the prayers, kind of reading them, but really not that tuned in. But if things are going rough, for whatever reason, the psalms and prayers seem to just pop off the page and touch me deeply. I was having a week from hell just recently, due to a lot of work pressures, and my little self, my ego, was fretting away.

After tossing and turning all night, I opened my prayer book and read "In the morning let me know your love for I put my trust in you. Make me know the way I should walk: to you I lift up my soul." (Ps 143) And then, two pages later, this from Paul's letter to the Romans, "The sufferings of the present are as nothing compared with the glory to be revealed in us." (Romans 8:18)

The point is that I've read these excerpts faithfully for 8 years now, but they only touched me when I was weak, vulnerable, yes, open. God can only become God to us when we stop being god. This is the answer to the question, "why do bad things happen to good people?" God allows the universe to be unfair, unjust, painful, and broken because it is in this weakness of the universe that God's grace can enter with power. It's not because God wants us to suffer, it's because God wants us to *listen*. God's message? My grace is enough. My grace is all that you need. You don't need money, alcohol, perfect teeth, a new BMW, a degree from Stanford, or a high-definition television. You need *grace*. You with me so far?

What does grace mean? What does a life of grace look like? If it's all that we need, how would our life look? To answer that, at least partially, go to the end of Paul's reading and uncover the second paradoxical statement he makes. Here's the description of a life of grace: "Therefore I am content with weaknesses, insults, hardships, persecutions and constraints, for the sake of Christ; for when I am weak, then I am strong." How is this true?

The life Paul is describing is a life of perfect freedom. Freedom! We all know how to live life when everything is going great. We seek it, work for it, drive ourselves to distraction to get there, and every so often, we actually taste it, don't we? That day when everything clicks. The traffic lights are all green, the kids are little angels, you get money in the mail, your body sings with nature. Ahh, you know how those days make you feel, right? Paul's insight, however, is that when you're having a truly awful day, you can be equally content, because in our weakness, we become *aware* that God's grace is working powerfully, just as it always is. Perfect freedom comes when nothing on this earth has any power over us. We recognize our place in the universe – we are children of God, and that is all we really need to know. This is a life of grace. And here's the truly amazing part, the final paradox explained. When nothing on this earth has any power over us, we are then the most powerful people on the earth. Do you understand that? When nothing has power over us, we are in perfect freedom, and nothing can affect us. This is the way Jesus walked the earth. He walked in apparent weakness, no money, no home, no place to lay his head. Yet in this apparent weakness, he had the knowledge that he was the beloved Son of God, and in that knowledge, nothing, not even death, had power over him.

If we can see ourselves for one moment as just that beloved, just that graced, we would experience perfect freedom through the power of the Holy Spirit and yes, change the world. If God is for us, who can be against?

Think back on the times in your life when God's presence has been particularly evident. Were you in a moment of weakness, of vulnerability? If you're going through a stressful time right now, whether economic or family or some other difficulty, ask yourself how God is trying to get through in your weakness. How is God making you aware of his grace? How is he speaking to you? If you're taking care of someone who is having a hard time, help them ask and answer the same question. Perhaps you're a key to their locked door. And if life is really good for you right now, that's great too! Rejoice and be glad! Thank the Lord for this time. But….understand, it won't last. This is what it means to be human, to be in this world. But if we learn to be equally content with the highs of life and the lows, then we've understood the power of Paul's paradoxical statements. Weakness, grace, strength, power – they're all tied together. Christ shows us how we can walk that path as well.

My grace is sufficient for you, for power is made perfect in weakness. On this July 4th weekend, we celebrate our country's *independence*, won at great cost. As Americans, we express our heartfelt gratitude to our forbearers. Christ offers the world something more – true *freedom*, which does not depend on nationality. The only prerequisite is our humanity – and to that end, we offer our thanks, our Eucharist, as celebrated today. Independence, freedom. We are truly blessed.

Relating to the Holy Spirit

Scripture Referenced: John 20:19-23

> Jesus said to them again, "Peace be with you. As the Father has sent me, so I send you." And when he had said this, he breathed on them and said to them, "Receive the Holy Spirit. Whose sins you forgive are forgiven them, and whose sins you retain are retained."

Today, Pentecost Sunday, is a day that we are invited to look very carefully at the third person of the Holy Trinity, the Spirit. All three readings mention the Holy Spirit specifically, but if I were to ask each of you to define the Holy Spirit, I'll bet I get a whole multitude of answers. We all have a sense of God the Father, mostly personified in our culture by Michelangelo's image of a large, floating, white-bearded guy in the sky, reaching out with His creative touch. God the Father seems a bit distant, maybe a bit fearsome for many of us. The second person, Jesus the Christ, is much more accessible, and clearly the focus of most of our prayer lives and meditations, particularly the Liturgy we call the Mass. Since Jesus is human as much as he is God, we feel a strong connection, an expectation that he understands us intrinsically, and through that connection we are made holy. All good stuff. But what about the Holy Spirit?

The image of the Holy Spirit that we typically see in art is what? Yes, a dove. Why? Because the bible specifically tells us that the Spirit descended upon Jesus during his baptism "in the form of a dove". Today's first reading is quite different in tone, equating the Spirit's arrival as a strong, driving wind that somehow morphs into tongues of fire resting on all of those present. Earlier in John, Chapter 14, Jesus talks about the Holy Spirit as the Advocate, perhaps better translated as a defense lawyer. But somehow, praying to God the Father, God the Son, and God the Holy Attorney doesn't quite cut it! So how do we relate to this third person of the Trinity?

We are told by theologians that the Holy Spirit exists through the relationship of God the Father and God the Son. The mutual indwelling in perfect love between Father and Son is so intensely powerful that a third person "proceeds" from this relationship, co-eternal, co-equal, and consubstantial. The Holy Spirit is the *action* of God the Father and God the Son, an incredible energy produced that affects the entire universe. Think of the scientific principle that drives the most important star in the sky for us, the sun. The fusion of hydrogen atoms ignites a blaze of fire that warms our planet 93 million miles away. Can you see how that analogy, although not ideal, gives you a sense of the Spirit?

Let's go a bit further with this idea. The Spirit proceeds from the relationship between the Father and the Son, so that invites us to probably the best definition of the Holy Spirit that I can muster. The Holy Spirit, by nature of that amazing love connection, comes to us as the God of *awareness*. You see, the Spirit connects the dots, the Spirit produces the "aha" moments in our lives, the Spirit blows where it wills and surprises us. The Spirit makes us aware that God is all around us, that God loves us immensely, and that God wants to work through us. Let me give you an example or two.

After the wild fires scorched East County in 2005, my wife and I took a trip to Julian one Sunday afternoon. We have every CD David Haas has ever produced, and we were playing his music in our car, with the music on shuffle – just playing songs randomly. We hadn't seen too much damage to the forest up to a point, when suddenly, we rounded a bend in the road and there spread out before us was a moonscape of destruction. Burnt trees, blackened earth, charred houses. We pulled off the road and just looked at the scene in shock, tears springing to our eyes. At that moment, David Haas began to sing, "Come Lord Jesus, send us your Spirit, renew the face of the earth!" We both laughed out loud, and knew God was here, amidst this disaster, and He was going to make it right. That was the Holy Spirit doing his thing.

When I write a homily, I invite the Holy Spirit to guide my words. One time, about 3 years ago, I wrote a homily about my younger brother, who died of cancer amidst a struggle with drug addiction. His journey was a journey of redemptive suffering, and I shared that story with some concern, because it was an emotionally wrenching story for me. After one of the Masses, a woman came up to me with tears pouring down her face, and I thought, oh no, what is this? I've clearly upset her. But her story astounded me. Her own brother, at that very moment in time, was living the exact same journey as mine did. My story gave her hope, gave her a path to walk, and we met twice more over the next few months, praying and talking about how to work with her lost sheep brother. It became a healing event. What did I learn? The Holy Spirit will use us in very direct, very specific ways, usually without our own knowledge. The Spirit of connections, working through His people, takes our meager gifts, offered in His name, and *glorifies* them.

Maybe one of the reasons why it is so hard to get our heads around the Holy Spirit is that God doesn't want us to! If we think we have God the Spirit defined, we immediately limit the Spirit, putting the Spirit in a little box on the shelf, rarely to be opened. The reality is that each of us comes to an understanding of the Spirit by how the Spirit manifests itself in us. St. Paul tells us that there are different kinds of spiritual gifts but the same Spirit, given to us for some benefit. In other words, your gifts, whatever they are, if offered to God, will be used by the Spirit to affect the world in some way, sometimes astonishing, but more often quiet and profound. The Spirit connects the dots, bringing awareness to someone who needs a question answered, who needs a smile today, who needs to be reminded that God loves, and loves, and loves, and especially, loves you!

And when we allow the Holy Spirit to work in our lives, to use our gifts in ways pleasing to God, the Spirit will leave a gift behind. Just as a torrent of water moving across the land leaves a channel carved in the earth, so will the Spirit leave a channel in our heart and mind, a channel lined with joy. That's how you can tell that your gifts are being used by the Spirit – if you feel joyful in the doing so. Healing, preaching, teaching, singing, smiling, building, comforting, holding, giving – if it gives you joy, you're on the right track. The Holy Spirit is connecting people, smoothing over the chaos, yes, renewing the face of the earth. The Spirit can't be held back, any more than you can dictate where a dove must fly, or where the wind must blow, or whether a person with inoperable cancer can be cured.

Come Holy Spirit, fill the hearts of your faithful, and kindle in them the fire of your love. Send forth your Spirit, and they shall be created, and you shall renew the face of the earth.

Faith and Healing

Scripture Referenced: Mark 5:21-43

> Jesus, aware at once that power had one out from him, turned around in the crowd and asked, "Who has touched my clothes?" But his disciples said to Jesus, "You see how the crowd is pressing upon you, and yet you ask, 'Who touched me?'" And he looked around to see who had done it. The woman, realizing what had happened to her, approached in fear and trembling. She fell down before Jesus and told him the whole truth. He said to her, "Daughter, your faith has saved you. Go in peace and be cured of your affliction."

Once one I was a child, I was riding my bicycle in the neighbor's driveway across the street and wouldn't you know it, the tire slipped on some gravel and I took a spill, scraping my knee bloody. All my friends hovered over me in concern, and I quickly got up, limped home and found my Mom in the kitchen. At her look of concern, I burst into tears and she did all of the correct "Mom" things, washing my wound, drying my tears, and applying a Band-Aid to the scrape. However, at the sight of the bandage, I didn't seem entirely comforted, so she, using that special Mother intuitive radar, took another look and said, "you know, I think this one needs a second Band-Aid…" That brought the smile she was looking for – for I was truly a wounded warrior now!

How does this simply childhood memory relate to the Gospel reading today? Isn't the gospel theme about life threatening illness and rising from the dead? Yes, but at a root level, the exact same thing is happening here as happened to me all those years ago, if we look carefully. Mark takes two healing stories and weaves them together in a most fascinating way, including a hidden number that is of great significance. Did you catch the magic number? (I'll tell you in a moment – now you have to stay awake!)

At first hearing, you think the story is about the poor hemorrhaging woman and the little girl who has died. No doubt they're the receivers of Jesus' healing. But that's not the real point of the story at all. The crux of the story is the interior disposition of Jairus and the hemorrhaging woman, what they are thinking, what they are feeling. We start with Jairus. As a synagogue official, he of all people would probably NOT be a fan of Jesus, who was known as a severe critic of the scribes and Pharisees. But there's something about the desperation of love that drives Jairus to Jesus, who immediately sets out to take care of his daughter. Jairus comes to Jesus out of desperation – remember this – he turns to God in crisis. This is typical of most of us, isn't it? We don't think of God when things are going great, but just wait until we fall off our bike…

Now we come to the second story, the hemorrhaging woman, who is literally a walking dead person in so many ways. Her bleeding makes her ritually impure, unclean, and she would be shunned by everyone she came in contact with. She has lost her health and her property both – you can't get much worse off. But amazingly, she comes to the certainty that by simply touching Jesus, she will be healed. She acts on her impulse and sure enough, she is healed. Jesus knows that power has gone out of him, and quickly confronts her, much to the astonishment of the apostles. The poor woman, trembling in the presence of God (as we all would, I suspect), tells the whole story and Jesus praises her faith. Note that he doesn't say, "Daughter, your faith allowed me to save you." No, simply put, "your faith has saved you". Apparently that is the key to the healing – her *faith*.

The touching scene, so poignantly told, is suddenly interrupted by the dreadful news that Jairus' daughter is dead. Why bother Jesus any longer? It's too late! Ever feel that way? Notice what Jesus says to Jairus at this moment. "Do not be afraid; just have faith." There's that word *faith* again. Somehow faith is linked to healing. But how? Keep on reading. Jesus continues to Jairus' house (don't you wonder what Jairus is thinking?) and there's a scene out of a bad movie. People wailing and acting hysterically, which is appropriate cultural behavior for the Middle East by the way. Jesus has none of it and gets rid of all the drama queens. Into the house they go – Jesus, a few close disciples and Jairus and his wife. Without any arm waving or loud cries to the gods, Jesus simply touches the girl and with a gentle word, she awakes.

Here's the magic number. How old is the girl? Twelve. How many years was the woman afflicted with bleeding? Twelve. What does blood signify in the Hebrew scriptures? Life. So in case you missed it, twelve is the perfect number (12 tribes, 12 apostles, etc.). Jesus stops the blood loss in the woman and re-invigorates the blood flow in the little girl. Both miracles were 12 years in the making – both stories are challenges to us to seek the inner depth of what's going on here – to drink deeply of these stories. The twelves are signs blinking out of the gospel reading. Pay attention!

So, let's look at faith and healing for a moment. A little boy, falling off his bicycle, runs to Mom. Why? He knows she will heal him. The hemorrhaging woman goes to Jesus and touches him. Why? She knows he will heal her. At the simplest level, this is faith. Is the healing permanent? No. The little boy will fall again, the woman will surely sicken and die one day. But for that moment in time, they had the perfect healing disposition. I approached Mom with the certainty that she would make it better. The woman did the same with Jesus. Can you hold on to that certainty as adults?

Alas, most of us are like Jairus, aren't we? When trouble hits, we quickly turn to God for help. But do we turn in faith? Or do we turn in desperation? There's a big difference. I distinctly remember that when my brother was on his death bed many years ago, my sister informed a priest friend that Steve was slipping, was definitely approaching death. The priest's response startled us all. He said, "Perhaps we're not praying hard enough!" I remember being surprised and a little irritated. My thought was an exact match of the villagers today – why bother Jesus? It's too late!

Are you ready for the really good news? Although faith is a wonderful facilitator of healing, you don't have to have much of it to be healed! Healing is not something you have to earn. Jesus will take even that turn to him in desperation, that mustard seed of faith, and use it not simply to heal, but to raise us from the dead. I doubt Jairus had much faith at all, and the little girl was simply a little girl. Jesus healed anyway. You see, brothers and sisters, in God's eyes, as the book of Wisdom tells us, we are imperishable, the image of God's own nature. The healing may not come in this life – have you thought of that? Some of us apparently need to die to be healed, in God's own mysterious way. The Church calls it *purgatory*. More often than not, it is not the person who is sick who needs healing, but the family around them, the onlookers, the doubters, who need healing. God's healing so amazing. We often ask for a drop of healing water and God says sure, why not, and sprays us with a fire hose. We get soaked and everyone around us gets wet too. When it comes to healing, God has lousy aim.

The little boy who ran home to Mom was sure of two things – home was safe and Mom was there to heal. Simple faith. God's home is safe, and Jesus is there to heal. Always.

A Life of Authenticity

Scripture Referenced: Luke 23:35-43

> Now one of the criminals hanging there reviled Jesus, saying, "Are you not the Christ? Save yourself and us." The other, however, rebuking him, said in reply, "Have you no fear of God, for you are subject to the same condemnation? And indeed, we have been condemned justly, for the sentence we received corresponds to our crimes, but this man has done nothing criminal." Then he said, "Jesus, remember me when you come into your kingdom." He replied to him, "Amen, I say to you, today you will be with me in Paradise."

I really love this feast day, this celebration fixed at the end of our Church year, this focus on Christ the King. It's a day of paradox and contrast, an invitation to ponder the mystery of Jesus the Christ and what we can learn and take to heart. Since it's a feast day, all three readings shine a different light on the occasion, each illuminating an aspect of Christ's kingship, and each casting a shadow as well. The first reading is a simple culmination of what has been a very long and dangerous journey for David. From simple shepherd roots, David slowly gains popularity and power, listening closely to God and dodging the increasingly violent King Saul, who is extremely jealous of David and his ability to always do the exact right thing at the right time. At this point in the story, Saul is dead, and David has consolidated his power to the point that the elders of Israel make him their new king. He goes on to rule for over 40 years, bringing Israel to the peak of influence and wealth. The point? This is what Israel considered a king, this is who the Messiah is supposed to be like, and this is still what we think about when we hear the word "king".

Paul's letter to the Colossians, our second reading, features a liturgical hymn, probably set to music at one time, that exalts Christ as the firstborn of creation *way back when*, the head of the body, the Church, *today*, and the preeminent firstborn of the dead, through which we all must pass in our final journey from heaven to earth. It's an amazing set of images, and seems to sum up all of the theological concepts around Christ in one tidy formula. Alas, this mind-blowing theophany is so far beyond our present reality that we can't get a handle on it. How does this image of Christ the King of the Universe impact our existence here and now? What does it call us to do as we exit Mass today?

Fortunately, the gospel brings it all home. Luke's depiction of Jesus in the final moments of his human life is horrendous in its detail. Jesus is alone in his agony, reviled and insulted by the rulers and soldiers, and even one of the criminals hung next to him joins in. Can you imagine a lower point for Jesus than this? This is a king? Are you serious? Now the delicious irony. A criminal, a sinner, a man deserving a death sentence, an absolute scumbag in the eyes of society, gets it right. He speaks the truth – this man Jesus is no criminal – and then audaciously asks for the *world.* Jesus, remember me when you come into your kingdom. And Jesus grants his wish without hesitation. What kind of a king is this? Light and shadow, exaltation and blood, power and helplessness, peace and forgiveness.

There's a word for this, a word we can take to prayer and pondering this day. That word is *integrity*. Integrity is the state of being whole, entire, consistent in actions, words, and deeds. It is *honesty lived out.* I recall an incident from my youth when I and my three brothers were called into the kitchen by my Mom and asked to explain why there were blobs of peanut butter on the wall. We all looked at the floor, none of us willing to admit that we had been engaged in a wonderful battle involving flicking peanut butter blobs at each other with the tip of a butter knife. Mom told us about integrity, which she explained as being honest at all times, even if we could be punished. My little brother then piped up and said, "In that case, Mom…" and he pointed at me, "he started it!" We all learned some lessons that day, one of which is that dried peanut butter doesn't come off walls very well!

Jesus lived a life of complete integrity. Integrity - the perfect match of word and action. *Integrity – the complete opposite of hypocrisy.* Is it any wonder that hypocrites drive Jesus crazy? They are the walking anti-Jesus people, evil twins, kryptonite. But wait, how do we know that Jesus had complete integrity? Because at his very worst point, the nadir of his life, he kept on doing what he always did. He forgave. Jesus forgave the thief on his right, forgave everyone who was killing him, returned love in the face of hatred, just as he had been doing his entire ministry. As he died is as he lived. The test of impending death revealed a core of pure, untainted gold.

I recently read about a woman named Rachel Remen. Rachel works with the dying as a counselor. One day a woman came up to her and confronted her, telling her she resented all this talk about death as something meaningful. Then she recounted the horrible death of her husband a number of years earlier. He had been diagnosed with cancer; and as therapy after therapy had failed, he became bitter, lashing out at everyone, rebuffing anyone who tried to comfort him. He regretted his life choices, and died angry and withdrawn. The woman ended the telling of this ordeal with the statement, "I do not want to die this way." Rachel asked her, "So how do you need to live?" The woman looked puzzled. So Rachel asked her again. "*How do you need to live to be sure that you do not die this way?*" This time she got it. The woman stared off into space for a moment, making eye contact with something intensely personal. Then she reached out, touched Rachel's hand and turned away into the crowd. Some months later, the woman contacted Rachel and told her that she realized at that moment that she was not living as authentically as she wanted. Contemplating her death started her on a process of discovering her own integrity.

Imagine. Move your death from somewhere in the distant future to right now. Many of us lead lives in the past, regretting past actions and poor decisions. We play the old tapes over and over again, pausing with perverse relish at our favorite parts, often dredging up old emotions – anger, fear, resentment, and embarrassment. Many of us lead lives in the future, imagining all of the things we are going to do some day, usually contingent on achieving some financial goal or magic age when we finally qualify for Social Security or a pension or an inheritance when the old bat finally kicks off.

Now consider that you, like Jesus, in the prime of life, are facing death. How does this knowledge test your life? What would you do if your days were a known number? How do we live so that whenever and wherever we die, our life is not just over, but fulfilled? Don't get me wrong, it's not about the bucket list, it goes much deeper than this. It's not about places you need to travel to, or cars you want to own, or skydiving out of airplanes. It's looking at your life and asking the key question, "*What do I need to rearrange so that I live a life of authenticity?*" Here's some questions to ponder:

If a stranger were to view one day of my life as a silent movie, how would they describe me at the end of the day? Do my actions reflect the person that I truly am, or would they be misled?

Does what I own, the things I surround myself with, convey the true me? Or is it a façade I hide behind?

Am I a thankful person? Who needs to be thanked in my life? What's holding me back?

Who needs to be forgiven? If you knew that tomorrow was your last day on earth, who is the one person you would desperately try to reach before it's too late so that you can reconcile with them?

Finally, fill in the blank. This group of needy people, this group who have touched my heart in some way again and again, this group I know I could make a difference by my action, this group called _________ is where God is calling me NOW. Fill in the blank.

Today is a day of paradox and contrast. Christ is king on earth, king of the cosmos, and king of mercy and forgiveness. Somehow all of these make sense because above all, Christ is authentic, real, and utterly integrated. Socrates said that the unexamined life is not worth living. Take a few moments this week and examine yours. Ponder life as if it's your last week on this earth. You might get an inspiration or two. *Make it count.*

Humility – What God Treasures Most

Scripture Referenced: Luke 1:26-38

> Mary said, "Behold, I am the handmaid of the Lord. May it be done to me according to your word."

If there is a perfect counterpart to the apostle Peter to be found in the Old Testament, it would have to be King David. These two are like peas in a pod. Each of them is impulsive, full of energy and brio, and suffer from the same tendency to open mouth and place in foot. We get a great example of this in today's first reading where David, presumably relaxing in his cedar palace, is suddenly stricken with guilt that he has neglected God. David has a great place to live, all the comforts possible for that era, and here the Ark of God is sitting in a tent outside. Using the prophet Nathan as his intermediary, David proposes to build God a cool temple. Well, the answer Nathan hears in response is not what either he or David expects! You can almost hear God chuckling at the proposal. "You want to build ME a house?" (You've got to be kidding) God then goes on to explain to David, in a gentle but firm way, that God's plan has nothing to do with temples, but a lot to do with people, people who are not even born yet, people who will come after David and carry on the kingdom. In so many words, God is saying to David, "It's not about you, David. It's not about buildings and palaces. It's not even about earthly kingdoms. I have a much bigger plan in mind."

Does David build a temple to God? No, he doesn't, but his son Solomon does. Was this a good thing to do? Well, the answer is yes *and* no. On the one hand, a temple is a powerful symbol of God's presence, an awe-inspiring reminder of man's humble position in the world. A temple focuses the attention of the people and provides a convenient place to gather in common prayer and praise. But, a temple has a down-side as well, because a temple can serve as a box in which God is held, a way to control God. If God is in the temple, then he isn't out here pestering me, is he? It's no different today, is it? Our church is a beautiful house of prayer, but it's so easy to box God in here, to simply come in and pay Him a visit on Sunday. If God is in here, we can keep God under control. It's then our agenda that determines when we set Him free. God is just too scary to let run loose, apparently.

Holding that thought, we move over to the Gospel reading for today, and ask why the Church connects these two passages on this 4th Sunday of Advent? Luke presents us with the story of Mary, a young virgin who is about as opposite to David as you can imagine. Unlike David, Mary is not telling God what she plans to do. Unlike David, Mary isn't full of herself and her position in life. Mary lives in simple openness, simple awareness, able to hear an angel speak. If you told David that the culmination of his kingdom, the birth of the ultimate and perfect heir to the throne, was dependent on the "yes" of a simple peasant girl in Nowhere, Galilee, I think he would have been a bit surprised. But then again, we know that our God is a God of surprises, don't we?

Was Mary in the temple when the angel "came to her"? Clearly not – the temple is in Jerusalem, not Nazareth. There are two beautiful, if competing traditions in Nazareth. One holds that the angel appeared to Mary at a well. It makes perfect sense since a young woman would have this as one of her duties. The other tradition has the angel appearing to Mary at Mary's home, equally likely in my opinion. It really doesn't matter much where the angel appeared. The key is that the angel came to Mary in the ordinary and everyday events of Mary's life. Not in Church, not in a temple, but in a simple setting. Mary was just doing what life required of her, and in one of those simple moments, God spoke to her.

Is the Church telling us that Mary is a vast improvement on King David? No, that would not be an accurate conclusion. Despite his documented foibles, murders, and shall we say, "passions", we must realize that God loved David very, very much. After all, God chose David specifically to be Saul's successor, and continually bestowed favored status on him throughout his long and eventful life. So no, we shouldn't look at David and Mary as opposites. But I'll bet that if I asked which one you relate to more, the men would choose David and the women would choose Mary. Right?

Is it simply gender identification or is there such a thing as a male and a female spirituality? Well, from the vantage point of a spiritual director,

I would say that men and women do indeed approach the spiritual side of their natures in very different ways. It's perhaps fashionable in this day and age to attempt to minimize gender distinctions, but I think that trend is largely dying out. Men and women are not the same, folks, and as the French would say, "Vive la difference!"

Some observations:

- Women love the relationship aspect of God, the inherent love that binds the Trinity, the way that love embraces the world.
- Men love the challenge, the creative energy God calls forth to make the kingdom come now, not later.
- Women love the beauty of a liturgy – the colors, the smells, the music, the sense of community. Women love the wholeness of things, the way it ideally ties together.
- Men love to be stirred – also possible through music and pageantry, but through homilies in particular. Men want a reason to keep coming back.
- Women tend to pray for people, especially family and friends. Men tend to pray for things to happen, for themselves and for others, and usually in very specific ways.

Thankfully, we have a God who delights in both types of spirituality, which should make us feel a bit more comfortable. There's room for boisterous sinners who think they know how things should be and there's room for the contemplative one who ponders everything in her heart. I think we each fall somewhere in between. However, there is a common thread that ties David and Mary together. Do you know what it is?

Humility. That's right – humility. When David gets caught with his hand in the cookie jar, he doesn't deny it or get defensive. He gets down on his knees and asks forgiveness. Read Psalm 51 if you'd like to get a sense of how David prays for forgiveness. And Mary simply exudes humility. As one of the poorest of the poor, Mary can expect nothing but a life of hardship. But never once does she complain – she simply says "yes" over and over, in perfect trust that God has indeed "done wondrous things for her, and holy is His name". So, whatever spiritual direction you lean toward, remember to stay humble – that seems to be the one thing that God truly treasures above all.

This is Love

Scripture Referenced: Mark 14:1-15:47

> At noon darkness came over the whole land until three in the afternoon. And at three o'clock Jesus cried out in a loud voice, "Eloi, Eloi, lema sabachthani?" which is translated, "My God, my God, why have you forsaken me?"

Today is a day of contradictions; truly a day of head-snapping paradox. Entering the city with cries of Hosanna, it is 5 short days later that Jesus is mocked as he hangs on the cross, desolate and alone. Isn't it interesting that the only people who really get who Jesus is are both pagans. Pilate, who asks the question we would seemingly ask, "Why? What evil has he done?" And a centurion who recognizes somehow that "Truly this man was the Son of God!" Everyone else, his disciples, even the women who cared for him, we are told, "looked on from a distance."

We, too, it seems, are looking on from a distance, the distance of time. How does this day resonate with you? Most of us probably fall into one of two camps. The first perspective, perhaps the most accessible one, is to take on the story in all of its realism, blood, pain, and suffering. The torture is gruesome, even by Hollywood horror standards, and we are buffeted numb. We feel an unaccountable guilt, as if we are somehow responsible, somehow in concert with these sadistic thugs. At some deep and dark level in all of us, we know that we are capable of inflicting great pain on another. It may not be with nails and hammer, but it certainly can hurt to an extreme degree. We are facing the shadow of humanity and we shudder at our own complicity.

The second perspective is more nuanced, more measured. We know that resurrection is a coming reality and our sorrow is thereby tempered by joyful expectation, by a knowledge that Jesus conquers death after all, and with it our greatest fear. Yet, despite this foreknowledge, this blessed assurance, we are still a bit stunned by the gruesome necessity of it all. Aren't you asking yourself, "Why did God let this happen? Wasn't there a better way?"

This question has challenged theologians over the centuries, as you can well imagine. The answer we usually hear is that Christ died for us, for our sins, to atone for humanity's history of free choices choosing evil. Please understand that this *does not* mean that God demanded an ultimate human sacrifice in a way to somehow get even. No, our God is not a vengeful God. The truth is much bigger than this. Understanding the wisdom of John the Evangelist, we know that God is love, and few of us get to the depth of that reality.

As Pope John Paul II said so well, "God is not someone who remains only outside of the world, content to be in Himself all-knowing and omnipotent. His wisdom and omnipotence are placed, *by free choice*, at the *service* of creation." And, since we human beings are our own worst enemies, the true source of most of the awful suffering in the world, the Pope goes on to say that "the crucified Christ is *proof of God's solidarity with man in his suffering*. God places Himself on the side of man" Jesus, the man-God, takes on the worst suffering the world can conceive at that point in time, and not only endures it, he transforms it from death to life. The message is clear if you pay close attention. Whatever pain and suffering you're going through right now, whatever pain and suffering is being foisted on a loved one of yours, whatever pain is being suffered by an innocent child in the world, Christ is present. Christ is fully alive in these moments of death. He'll take us through the pain. In the midst of the paradox of Hosanna and despair, Christ holds it together.

This is love. This is love.

Chapter 10 – Service

St. James tells us that faith without action is useless. We nod our heads, exit Mass, and take care of our families and our jobs, thinking that we're doing all we can possibly do. And that's the problem. For some reason, we think that doing acts of service is all up to us as individuals, and as such, we simply don't have the time or energy. But what if I were to tell you that service in the name of Christ is one of the most energizing things you'll ever do? It starts with a simple concept, *encounter*. Then look out!

The Christian Walk

Scripture Referenced: Matthew 28:16-20

> Then Jesus approached and said to them, "All power in heaven and on earth has been given to me. Go, therefore, and make disciples of all nations, baptizing them in the name of the Father, and of the Son, and of the Holy Spirit, teaching them to observe all that I have commanded you. And behold, I am with you always, until the end of the age."

Each year on this feast of the Ascension, we hear the same first reading from Acts of the Apostles. It's easy to see why. This beautifully depicted scene from Luke is meant to help us understand clearly that the bodily Jesus has moved on, but at the same time, the story is not over. There's much more to follow, and an entire book, The Acts of the Apostles, continues on from this point. Yes, the apostles seem a little uncertain at this precise moment, but that's explainable. They're missing something, something that's yet to come, something that will turn their puzzled sky-gazing into galvanic action. We all know what that is, right? If you're not sure, come back next week and you'll hear all about it!

As much as the first reading is the same each year, the Gospel reading is different each year. Appropriate to this year, we hear Matthew's version, which is short and to the point. As is typical in Matthew, he places this scene on the mountain, once again triggering in his Jewish audience the connection between Moses and Jesus. The apostles worship Jesus, but they doubt. Jesus doesn't try to convince them of anything – he simply states his reality – all power has been given to him – and then gives his final commandment. "Go and make disciples of all nations, baptizing them in the name of the Father, and of the Son, and of the Holy Spirit, teaching them to observe all that I have commanded you." Put yourself in that scene for a moment and listen to that command. Does that make you a little nervous? How do I do that? What does he mean? How does he expect me to take on such a job? I've got some fishing to do. So Jesus changes his tone from commanding to consoling, and in one of the most beloved sayings of the gospel, ends with this: “And behold, I am with you always, until the end of the age.”

Here we are, two thousand years later. We come to worship, but we still have doubts. We hear the commands of Jesus, and we make some effort, but let’s face it. We know that we don’t measure up. We are consoled by the words of Jesus, and they certainly help, but in the end, there’s a lingering sense of incompleteness. Does that fit your sense of things? Pope Francis speaks about the “joy of the gospel”. He certainly exemplifies this attitude in everything he does. He doesn’t seem discouraged or incomplete, nor does he seem full of doubts. What’s the secret? Special prayers? Drinks holy water? Has God’s phone number? Hmmm, maybe not. Maybe it’s something else.

The spiritual life is a never-ending cycle of four connected states of being, and one must follow the other. These four states are *encounter, conversion, communion,* and *mission.* You can’t start in the middle, or the end. You have to go in order. The first stage is *encounter*, and not just any encounter, but an encounter with the person of Jesus Christ. We may seek it out, we may not, but Jesus decides how and when to grant that encounter. I would venture to say that every person here over the age of 40 has had at least one encounter with Jesus Christ. You wouldn’t be here otherwise. What do I mean by encounter? Simply put, an encounter with the person of Jesus Christ shifts your being, your core you. It wakens something in you, and calls you to stop, ponder, and wonder. It come from outside of you, and you are pulled in a direction you don’t expect, nor necessarily want. It fascinates you. Do you understand? I remember the time back in 1991 when my wife and I were invited to help out on the RCIA team for St. James. Note, we were asked – we weren’t looking for this. But I was intrigued. Oh boy, we can convert people! Little did I know that God had someone else in mind to convert, namely, *me*!

What you do with that encounter is the second stage, *conversion.* You have a choice. You can pass that encounter off with a shrug, or you can act on it. Conversion simply means that you act. It can take many directions or forms. Perhaps you tell a friend about your encounter. Perhaps you wander into a church and sit quietly in a pew, pondering the meaning. Maybe you journal about it. Maybe you do all of that. Maybe you ask a person with a reputation for holiness. You act.

Once you're in conversion mode, you seek out people with similar experiences of encounter and conversion. This stage is called *communion.* You realize that you're not alone, that many others have been touched by Christ, and that you belong to them. It is a good feeling, a sense of community, a sense of rightness, a sense of shared vision. In short, you start appreciating Church. If the Church is doing its job right, the Church welcomes you, helps you to understand your encounter and conversion, and offers you friendship, Eucharistic food, and support. You're becoming part of a family. And then, and only then, are you drawn into the fourth stage, *mission.* You feel the need to reach out to others who are struggling, who are hurting, who are far from peace, and you begin to share with them the good news. With words yes, but more often with actions of love and caring, that are hopefully received gratefully, but maybe not. That's okay too, because you don't need their gratitude – Christ is more than enough. *Mission* completes the cycle of the Christian walk.

Do you understand the sequence? Encounter, conversion, communion, mission. Here's the interesting thing. You can move through each stage more than once! In fact, you have to in order to stay on the path. You've heard me say up here (more than once!) that the best place to encounter Christ is where? Yes, the poor, the imprisoned, the sick, the helpless, the broken. If your spiritual life needs a boost, that's where to restart the cycle. Enter the arena where Christ can most easily find you! Then you'll once again ponder the encounter, act on it, mediate the experience through the Church, and go out on mission again. It's a beautiful cycle of energy and enlightenment and peace. So many of you come to me and ask, "how can I get my kids to come to Mass?" Ask it differently. Where are they on the cycle? Have they had an encounter with Christ? Ever? Note that going to Church is the third stage. You can't jump them to that stage if they haven't experienced encounter and conversion! So, the better question to ask is, "How can I give my kids an encounter with Christ?" Yes, it could happen at Mass, but if they've been dragged to Mass for the past umpteen years, I don't think they're going to encounter Christ in this environment anytime soon. The simple reality is that you have to take them to where Christ is the most obviously present and let Christ do the encountering. Where's that? I think you know the answer. The poor, the imprisoned, the sick, the helpless, the broken. Let Christ do the work – you just need to prepare the soil.

When Jesus was up on that mountain telling the apostles that their mission was to baptize, note, ALL nations, I'm sure that some of the apostles were shaking their heads. Others were intrigued, and still others were willing but unsure. They were certainly encountering Jesus the person, but they needed something a bit more. They needed to encounter the Christ, and that is only possible through the power of the Holy Spirit. Thankfully, that came shortly thereafter, or we wouldn't have the Acts of the Apostles. Once the apostles moved from encounter to conversion to communion, the mission was straightforward. They not only had Christ's promise to be with them until the end of the age, they had the Holy Spirit to inspire them, help them remember the words of Jesus, and move them from uncertainty to acts of courage and conviction. Were they re-inspired at different times, renewed, reawakened to deeper truths? Yes, yes, yes! Read St. Paul, read the Acts, read the letters of John – note the active seeking, understanding, and mission actions. Pope Francis moves through these stages almost daily. You've got the same opportunity. Go for it!

Comfort Zones

Scripture Referenced: Matthew 15:21-28

> At that time, Jesus withdrew to the region of Tyre and Sidon. And behold, a Canaanite woman of that district came and called out, "Have pity on me, Lord, Son of David! My daughter is tormented by a demon." But Jesus did not say a word in answer to her.

I was at a family reunion last weekend and as usual in such settings, you spend a lot of time catching up with people's lives. You hear about jobs, kids, illnesses, and who's not talking to who. You hear about births, graduations, and new beginnings. You hear a lot about the old days, when things were so much simpler. The younger kids roll their eyes, finding it hard to imagine a time without video games and cell phones. One of the favorite topics of adults in my era is trips – vacations especially, and where we've all been. You quickly realize that people fall into two camps – those who prefer to stay in familiar territory, and those who relish going places that few people visit. One woman, who was the wife of my wife's older male cousin (did you get that?), told me that she had no desire to go to Europe, or anywhere overseas for that matter. It was simply outside her comfort zone. For some reason, that phrase stuck in my head, and when I pondered today's Gospel reading, I suddenly realized why.

Note that Jesus, as we are told, is in the region of Tyre and Sidon, apparently by choice. Tyre and Sidon are in present day Lebanon, quite some distance from Jerusalem, and definitely outside of the region where Jesus would feel at home. We're not told specifically why Jesus is here – the Gospel says he *withdrew* here, an interesting word choice that suggests that he was on a little vacation perhaps, heading to a place he would be unknown, or at least left alone. Like all of us who go off to a different place, whether by accident or on purpose, he's probably not entirely comfortable. He may be a little out of his comfort zone.

Many years ago, I was sent to Cairo, Egypt on a 3-week business trip. It was definitely a unique experience, my first time in an Arab country, and I was intrigued and on edge at the same time. My senses were heightened; it was a time of what I would call *focused* living, when I noticed *everything* because, well, everything was different. The people spoke a foreign language, they were dressed differently, and I of course, received many interested looks, given that I was obviously Western. Most of the time, I was addressed in French, since at one time Egypt was a French colony. When I was shown to be unable to converse in either French or Arabic, communication ground to a halt. It was a bit frustrating, and I definitely felt out of my comfort zone.

Here is Jesus in a foreign land, and in what seems an amazing coincidence, a Canaanite woman somehow gets word that Jesus, the miracle worker of Galilee, is in her neck of the woods. Defying all cultural norms of the day, she calls out to Jesus in public, utterly embarrassing the poor apostles, who try to shush her up. Undeterred, she keeps calling out until she gets Jesus' attention. The verbal exchange that follows is fascinating, for Jesus seems unable to see beyond her ethnic background. He tells her that she is not of the house of Israel, in fact, is as low as a dog in the view of any good Jew of the time. It's shocking to us since it seems so unlike Jesus to say these things. You can see the disciples in the background, nodding their head in agreement. Is he simply parroting their thoughts perhaps? Trying to make a point? It's not clear. But the woman is persistent and clever, forcing the traveling band of Jesus' followers to see that she is not a foreign dog, but a woman with a sick child, a woman who is just like the wives, mothers, and sisters of these men back home in Galilee. Jesus now responds as we knew he would – with praise and healing.

One afternoon, after I got off work in Cairo, I borrowed a friend's binoculars and took an elevator ride to the top of the Cairo Tower, for 50 years the tallest structure in Africa. The view from the top, some 600 feet up, is quite striking, and I spend many minutes peering through the binoculars at various landmarks, from the pyramids to the hotels to the dusty streets of the city. All at once, I notice a group of school-age girls who are gathered to one side of the viewing area, chattering away, and taking in the sights. I suddenly think of my own younger sisters, and catching the eye of one of the girls, I hold out the binoculars and gesture for her to try them out. After some shy giggling, she approaches me with great care, takes the binoculars and looks out at the city. Suddenly, she shrieks with delight, and in a nano-second, I am surrounded by a dozen jumping girls who can't wait for their turn. Fearing that one of them would fumble the binoculars over the side, I carefully show them how to put the strap over their heads and then take a look. For the next 30 minutes, I'm the most popular person on the Cairo tower. The girls, their teacher, the other tourists, everyone surrounds me and gestures for their turn. For those brief moments, I'm no different from them, no longer a foreigner, some Western man amid Arab people, who can't speak their language. We are simply sharing an experience, a human touch. Once they all have their turn, the first girl who had shyly started the mad rush comes up to me, with her classmates gathered behind her, and solemnly says to me "Zank you". I bow to her, and she runs off in another fit of giggling. I think giggling is the universal language.

I think the message for us today is two-fold. First of all, despite the inherent anxiety, it is important to get outside of our comfort zone. You don't need to go to Egypt to do this. It can be Tijuana, it can be a soup kitchen. It can be a hospital, it can be the home of an elderly neighbor. It can be a prison, or it can be the room of a lonely 10 year old. It can be Mexican outside of Home Depot, or it can be a woman in a fancy car who looks lost. Seek a little discomfort this week. The second part of the message is just as important – when you're in that uncomfortable place, ask God to show you the humanity that exists there, the face of Christ you haven't seen before. It may be a shock when it comes – it may rattle your preconceived notions. Open your hearts to the possibility that we are all one family at our roots. That's certainly the way God sees us.

But to really take this reading seriously, ask yourself who is no more than a *dog* to you, a person or a group of people who you equate with animals. You'll be tempted to say, "no one", because look, we're in Church, and that kind of thinking is not allowed. But take an honest inventory and see if someone or some group comes close. Now ask Jesus to show you a truth about this person or group that humanizes them. It may take a little effort on your part – reading something you'd typically skip, or seeing a movie that makes you uneasy, or perhaps taking a trip to another land where you won't feel comfortable. The important point is to get behind the label to the person who is in there, a person who God made. Years ago, Zenith ran a bunch of ads with the slogan, "the quality goes in before the name goes on". I think that's how God views his creation too, don't you think?

Distilled Christianity

Scripture Referenced: Mark 12:28-34

> One of the scribes, when he came forward and heard them disputing and saw how well he had answered them, asked him, "Which is the first of all the commandments?" Jesus replied, "The first is this: 'Hear, O Israel! The Lord our God is Lord alone! You shall love the Lord your God with all your heart, with all your soul, with all your mind, and with all your strength.' The second is this: "You shall love your neighbor as yourself.'"

As many of you know, I was in the state prison from Thursday through Sunday last week for the *Kairos* retreat, an intensive Christian experience for inmates designed to show them a new way of thinking and living in spite of their surroundings. One of the challenges in the weekend is to keep it simple and focused – there's not much time or appetite for intensive theological discussions. Many of the inmates have a very warped view of Christianity, if they have any view at all. Each of us who go into the prison must be prepared to deliver what I call "distilled Christianity", that is, a brief yet sincere testimony of what it means to be a Christian. Some call it the Christian elevator pitch – what can you say to summarize Christianity in less than 90 seconds? Try it sometime – it's harder than it sounds.

The scribe in today's gospel is asking Jesus to do this exact thing with respect to the Jewish Law. C'mon, Jesus, let's hear your summation of the 613 laws of Judaism. Jesus promptly answers the question by quoting the *Sh'ma*, the love of God as expressed in the first reading today from Deuteronomy. Every Jew knows this beautiful phrase and would agree with Jesus. But then Jesus surprises them by giving them a second law, to love one's neighbor as oneself. This is one of the most important teachings of Jesus – for the first time ever, love of God and love of neighbor are put on *equal* footing. St. John goes even further by saying, "If anyone says, "I love God," but hates his brother, he is a liar…" (1 John 4:20) Clearly, love of God and love of neighbor is fundamental to our Christian walk and quite frankly, is a great way to start your elevator pitch.

One of the inmates who was on the "inside team," that is, who had already gone through Kairos and was helping to put on the retreat from the inside, spoke to all of us on Saturday. He was *sent down* to prison when he was 19 years old for murder. Due to some mitigating circumstances, he escaped death row. His sentence was 29 years to life, which means that he was eligible for parole after about 25 years. When he first came up for parole about 7 years ago, he was denied. He was depressed and angry. Shortly afterward, he was invited to attend a *Kairos* weekend. He wasn't a Christian, but he decided to attend the retreat for two reasons – he thought it would look good on his record, and, there were cookies offered. Lots of cookies. So he went to the retreat. The third day into the retreat, he said to God, "I don't know if you're there or not, but I'm willing to give your path a try. My path is certainly not working." Good choice. For the past 7 years, this guy has been on fire. He started Bible study programs, edits a prison newsletter on the Christian walk, gave his testimony to anyone who would listen, and was even put on Christian television. He has brought men to Christ, encouraged the newbies, and shined a light in many dark corners of the prison. Two weeks ago, at the age of 52, he was granted a parole date – he will be released in February. He has reconciled with the victim's family, he is a model of how Christ's love can change anyone, and he is the first one to tell you that cookies save lives. If you're one of our beloved cookie monsters, er, Masters, out there who baked over 400 dozen cookies for the weekend, my heartfelt thanks go out to you. Cookies bring them in, and Christ uses the retreat team to do the rest. What a great combo!

Not everyone is called to work in the prisons. We have a hard task filling the outside team each time the weekend comes around. Prison is a dry, ugly, and depressing place, filled with many angry men. I go in because I love to watch the Holy Spirit do that Holy Spirit thing –for as St. Paul tells us, "Where sin abounds, grace abounds all the more…" You focus evil in a particular place and great good finds a way to burst through – "the light shines in the darkness, and the darkness has not overcome it." (John 1:5) If any of you men would like to join me and see for yourself, let's talk.

It's not easy loving God and loving neighbor in an equal way as Jesus asks. Most of us who take the Christian walk seriously have a well-developed prayer life. We attend Mass faithfully, we have our prayer practices well ingrained, we have the love of God in our lives. This is of paramount importance. But we all need to look hard at this "love of neighbor" concept from time to time. It's easy to love our neighbor if we define it the way the Scribes of Jesus' time did – love of neighbor meant love of one's family and tribe, that is, love of those folks you know well. But that's not what Jesus challenges us to do.

Peter Maurin, a partner with Dorothy Day in founding the Catholic Worker movement, expresses the challenge of loving God and neighbor in this way: "If I cannot find the face of Jesus in the face of those who are my enemies, if I cannot find him in the unbeautiful, if I cannot find him in those who have the 'wrong ideas,' if I cannot find him in the poor and the defeated, then I will not find him in the bread or the wine. If I do not reach out in this world to those with whom he has identified himself, why do I imagine that I want to be with him, and them, in heaven? Why do I think I want to be for all eternity in the company of those whose companionship I have avoided every day of my life?"

These words are hard to hear. Most of us want to serve our neighbor, but mostly in an advisory capacity. If they would only listen! But here's a not so surprising observation – people only listen, truly listen, to another person if that person has walked on the same path that they are on. I will tell you that the most effective addiction counselors are ex-addicts themselves. I will tell you that the most effective witnesses of God's grace are those who have needed it, found it, and been transformed by it. The only reason that any preacher is credible is the extent to which you identify with their walk. Preachers simply put words to the walk – you're walking the walk too.

Let's get specific, shall we? Look back on your lives. Have you suffered at one time or another? If you've over the age of 18, I'll bet the answer is yes. What was the nature of that pain in your life? Did you lose a job? A baby? A loved one to cancer? A parent to Alzheimer's? Were you the victim of a crime? Were you defrauded? Suffer the pain of a separation or divorce? Been addicted to alcohol or gambling? Whatever that pain was for you, can you accept the possibility that God might want you to use that pain to help someone else? This is one of the notions inherent in the term *redemptive suffering*. It sure doesn't feel very redemptive when you're going through it, but it can be transformed into a positive by your decision to help the next poor soul navigate that path. That's the love of neighbor that Jesus is challenging us to see. He did it through the cross. Can you use your cross in the same way? Every single "pain" that I listed just now has a corresponding charity or justice organization out there that could use your help. Transform your pain – and you'll be walking the path of life.

Jesus Christ is the way, the truth, and the life. All life begins in him, abides in him, and lives on in him. He is the human face of God on this earth, and he calls us to follow him into the darkness so that we can shine a light on the poor and desperate and bring them to new life. It's a joyful task.

By the way, that was my elevator pitch.

Christian Farming

Scripture Referenced: Matthew 13:1-23

> [Jesus] spoke to them at length in parables, saying: "A sower went out to sow. And as he sowed, some seed fell on the path, and birds came and ate it up. Some fell on rocky ground, where it had little soil…Some seed fell among thorns, and the thorns grew up and choked it. But some seed fell on rich soil, and produced fruit…"

When I was a kid growing up in upstate New York, we had a family garden. There were nine of us in the family, so the garden wasn't simply a hobby, but a necessity. Fortunately, the soil was good for farming, and my Dad went at it with enthusiasm, tilling the soil carefully in the early spring, adding abundant horse manure from the local farms, and carefully watching the calendar to choose the right weekend to finally plant the seeds. I remember when the seed packets came in the mail, always astonished that this little packet of seeds would presumably deliver a crop of beans or peas or carrots or corn. On the appointed day, Dad would create a furrow in the soil with his hoe and we would carefully drop a seed every 5 inches in the rich earth, cover it up and carefully mark what was in each row. Not a seed was wasted.

Now the sower in today's Gospel reading is quite a different sort of farmer, isn't he? None of this soil tilling stuff for him, no careful furrows, just a random tossing of seed every which way. The sower doesn't seem to mind that some of the seed is almost guaranteed *not* to produce a harvest – he just keeps on tossing seed. And, as expected, the seed falls in all sorts of places – the path, rocky ground, amid thorns, and fortunately, on some good soil as well. So let's pause a moment and ask some questions:

- Who is the sower? Some people are quick to answer Jesus, but I think not. The sower is God the Father. The first reading from Isaiah clarifies that point. The word that comes from the mouth of God shall do His will, achieving the end for which He sent it. Which leads us the second question.

- Who is the seed? Hint, the word became flesh and dwells among us. Yes, this time the right answer is Jesus. Jesus is the seed, the grain of wheat that must die to achieve new life. And clearly, there's plenty of Jesus to go around!

But that still doesn't explain why God is such a lousy farmer. Why doesn't he be a bit more careful? Wouldn't it make sense not to waste Jesus on people who really don't care? You know the types I'm talking about, right? The atheists, the radical Muslims, the abortionists, the child molesters, the thieves and the robbers? Why bother? Pearls before swine.

The parable goes on to state exactly how the seed is wasted, as if this is really important. Listen to the reasons why the seed fails to produce:

- The person hears the word but does not understand it
- The person hears the word, rejoices, but doesn't use it in times of trial
- The person hears the word, but anxiety and the lure of riches chokes it off

And after a brief statement that the seed that falls on good soil produces a huge bounty, the parable ends. Well, thank goodness for the good soil, I guess. But we're left with a very uneasy question, aren't we? What are we supposed to do with this parable? If we're not the sower, and we're not the seed, does that mean we're the soil? And, as it must seem obvious because here we are in Church on Sunday, I guess we're the good soil, right? So congratulations and have a nice day? I think there's more to it than that, don't you?

Back in upstate New York, a couple of weeks after planting, the first shoots peep through the ground, much to our delight. By the end of the first month, the plants are definitely showing their stuff, but there's also these other plants that are growing too, these weeds. And here come the bugs. And the rabbits. And the birds. Do we just stand by and watch? Nope. Dad is out there on his hands and knees, pulling up weeds. We get our chores as well, because Dad can't be there every day. We weed, we chase off the birds, we fence off the tender crops, we take care of the plants. It's a grind, not much fun, and sometimes we accidentally yank up a promising plant. Ouch.

Do you get it? Our job begins as the parable ends. We're the farmers, the field hands, the workers in the vineyard. Jesus tells us exactly what to watch for in our cooperative efforts:

- For people who don't understand the Word, we are asked to educate and explain how God works. We catechize, we teach, we listen to their questions.
- For people who hit a rough patch and turn to worldly solutions, we are asked to show them how to pray, how to see God in the pain, how to be God "with skin on" to soothe their suffering.
- For people who are anxious and lured by riches, we are asked to show them how to detach from their worries and trust that God's peace far outweighs any material thing.

And occasionally, as God chooses, we sometimes get to see the harvest. It's a beautiful thing to behold when a person we've helped blooms into abundant flower. I never get tired of it – outside of my marriage, it's the most satisfying part of my life.

When we go into the prison for our Kairos weekends, this parable plays out in real life. 36 inmates enter the room. God the Father, through his servants, us, scatters Jesus around the room with reckless abandon. Over the course of the three days, all of the inmates hear the Word of God, and by the end of the weekend, you'd swear you had 36 bountiful harvests. But us farmers know better. The seeds are definitely planted, but now the real work begins. Outside guys volunteer in the prison every week to continue evangelizing. I go in once a month for a reunion of all of the inmates. They don't all make it. It's sad, but we don't lose faith, we don't lose hope. Some of the guys, just like us, need to hear the Word not once, but 2, 3, 4, 100 times before it strikes a chord. As farmers, we simply work the field. God's grace, the person's receptivity, life circumstances, all conspire together to encourage a blossom. As one inmate said to me, "It took me 30 years to understand what this Christian stuff was all about!" Thirty years is a long time to wait for a plant to blossom, isn't it?

Are you tending some plants right now? Wherever they are on their growth, I invite you to consider what the next best step is for these important people. Do they need a little more education? Perhaps a dash of hope or encouragement? The key is to be *intentional*. Far too often, we wait for them to come to us. If only they would tap this fountain of knowledge that is *us*, we think. Maybe we need to jump off our pedestal and ask what they need right now. That's what a good farmer does, right?

Remember, we're not called to perfection, we're called to faithful persistence. We don't keep score as to how many plants make it. That implies that it's up to us to somehow make the plants thrive. Baloney. We're called to engage the people, to witness our faith, to be seen as different because we're Christians. Whatever you do, remember that the point of today's parable is *cooperation* with the sower and the seed. We work together with God the Father and Jesus the Son. Welcome to the art of Christian farming.

God is Sooooo Good

Scripture Referenced: John 13:1-15

> So when he had washed their feet and put his garments back on and reclined at table again, he said to them, "Do you realize what I have done for you? You call me 'teacher' and 'master' and rightly so, for indeed I am. If I therefore, the master and teacher, have washed your feet, you ought to wash one another's feet."

Eleven days ago, on the 5th Sunday of Lent, we heard from the prophet Isaiah in our first reading. You can be forgiven if you don't remember exactly what he said – it kind of flew by. Written to the Israelite people who were depressed and forsaken in Babylonian exile, Isaiah sounds a very upbeat note. Listen to his words: "Remember not the events of the past, the things of long ago consider not; see, I am doing something new!" (Isaiah 43:18-19a) Tonight, part one of the Easter Triduum celebration of the church, we are indeed doing something new. Can we for just a moment consider not what we do each Sunday and see tonight with new eyes? This is the challenge and joy of not just Holy Thursday but Good Friday and the Easter Vigil as well. Take a moment to really take in the fresh symbolism, the beauty of the music, the poetry of the Liturgy.

Consider this. The first reading describes the Passover feast, memorialized annually through the actions of hundreds of Jewish generations, down to today. Jesus, the good Jew that he is, gathers with his disciples in anticipation of the feast. The symbols are rich and deep. The Passover celebrates the last day of the Hebrew people in slavery – they are preparing to flee with Moses. Something new! As Paul tells us in the second reading, Jesus takes the bread and the wine and invites his disciples to see a connection between himself and the innocent lamb to be slaughtered. It must have shocked them and yet intrigued them as well. But Jesus doesn't stop here. He answers the question that must have been raging in their minds – what does he mean? What is he calling us to do? Something new! It's not about law and right thinking and boundaries and purity codes. Jesus demonstrates that following him is about action, and not the action of battle and argument, but the action of service, one to the other.

Imagine if, 2000 years ago, the Church fathers decided that every Sunday liturgy should feature a re-enactment of the washing of the feet? A person would be selected at random, and the priest would solemnly wash that person's feet, reciting the words of Jesus, "If I have washed your feet, you ought to wash one another's feet. As I have done for you, you should also do." Now that would be something new, wouldn't it? Clearly, John the Evangelist thought much more of this action of Jesus than he did the institution of the Eucharist. He doesn't even mention bread and wine, body and blood, at all! So, we can spend a lot of time speculating about this, but here's the reality. We cannot in good conscience take the body and blood of Jesus into our bodies and then ignore our neighbor. They are completely linked, one action following another. We taste Jesus, we serve our neighbor. A, B., 1, 2. You know, this might be on the final exam! Let's see, you received Eucharist 40,000 times in your life and you helped another person in need, um, 40 times? Because helping those who already love you doesn't count, you see. Oops.

Now, to be honest, outside of Mother Teresa, there may not be many who pass that test! Luckily, God recognizes exactly how weak and self-centered we are. In fact, as Jesus tells us in parable after parable, God would be perfectly happy if we simply helped one person in need, if we simply performed one selfless action, if we acted like Jesus just once in a while. The good Samaritan, the prodigal Father, the thankful leper – simple actions, simply done, but performed with love.

Last week, I was in Oakland waiting outside my hotel for my ride to dinner. A skinny older woman of color, dressed shabbily, came up to me and smiled. I politely nodded, and she then launched into an elaborate story about how she was quite frustrated to be just $11 short of enough cash to buy her monthly supply of insulin for her diabetes. My first reaction? Well, to be honest, I was annoyed, mostly because I hadn't seen this coming. But something told me to pause a moment, and not react too quickly. So I asked her some questions about where she lived, how long she had been in California, where she had come from, about her family. She answered very cheerfully and readily, and told me that she was from Leavenworth, Kansas. She then added that her father had been a prison guard at the federal prison there. When I then told her that I did prison ministry, she absolutely lit up and proclaimed, "God is soooo good!" I think she felt that she had hit the jackpot with me. She told me her name was Rhonda and we shook hands. I then looked her in the eye and said, "Rhonda, are you telling me the truth?" She quickly nodded, but it wasn't sincere. There was no truth in her words. And then the Spirit opened my eyes and I *saw* the truth. I saw a poor black woman with about 3 teeth, undernourished, and most certainly living in poverty. I saw a person who was begging because there weren't any other options. I saw a soul who would have much preferred to be home with her feet up watching some silly TV show. So I took out my wallet, gave her a twenty and said, "This isn't for your insulin, this is for you. Go get something to eat." She thanked me profusely and skittered down the road. Perhaps we both saw something new that evening. That's what you get when you wash each other's feet. So I challenge you to look for an opportunity to serve another in the days ahead – and try a new response! God is soooo good!

Servant Leadership

Scripture Referenced: John 10:11-18

> I am the good shepherd, and I know mine and mine know me, just as the Father knows me and I know the Father; and I will lay down my life for the sheep.

The seven Sundays following Easter that culminate with Pentecost Sunday are designed to help us answer the question, "who is this Jesus anyway?" In many ways, we are pondering the exact same question that the early disciples did just after the Resurrection event. You can imagine them sitting around the dinner table trying to make sense of it all. The Messiah they got was not the Messiah they were expecting. What did they miss in the words of the prophets? What was written in the Scripture that was confusing or vague before, but now makes sense?

A good example of this Scriptural discovery can be found in the first reading from Acts. Peter, no longer the coward hiding from servant girls in the courtyard of the high priest, is now speaking in public under the inspiration of the Holy Spirit. Proclaiming the power of the name of Christ, despite the fact that Jesus was crucified as a common criminal, Peter makes a connection to Psalm 118: "The stone the builders rejected has become the cornerstone. By the Lord has this been done; it is wonderful in our eyes." It's an inspired connection, particularly for an uneducated fisherman. Many scholars point to the gospel reading from last Sunday to explain this revelation. We are told that the resurrected Jesus "opened their minds to understand the Scriptures." (Luke 24:45) Perhaps Jesus himself connected the dots for them in ways they would never have considered.

Our gospel reading from John takes a slightly different approach. The theological depth of John's account is a testimony to 80 years of meditation on the words of Jesus, words that were puzzling when he first spoke them, but now taking on a completely new meaning in the light of his resurrection. This beloved reading is one result, in which Jesus takes a very common labor category, shepherd, and weaves a beautiful metaphor of servant leadership around the very mundane task of tending sheep. Who would have thought that such a simple activity could have such hidden depth?

Now I don't know about you, but the last time I saw a shepherd in action was about six years ago when I was visiting a farm in New Zealand. Maybe it's time to update this gospel a bit. How do these sound? Jesus says, "I am the good cop." "I am the good waiter." "I am the good bartender." "I am the good CFO." "I am the good teacher." "I am the good systems analyst, grade 3." "I am the good (please fill in the blank with your calling in life)" Some of these are kind of amusing to think about, but if we don't think about it, we've completely missed the point of today's gospel. You see, even though the gospel seems to be about Jesus, if we leave it there, it's just another "oh yeah, I've heard this before" reading. What does it mean to be the "good" cop, waiter, bartender, CFO, teacher, system analyst grade 3, or ditch digger?

Notice how Jesus frames the description of the good shepherd. First of all, a good shepherd is not motivated by money, by how much the job pays. Second, the good shepherd personalizes what he does. He knows his flock and by extension, his flock knows him. Thirdly, the good shepherd thinks beyond his own present responsibility. Can we take these qualities to our present world? Let's take an easy one first, a teacher.

Think about a *good* teacher. Does a teacher teach because the pay is fantastic? I don't think so. Does a good teacher personalize the work they do? Do they know their students well? Do they make every attempt to uncover what makes each student tick, especially the annoying ones? And finally, do they end the school year with the thought, "Well, that class is over. I couldn't care less what happens to them next year." (?!) Well, maybe a little! But the good ones do care, right through to adulthood. If you doubt me, contact an old teacher of yours and let them know how you're doing and what they meant to you. They care.

Okay, let's take a harder one. Jesus says, "I am the good short order cook. I sling eggs and hash at Denny's." Is the money a key factor? Not likely. I'll bet even Emiril and Rachel Ray started cooking at low, low wages. Does a good short order cook personalize their work? Do they know their customers? The good ones do. They know that you like your eggs a little runny. You like them with a little bit of chopped red pepper. You like yours fried in bacon grease. You like yours cooked until they bounce. Right? Does a good short order cook think beyond their current circumstances? Do they aspire to reach and touch many others with their good cooking? Sure they do! Every restaurant cook I've ever met has this thought running through their heads, "When I open my own place, it will …"

Now think about what you do, whether it's for a living, or as a hobby if you're retired. No one is off the hook here. You could be a student or a car mechanic, a full-time Mom or crossing guard. Own your own company or sweep the floor at Mickey D's. A priest or a baseball coach. Think about your day. Now put Jesus in your shoes. You're going to let him do your job for a day. He's going to look just like you in every way, but it's Jesus speaking and doing your job. He and you are one.

Would anyone notice? Would anyone notice a difference?

Well, unless you're a walking saint, I suspect the answer is yes. But here's the key question. In what way would there be a difference? Do you do your job strictly for the money? I'll bet that shows up in ways you never imagined. Do you really care about your co-workers and your customers? Do you care about your suppliers and your patients? Do they know you as well as you know them? Do you give a hoot about what happens to them? Their pains, their struggles, their humanity? Would you lay down even a little bit of your life for them? Or is every favor granted with a grudge and the unspoken warning to never ask for that again? Finally, how do you look beyond your present circumstances? What is your aspiration? If it's about power, possessions, and pride, the typical goals our society sets, then you're wandering far from the model Jesus gives us today.

In the end, it doesn't matter a bit what job you have, does it? Jesus is simply showing us how His spirit can infuse every part of who you are. It's not simply spiritual! When Jesus runs your life, it will come out in everything you do, whether it's cooking, cleaning, writing novels, or counting money. You'll be a servant leader, a compassionate co-worker, a light in the darkness. You'll draw people like sheep to a good shepherd. They'll come to you not because of your job title, but because you *care*.

Chapter 11 – Justice, Mercy, Compassion

Despite our best efforts, we all fall into sin. It's elemental to the human condition, built in from day one, so pervasive and obvious that the Church fathers called this propensity to do wrong *original sin.* It can be depressing to the point that we simply decide to crawl up under a blanket and feel sorry for ourselves. But here's the good news. God knows all about our sinfulness, and even though he is disappointed in our actions, he is always ready to forgive and nudge us in a new direction. Justice, mercy, and compassion – the three most important words we need to get our heads around if we dare to call ourselves *Christians*.

Forgive and Learn

Scripture Referenced: Luke 21:25-36

> Jesus said to his disciples: "There will be signs in the sun, the moon, and the stars, and on earth nations will be in dismay, perplexed by the roaring of the sea and the waves. People will die of fright in anticipation of what is coming upon the world, for the powers of the heavens will be shaken."

As we launch into a new Church year, the year of Luke to be exact, our readings seem to be a bit schizophrenic. We have the hopeful vision of the first reading from Jeremiah, a prophecy of peace and security to a people who are being assaulted from every direction. We have a selection from the oldest book in the New Testament, 1st Thessalonians, in which Paul encourages his readers to keep up their good work, as they are indeed pleasing God. But the gospel rings a discordant note. Jesus is describing the end times to his audience, and the picture is not a very pretty one. Signs in the heavens, roiling storms, people dying of fright – I had to double-check that I was in the right place in the Lectionary. Aren't we supposed to be starting Advent, the season of anticipation and hope? This sounds like a bad dream. What are we supposed to do with these contradictory visions?

In truth, we live in contradictory times, don't we? Despite our best efforts to find security, happiness, and peace for ourselves and our loved ones, most of us don't achieve such an elusive goal. We certainly have come a long way from Thoreau's comment that "The mass of men lead lives of quiet desperation." But our very search for a perfect world has spawned an equally debilitating vigilance that manifests itself in paranoia. Have you noticed that every "good" thing we have discovered as a society seems to have a corresponding "bad" effect? If not immediately clear, it shows up soon enough. Antibiotics and hand sanitizers kill the bad germs – hurray! The overuse of antibiotics is now fostering the rise of super-germs that resist all treatment. Yikes! Coffee is good for you. No, coffee is bad for you. No wait, *organic* coffee is good for you. No wait… Let's have a glass of wine. Of course, parents are the worst offenders of all, helicoptering over their children with grim determination that nothing evil will come within 10 paces. There's a new book that just came out called the *Encyclopedia Paranoica*. I'm going to get a copy for the bathroom.

So, far from missing the mark, our readings today hit the nail right on the head. Advent is about beginnings, about promises kept from prophecies long ago. Advent should call to mind birth – not just our birth, but the birth of hope into the world through Jesus. But Advent is also about reflection – about where we are in this journey to our inevitable end. This reflection could either frighten you to death, as Jesus notes wryly, or cause you to stand erect and raise your heads because your redemption is near. Which is it? The truth is that we'd rather not think about it at all, especially if life is going reasonably well. But this is the exact purpose of Advent. Here's an opportunity, a good excuse, to indeed think about it. How do we do that in a new way? Here's some suggestions:

Visit the boundaries. Yes, that's right. Visit the two edges of existence, birth and death. Every one of us here was born, every one of us here is going to die. Through the experience of others, we have an opportunity to visit our entry and exit doors. There's something very, very special about childbirth. Expectation, discomfort, hope, pain, drama, exhaustion, exhilaration – and I'm only referring to the Dad's journey here, of course! If you have the opportunity to hold an infant this season, welcome it. If you have the opportunity to visit a maternity ward, don't miss it. Strive to see the creative wonder of God – it's right there for us to see. Equally important, visit a dying person if you have the opportunity. Yes, it can seem a sad and dismaying time. But look beyond the immediate reality and see the invitation to eternity, the beckoning door. If you're lucky, you'll see the dying person strive to get across, ready for the change, helped by angels. Why visit the boundaries? By demystifying the beginning and the end, we remove the power of ignorance, and we begin to see that the time we have in-between is the time of our life.

Look around. Take a good look around. Many, if not most of us, fall into traps. It's not surprising that the Church uses the term "falling into sin". Because sin is simply another word for a trap. The great illusion is that *we think we know* all of the sins we commit. We know about our selfish attitudes, our temper, our impatience, our over-indulgence in eating and drinking. We "tsk tsk" ourselves and swear we're going to turn that around and sometimes we even do so. Hurray, we think. I'm definitely on the right road now! Well, you're on a road alright. I'm not sure it's the right road. Here's the challenge for you. What trap are you in right now? What do I mean by a trap? What is stopping you, or slowing you, from becoming the best "you" that you are capable of becoming? Yes, and by "best", I mean the best in God's eyes. What is stopping or slowing you from becoming a true disciple of Jesus Christ? Is it worry? Fear? Obligation? Here's a tip – look hard at any obstacle being imposed from the outside world. You see, a well-functioning trap is always disguised, often disguised as something that seems good on its face. For many of us, it's material goods. House, car, toys, furnishings – things we actually go into debt for – these are responses to outside expectations. Society defines happy families as having lots of things, especially at Christmas. And we never, ever, get to the point where we have every *thing*. That's a trap. I have a plaque at home that reads "The best things in life aren't things". See the trap and plan your way out of it. That's what so many of Jesus' teachings are about. Blindness, deafness, hypocrisy – all signs of being stuck in the trap. What trap are you in right now?

Last piece of Advent advice – forgive someone. You know who. Someone has really ticked you off. They broke a promise. They stabbed you in the back. They made you feel small or embarrassed. Maybe they voted wrong. Somebody has really irritated you. Take a quick inventory. Who comes to mind first? Now before you say, "OK, I'll forgive so and so," it's important to think it through. Yes, more reflection time here. This is one of the truly important and overlooked reasons to forgive. If we ask ourselves why this person has upset us so much, it is an invitation to understand something about ourselves. Is our anger and resentment disguising a trap we're in? Is our resistance to forgive this person a reflection on us? What if we thought of not one person, but several persons we need to forgive? Are we so easily offended? A true measure of our progress on the spiritual journey is the thickness of our skin. I can tell you that the most peaceful, spiritually whole people I know are virtually immune to poor treatment by others. They are so secure in themselves that they simply laugh when faced with behavior we would find infuriating. Forgive and learn. Forgive and learn.

Advent, a reflection of beginnings and endings, of the space in between we call life. Look at all aspects and simply try to grow a little this season – reflect, learn, forgive, and reflect a bit more. That's a gift that will never tarnish, and one that our Lord truly treasures.

Judgment or Mercy?

Scripture Referenced: Matthew 3:1-12

> John the Baptist appeared, preaching in the desert of Judea and saying, "Repent, for the kingdom of heaven is at hand!"

The sure-fire way to tell you're in the Advent season is to listen for one name, called out in all four gospels, of a person who is utterly bound up in the early pre-ministry days of Jesus. That person, of course, is John the Baptist. In Matthew's gospel, which we just heard, John the Baptist appears out of nowhere, speaking from the desert fringes of society, dressed in weird garments, eating symbolic food of locusts and honey, and proclaiming repentance. He must have been quite a sight, and undoubtedly some people came out to see who the lunatic was. At least at first… But the lunatic surprised them. He spoke with authority and clarity, with an urgency that moved his listeners to symbolically wash themselves clean. Eventually, the religious authorities felt obliged to see who was drawing people away from the temple, and they too approached the river Jordan. They did not receive a warm welcome. John insults them, calling them snakes, and challenges them to not simply go through the motions of baptism, but to produce good fruit as evidence of their repentance. We know from subsequent run-ins with Jesus that their presence here is just as John claimed - all a sham.

John the Baptist is often called the last of the Old Testament prophets. Remember that a prophet is not someone who sees the future so much as someone who speaks for God. Being a prophet was very difficult because the prophet often felt called to speak words of warning, particularly to those in power. As you can imagine, this rarely went over well. The other characteristic of a prophet is an almost irresistible need to speak out regardless of the danger – and this is usually a poor idea as well, if you wanted to have any kind of a long life! Alas, John met the same fate that most Hebrew prophets did – death at the hands of a tyrannical king.

Many bible scholars and theologians have remarked on the very different prophetic voices of John the Baptist and Jesus. Both preached repentance. Both preached the need for a radical transformation from an old life that served no one and a new life of good fruit. But John seems to speak for a God who punishes, who is angry, who is going to sweep the world clean with a flaming scythe. Jesus speaks words of mercy and forgiveness, of a loving father who pursues us in our folly and rescues us from our worst impulses.

As we continue our Advent theme of spiritual renewal, a good question to ask yourself is where you are on the spectrum between John and Jesus? Do you believe in judgment or do you believe in mercy? Do you believe in rules and moral codes or do you believe that love conquers all? Do you believe that most people are in hell or most people are in heaven? Or, do you feel kind of in-between, hoping that God is more like God the loving father, but sort of expecting a very uncomfortable judgment day just the same?

You've got to start your spiritual walk somewhere. Most educators will tell you that the best place to begin is with the basic simple truths. When it comes to moral development, nothing works better than the ten commandments. That's why we start children here. The ten commandments govern basic social interaction, the essential grease that allows us to move through life with shared expectations. We *should* expect people to keep their word, to not steal, to honor their parents, to refrain from killing. These are good, basic rules to live by. But if we stop here at phase one, the rules, we'll never experience the kingdom in our very midst, as Jesus calls us to. We'll never move on to the Beatitudes.

If religion to us is nothing but a bunch of rules, a bunch of dos and don'ts, it can't bring life. This is what Paul came to understand in his conversion experience. The law in and of itself, cannot bring us to life, it simply leads to death. Rigid rule following leads to only two possible outcomes – rebellion against the rules in subtle or not so subtle ways, or, becoming a Pharisee, a morality cop, a judge above the rest of mankind. Jesus offers another way – he speaks of *fulfilling* the law, a very different concept. Fulfilling the law honors the intent of the law without breaking the law. Fulfilling the law acknowledges that life is not black and white, no matter how much we'd like it to be, and that there is always an overriding context that makes almost any situation nuanced and subtle. Fulfilling the law is a very different practice.

What does this look like in real life? A number of years ago, a young Catholic couple asked me to preside at their wedding. I was quite happy to oblige, and they told me that the chosen venue was a fancy hotel overlooking the ocean, with the ceremony to be performed in the great outdoors before 200 guests, a string orchestra, and well, you know the picture. Sounds great, but here's the catch. By canon law, without prior dispensation by the bishop, two Catholics must be married in a Catholic church. It's quite clear, and I know, since I've asked in the past, that our bishop does not grant such dispensations unless it is highly unusual, and losing one's deposit is not a good enough reason. Now, you can say that the couple should have known better, and you could say that I was in my rights to tell them that they would have to change all of their plans. It's in the law. And it's a good law – sacramental moments are particularly heightened when celebrated in our Church building, before the blessed sacrament. But one look at this couple, and I knew that this law was not giving life at this point – quite the opposite. So how do we work within the law to fulfill it?

The solution was surprisingly simple. Since the big bash was at 1 PM in the afternoon, I asked the couple to come to St. James at 10 that morning, with close family and friends – no fancy clothes, no music, no grand entrances, and gather with me in the prayer chapel. The Catholic marriage ceremony is a masterpiece of simplicity. A couple of readings, some shared wisdom, the perfect moment when they look at each other and agree to love and honor for the rest of their lives. In the morning quiet, birds chirping in the fountain outside, the tabernacle five feet away, the marriage was exquisitely sacramental. There wasn't a dry eye in the house. This was a God moment, a sacrament in the fullest sense of the word. Later that day, at the big venue, we *renewed* their vows, and the sun shone down in all its glory, and the music welled, and the bride whispered to me, "I liked this morning much better…"

Or, consider this situation, which I know will arise in 17 days. You're at Christmas Mass and someone you know for a fact has not been to Church in a year or more, and leads a life that is hardly Christian, let alone Catholic, goes up to receive communion. What's going through your mind? Part of you is screaming, "You shouldn't receive communion! I'm going to tackle you right now!" What does the law say? Yes, that person should definitely not receive communion.

What does "fulfilling the law" ask you to do? It asks you to assume that this person has just received a compelling call from the Holy Spirit to turn their lives around starting today, starting with *this* Eucharist.

You see, what Jesus does is to take the hard reality of the law and dose it with the baptism of love, and that makes all of the difference.

You've got to turn off your worldly cynicism and believe in the power of the Spirit of God. When I'm working with the guys in the prison, where they are from is hugely influential on what they did, why they did it, and who they are. The key to repentance work is to realize that all of one's past behavior is just that – *past behavior* – and the future is one of endless potential for happiness and peace and moral behavior. Basically, you have to believe that people can change. This is the heart of Jesus' message as told in his parable of the Prodigal Son. This is why Dickens story of Ebenezer Scrooge is so compelling even today.

Ponder this dilemma. Law and love. It's at the heart of the spiritual journey we're all on this Advent. How can you honor the words of both John the Baptist and Jesus the Christ?

God's Invitation

Scripture Referenced: Luke 13:1-9

> [Jesus said:] "There once was a person who had a fig tree planted in his orchard, and when he came in search of fruit on it but found none, he said to the gardener, 'For three years now I have come in search of fruit on this fig tree but have found none. So cut it down. Why should it exhaust the soil?' He said to him in reply, 'Sir, leave it for this year also, and I shall cultivate the ground around it and fertilize it; it may bear fruit in the future. If not you can cut it down.'"

It's hard to hear the first reading and not picture Charlton Heston on the mountainside puzzling at the cheesy Hollywood burning bush in the movie The Ten Commandments. It brings a quick smile, but don't dismiss this event too quickly. This is an archetypical moment in God's relationship to mankind. What I mean by that is that what Moses goes through is in some way a stand-in for all of us, a model of how God calls each of us. But don't stop here – note the Gospel reading today. Jesus seems particularly harsh – his message seems to distill down to two words – repent or perish! It's the only time I've ever felt sorry for a fig tree. So what's the link here? What's going on?

Our friend Moses has lived a pretty interesting life up to this event. It is only through the daring ingenuity of his mother that Moses escapes an early death at infancy. Raised in Pharaoh's court, he has a pretty good life going for himself until he has a pang of conscience, an awakening that he is no more an Egyptian than you and me. He acts in defense of a Hebrew slave being beaten by an overseer, kills the Egyptian, and runs from the law, out to this very desert where Yahweh God has set some bait for Moses to investigate. God isn't done with Moses, is he?

Isn't that just like God? He loves to intrigue us. An early awareness of God is common to most of us. But God doesn't stop. An invitation here, an interesting opportunity there, a phone call, a magazine article, a good homily, a friend with a question. Like Moses, we think, "I must go over to look at this remarkable sight..." When we take a closer look, we see that the "remarkable sight" is actually an invitation into something bigger. Yahweh reveals to Moses that Yahweh is a God of compassion – a very unusual stance for a god in the time of Moses. Yahweh invites Moses to accompany him on the journey into compassion by playing a critically important role as intercessor between Yahweh and the people. Moses is being offered the job as Israel's first prophet.

What would you have done? Moses is clearly uneasy about this offer – it sounds dangerous and unlikely to succeed. Are any of you facing such a decision? A call to use your gifts in a new way? A way that seems unlikely to succeed? A heckuva stretch?

In the gospel, Jesus tells the story of a fig tree. The tree seems healthy enough. It has leaves, it grows, it would look to anyone like the tree is doing just fine. But the landlord knows that the tree is not living up to what it *can* be. The fig tree, if you'll excuse the expression, doesn't give a fig! It seems content to just be a regular tree, planted firmly, but not of much use, just taking up some space and some fertilizer. And when you get right down to it, what's the problem with that? The tree isn't harming anyone. Who cares?

Here's the hard reality, folks. A plant that doesn't flower or produce fruit is doomed. It will wither and die – perhaps not immediately, but soon enough. You gardeners out there know this. Why keep a flowering plant around if it never flowers? Better to yank it out and replace it with a better, more suitable plant. Of course, carrying this analogy to human beings is a bit difficult. Is God really standing there with a big scythe waiting to see if we bear fruit? No, not exactly. But don't let the image confuse you. If we are not being the best person God knows we can be, we are not bearing fruit. And the reality is that when we don't bear fruit, we will be unhappy. We will always feel like we're missing something. We will always feel anxious and depressed. We will feel like we're withering, that we're wasting our time. Pay attention if that describes you.

Note that the parable doesn't end with the landlord tearing up the tree. The gardener intercedes and says, "Let me work on this one a bit longer. Maybe I can coax it into a fuller life." So who's the gardener in the story? Yeah, Jesus. He's going to keep on trying for a while. But not forever it seems.

Does Moses accept the invitation? Well, sort of. He squirms and dodges, coming up with several lame excuses that we don't actually hear in the reading today, but check out all of Exodus, Chapter 3 to get the entire story. Then, in what seems a sly trick, Moses asks Yahweh's name, which seems a curious question at this juncture, but actually is quite meaningful on several levels. Knowing another person's name implies a familiarity that may or may not be warranted. Moses is angling for that insider knowledge. But more than this, Moses is demonstrating a very human trait – a desire to put God in a box, to get some boundaries around God, to get a leash on this dangerous power. If Moses knows God's name, Moses can call God and God will come. Do you see how manipulative this is? What follows is probably one of the most profound God moments in the entire Bible. God answers Moses with a simple two-word phrase that is utterly baffling, utterly confusing, utterly bizarre, and utterly perfect. God's name? I AM. Present tense. Now. Existing now, back then, and tomorrow. Un-made, un-named, inescapable. I AM. Deal with it, Moses. Deal with it, my friends. You aren't getting this God in a box, no matter how hard you try.

Jesus is right here next to us, cultivating the ground, adding some fertilizer, checking if we're being watered enough. Do you feel like you're flowering yet? Are you producing fruit? Or are you resisting? What holds you back? Worry about what people will think? Afraid to try something new? Michelangelo once said, "The great danger for most of us lies *not* in setting our aim too high and failing, but in setting our aim too *low* and achieving our mark." Our God is a God of abundance, do you realize that? You know, he could have made just one type of dog, and that would be it. I was watching the Westminster dog show the other day and I was astounded at the different types of dogs. God seems to absolutely relish abundant life. He wants us to live that kind of abundance, too. When Jesus says repent or perish, it sounds like a threat. But that's a misreading. It's not a threat, it's a statement of fact. If we do not flower with all that we are, we will be unhappy, unfulfilled, and live a life of lack and addiction, constantly seeking to fill the hole in our soul.

Here's five ways to open yourself to the gardener:

- Worship – prayer, Mass, meditation, contemplation. Worship always puts us in a humble stance, a receptive stance before God.
- Knowledge – attend an adult faith formation event – grow a little. Add a little weight to your spear!

- Serve – consciously share your gifts in service to others. This is a well-traveled route to happiness.
- Connect – meet someone new – maybe as you're walking out of Mass this morning. Look around and introduce yourselves.
- Give – when you give, you detach – it's the only way to put our money and goods in proper perspective.

Repent or perish? What Jesus the gardener is really saying is "Please listen to me. I don't want you to die. I want you to thrive!"

A Compassionate Response

Scripture Referenced: Mark 6:30-34

> When he disembarked and saw the vast crowd, his heart was moved with pity for them, for they were like sheep without a shepherd; and he began to teach them many things.

The gospel seems like a good summer time reading. The disciples are back from their first big mission trip, full of news about the healings, the encounters with demon-possessed people, the bravery they demonstrated walking into strange villages with nothing but the clothes on their back and an offer to tell the good news. Jesus suggests a brief vacation – come away by yourselves and rest a while. It seems like a pretty good idea for all of us "do-gooders". We've been reaching down to help others get better, get fed, get a job, get educated, you name it. We all deserve a break with Jesus now and then – a nice little retreat to "anywhere but here."

But Jesus has an interesting plan. He clearly sees that a teaching moment is at hand. Notice the destination he proposes for the apostles. A deserted place. Why? Why not the seashore? Why not Jerusalem? Why not a nice hotel in Jericho? Why a deserted place? Understand first of all that the desert was the place of Jewish mysticism – all of the great prophets, most recently John the Baptist, came out of the desert. The desert was associated with Yahweh God, with Moses and the Sinai. The desert is a place of power amid the barren lands. It is a paradoxical place. Dry and lifeless for human bodies, full of life for the Spirit. Jesus' choice of destination may have raised an eyebrow or two, but the apostles would likely get the point. They were vacationing in God's land.

How did the big plan work out? Off they go, across the sea (another metaphor for the spiritual journey), and they reach their destination – a deserted place. NOT. Expecting nothing but rocks and the quiet of deep nature, they instead come upon a whole lot of needy people. You can imagine the apostles turning to look at Jesus in the boat. What do we do now? Do we keep on sailing for another shore? Do we beat them back with sticks? What do we have to do to get a little peace around here?

Now Jesus acts. Rather than being angry or frustrated, he is moved with pity. Rather than showing impatience with their endless needs, he wades in once again, seemingly in complete calm. He teaches and preaches and heals, and the apostles can be seen sitting by the boat, trying to understand.

Have you ever met someone who just seems to have a boundless energy to serve? Do you ever wonder what makes them tick? In just this past week, our diocesan newspaper featured an article on Fr. Joe Carroll, who I think would fit this category well. He's been serving the homeless for 30 years, and if anyone could be seen as a good shepherd, it's him. How does he do it?

We hear a lot of talk about burn-out in today's world, especially among people who are care-givers. The story goes something like this. The more of a caregiver you are (nurse, teacher, doctor, clergy person, social worker, etc.), the more cautious you need to be about burning out. I guess the opposite is true as well if we hold to logic. The more self-centered you are (dictator, Internet mogul, professional athlete, movie star, pop singer), the less likely you'll burn out. Well, neither generalization is correct, so we're missing something. I know many caregivers who have a seemingly endless fountain of energy and good will – far from burnout. And you don't need to read much of Entertainment Weekly to come across some sorry movie stars who are as burned out and depressed as you can imagine. What are we missing here?

The key to the story is in the final sentence of today's Gospel: "When he disembarked and saw the vast crowd, his heart was moved with pity for them, for they were like sheep without a shepherd; and he began to teach them many things." Did you get the connection? Jesus tells the apostles that we're going out to a deserted place to commune with God. They get to the place and alas, they find not God, but people. Translation: guess where you find God? In people. Surprise! The apostles are understandably annoyed to find the people, and here is Jesus' final point. If you see the people you serve as somehow beneath you, which is a very easy trap to fall into, you will most certainly burn out eventually. You will become frustrated that they don't "get it", you will be irritated at having to solve the same old problem again and again, and you will eventually resent their very existence. What does Jesus show these people? Is he frustrated? Irritated? Resentful? No. He is moved with pity. In other words, he is filled with *compassion.* This is the teaching moment Jesus offers the apostles. If you want to remain energized while working for the Lord for a long time, the only way that will happen is if your motivation is compassion. If you're motivated to help because you're smarter, or more organized, or richer, or feeling guiltier, or want to make the whole world Catholic – well, it's not going to last long. As long as your motivation comes from something you need to do or prove, you'll burn out. If, however, you are motivated by a heart moved to pity, by a compassionate desire to spread a little grace around, then you'll never burn out. Why? Because the *compassionate* response is a *God* response, and God's power, grace, and peace are eternal fires. They can't burn out. Tap into these and you have the secret to a long life of true giving.

Back to Fr. Joe. When asked what he considered his greatest accomplishment, he said it was helping others to see that the homeless are really just neighbors who need our help. Do you hear the compassion in that statement? Compassion – suffering with someone else. He goes on to say, "When you take the name 'homeless' out of it, it seems to take the fear out of working with our neighbors in need." That's the key to service, to see that those you serve are just like you are, and all you're doing is being Christ to them. Is that so hard?

When I go into the prison or the jail with people for the first time, inevitably they come out and say, "they're just like you and me." Yes, and that's what Jesus was teaching his apostles. These people are just like you and me, as indistinguishable as a flock of sheep. There's no need to be the Messiah, that job has been taken. We simply need to follow the Messiah into the pain of the world and let Him work through us. No pressure, no expectations, no grades. Just compassion. That's all it takes.

Justice

Scripture Referenced: Matthew 20:1-16

> The landlord said to one of them in reply, 'My friend, I am not cheating you. Did you not agree with me for the usual daily wage? Take what is yours and go. What if I wish to give this last one the same as you? Or am I not free to do as I wish with my own money? Are you envious because I am generous?'

When I was a kid growing up in upstate New York, I lived out in the country. Our house was modest in size, but we lived on an acre of land, which allowed room for a large lawn and a garden in the back. My grandfather planted raspberry bushes when we first moved in – a lot of them. Two one-hundred foot rows of raspberry bushes in fact. The bushes matured at about the same rate as my brothers and sisters did and by the time I was 13, the bushes were producing a prodigious crop. We had raspberries everywhere! My mother, after much prodding from us kids, finally agreed that we could sell raspberries to cars passing by the house – a little mini farm stand. The deal was simple - for every pint of raspberries each of us picked, we would get the benefit of the profit when they were sold. So the next day, after a leisurely breakfast, I and my younger siblings headed up to the raspberry patch to pick some berries and make some money. Imagine our shock to see my older brother already there, proudly displaying 20 pints of picked raspberries! The bushes were virtually empty of berries. He had arisen at dawn and taken matters into his own hands. Of course, we went howling off to Mom, accusing my brother of dirty pool. But Mom simply acknowledged that my brother had worked hard and smart, so we had nothing to complain about. Our indignant response? It's not fair!

Imagine today's gospel overlaid on this same story. Imagine my mother taking the raspberries from my older brother, paying him in full, and then turning to the rest of us and paying us the same amount! How do you think my brother would have responded? Much like the full-day workers in the parable, don't you think? His answer would have been, like theirs, "it's not fair!"

This parable, like all of the parables of Jesus, is designed to shock us. The predicted outcome is tossed aside, and we're forced to think. The fact that to this day all of us (be honest now!) are irritated by the generosity of the landowner, tells us that this parable is still working its magic over 2000 years later. We're forced to ask two questions – what does this parable say about God, and more importantly, how do we respond to it as Christians in today's world?

At its root level, the topic of this parable is justice, or at least, our notion of justice. Justice, to us, is about fairness and impartiality, about being treated in exact conformance to our conduct. It's a simple concept really. I do good things, I get rewards. I do bad things, I get punished. I work harder than you, I get more than you. If I'm a better person than you, I should go to heaven and if you're bad enough, you should go to hell. Or if that seems a bit too strong, I would expect that there would at least be different levels in heaven, with the saints and martyrs living in the high rent districts, right?

My thoughts are not your thoughts, nor are your ways my ways, says the Lord.

Let's dig a little deeper. Why do we need the concept of justice anyway? Why is this necessary? The shameful reality is that at the depth of our being, we are all incredibly selfish people. In a world that has no justice, it is simply dog eat dog, Lord of the Flies anarchy, a dystopian reality that we shudder to ponder. The notion of justice is universally understood, regardless of religious awareness – it is part of what we call natural law. God imbues all of us with this sense of justice, for without it, the world would indeed collapse in never-ending warfare.

In this parable, Jesus asks us to imagine a reality where justice is *unnecessary*. This is the world that God calls us to – a world where *sharing* is the driving force. What if your first thought in the morning is not "How do I get ahead today?" What if your first thought is "How do I make someone else's life a little better?" The interesting thing is that we *can* imagine a world like that, but, we shake our heads internally, because all it takes is one selfish person and that beautiful notion breaks down. So why bother trying?

I'll tell you why. Because Christ *in us* can make this happen. We can't do it by ourselves – it would be discouraging and exhausting. But, as St. Paul tells us, Christ is *magnified* in our bodies, somehow taking our pitiful efforts and turbo-charging the results. This is what it means to be a Christian.

Back in upstate New York, umpteen years ago, it's the next morning. I get up at 4 AM, and run out the backdoor with my flashlight, determined to get my share of the profits. Alas, brilliant ideas run in the family and I am soon joined by my other siblings, stumbling in the dark, each of us glaring at the other. Moments later, my parents come to the backdoor, call us in sternly, and send us back to bed. New rules: no one could pick before 8 AM – and, for every 2 pints we older boys picked, we had to help our little sisters pick a pint as well. The raspberry wars were over.

Let's not be naïve – this world still needs justice. But let's be Christian too. There are two directions we need to go. One is toward sharing – simply sharing. We share with the vulnerable, we share with those who are not as gifted as we are, we share simply because we're all human beings made in the image of God. Share. Second direction – much more difficult – work toward that imagined world where justice is *unnecessary*. That takes imagination, courage, and asking challenging questions. You see, the question is not simply how much money we give to the beggar on the street, but why is that guy begging in the first place? The question is not how much food is needed to be sent to Africa, but why do we keep having to do this? The questions keep coming. Tough questions. We recoil at the horror of abortion, the false promise of euthanasia. Yes, it is good to fight these evils – but we need to ask, why are people drawn to these actions in the first place? It's not because people are inherently evil, it's because for whatever reason, these people feel that they have *no other option*. That's where true Christian action needs to focus. Can we make abortion and euthanasia completely unnecessary? A world where everyone is fed, everyone has a roof over their head, everyone feels love and care from the beginning to the end? That's the world that God is asking us to imagine – and Jesus will work with us to achieve.

As high as the heavens are above the earth, so high are my ways above your ways and my thoughts above your thoughts, says the Lord. That beautiful phrase from Isaiah is certainly true, but remember – that's from the Old Testament. With Christ working in us, we are privileged to get a glimpse of God's thoughts and His ways. Let's work together and see if we can re-imagine a new world, a kingdom where there are no tears, no suffering, and plenty of raspberries to go around.

Seeing With Christ's Eyes

Scripture Referenced: Luke 18:1-8

> [Jesus said:] "There was a judge in a certain town who neither feared God nor respected any human being. And a widow in that town used to come to him and say, 'Render a just decision for me against my adversary.' For a long time the judge was unwilling, but eventually he thought, 'While it is true that I neither fear God nor respect any human being, because this widow keeps bothering me I shall deliver a just decision for her lest she finally come and strike me.'"

A few weeks ago, we had a gospel reading with a similar theme – the need for us to be persistent in prayer. At that time we heard about the homeowner who was asked by his neighbor to provide him 3 loaves of bread in the middle of the night. We are told that the homeowner will accommodate the neighbor because of his persistence, not necessarily because he's a nice guy. So what's different in today's reading? The ante is a bit higher. The widow, who represents a person with no power whatsoever, is up against a judge who is not simply indifferent, but apparently corrupt. Total powerlessness versus unyielding authority. She doesn't have a chance.

Now if this were a Hollywood movie, what would happen next? On being thwarted, she would seek out the local Mafia chief, come to some sort of arrangement, and the judge would be "convinced" that he should find in her favor. Might overcomes might. Or, she would find a way to seduce the judge, threaten to embarrass him in public, and therefore get her way. Deviousness overcomes deviousness. Anyway, you get the picture. According to Hollywood, the way to overcome injustice is to (temporarily of course) resort to violent or devious tactics until you get your justice, and then go back to being a good person again. We see this theme played out so often that we hardly blink an eye. Practically every action picture you see features *righteous revenge* as the main motivation that drives the character and plot. Check it out – it's truly amazing.

Now, despite all of this good Hollywood advice, the widow uses the only thing she has going for her – a willingness to ask for justice, not once, not twice, but over and over. This is her plan – that's all it is – to just keep asking, in person, firmly and politely, for justice. Not much of a plan, huh?

In the early part of the 20th century, this was essentially the same plan that Mahatma Gandhi came up with to rid his country of British colonial rule. Non-violence, protest marches, appealing to the best side of human nature, relying on the simple fact that he had truth, time, and many like-minded people who had nothing to lose marching with him. In 1963, Martin Luther King Jr. adopted these exact same tactics in his leadership for Civil Rights in America. Despite often violent response to his organized marches, he knew that as long as he did not resort to violence in return, the cause would be his. Unfortunately, it cost him his life to prove the point. In 1994, Nelson Mandela did the same thing in South Africa. What do all three of these men have in common? A deep spirituality, one Hindu and the other two Christian, that allowed them each to seek the moral high ground and operate from a stance of fearless and persistent calls for justice, never lowering themselves or their followers to violent acts.

We're told that the widow wins her case from the corrupt judge, and Jesus makes a point of saying, "Pay attention to what the dishonest judge says." Note that the judge does not rule in her favor because it is the right thing to do – no, the judge rules in her favor because he wants to get rid of her. He's a little afraid of her, actually. He simply wants to get out of the uncomfortable spotlight this woman is focusing on him. Isn't that interesting? The judge doesn't have some Hollywood conversion experience – he simply wants out! He's afraid of getting embarrassed – of looking bad.

If we update the gospel, who represents the powerlessness of the first century widow today? Who can claim the unfortunate label of "most vulnerable"? The homeless? Certainly. The undocumented immigrant? Yes. How about the unborn? In a very distressing way, yes, they qualify too. How about the prisoner? Sure – and even more so, someone who has done their time and has a criminal record. Try getting a job with a felony on your record – you learn quickly the meaning of un-forgiveness.

A few years ago, I was at the end of a business trip, heading home to San Diego. As I waited to board the plane in Dallas, I noticed a large number of young men in the waiting area. They didn't seem to know each other, but all had that certain look to them – 19 years old, kind of fidgety and nervous, and it struck me immediately – Marines! Or more accurately, new recruits to the Marines – all on their way to boot camp. Since I was a Platinum card holder, I get the aisle seat just behind the exit row. A well-dressed woman gets the window seat. Who gets the middle seat? You guessed it. A young Afro-American man politely settles in, and off we go.

I strike up a conversation with him and he confirms that yes, boot camp awaits. We discuss his hopes and aspirations and it strikes me that this young man is starting out life from a ten-foot hole. He's only got a high school education. He comes from a very poor neighborhood in the Midwest, and his skin color is not going to open any doors for him. My first reaction was a sense of superiority – much like the judge in the Gospel. But that quickly passed as he chatted, and soon my reaction to him became more akin to compassion. You see, I began to remember what it was like to be 19, to see the world with an idealistic eye, to have hope and expectations, to see more friendly faces than frowning ones. Ultimately I gave him my business card and told him to give me a call when he got out.

You see, what really won the day for the persistent widow was that she *personalized* the quest for justice. She made herself known to the judge. He became fully aware of her, uncomfortably aware of her, in fact. As long as the most vulnerable are simply labels – homeless, undocumented, unborn, criminal, poor black man – we aren't motivated to do anything. But if we crack through the veneer and see what it means to be marginalized, to have no power, to see that behind the label is a person just like we are, a person who wants the same things we do out of life, then all of a sudden the request for simple understanding and acknowledgement becomes not only easy to hear, but easy to respond to. We see the spark of God in that person. That's why compassion – remember the meaning of the word – to "suffer with", is such an important prerequisite to justice. We only squirm in our chair when it becomes *real*!

I ask you to take a look around this week. Who are the most vulnerable around you? Who are the invisible people with labels that you barely notice? I've got news for you – most of us are more like the judge in today's gospel than the widow. But the good news is that you're not corrupt, you're not completely selfish. You simply need to open your eyes and let the *Christ in you* look out in compassion. Start the conversation with a vulnerable person, a powerless person. As the widow shows us, justice begins one person at a time.

Presence, Compassion, Peace

Scripture Referenced: Luke 16:19-31

> Jesus said to the Pharisees: "There was a rich man who dressed in purple garments and fine linen and dined sumptuously each day. And lying at his door was a poor man named Lazarus, covered with sores, who would gladly have eaten his fill of the scraps that fell from the rich man's table."

When I saw the readings for this Sunday, my reaction was probably a lot like yours right now, namely, "Oh great, the parable of the rich man and Lazarus. Time for the guilt trip!" Now I'm sure that Fr. John wouldn't mind a few extra bucks in the collection basket so you'll feel better, but I'd like to get beyond the guilt for a moment and look at the real message of this gospel.

By the description of the life the rich man leads, it is clear that he is *very* rich – purple garments, fine linen, eating sumptuously – practically unheard of in a largely agrarian society where most people did not know where their next meal was coming from. By contrast, Lazarus is dressed in rags, seemingly unable to walk, and covered with sores. After both die, the rich man finds himself in hell, and Lazarus in heaven. The interesting dialog that ensues between the rich man and Abraham reveals that what has condemned the rich man is not that he mistreated Lazarus. In fact, we'd probably feel better if the rich man had actually abused Lazarus. No, what condemns the rich man is that he *ignored* Lazarus. Lazarus was virtually invisible to him, beneath the level of a dog. The rich man is not condemned for being rich. He is condemned for lacking a simple virtue – *compassion.*

We have a fuzzy notion of compassion as being nice to others who are hurting, or being charitable (whatever that means), or being kind to someone who lost a loved one, but this isn't really compassion. To understand compassion, it's useful to consider the opposite of compassion. Any idea of what that word would be? No, it's not indifference, or hate, or anything simple like that. According to Henri Nouwen, it's *competition.* Yes, competition.

Some years ago, I heard a speaker address this topic and he made a point that in the Christian life, we needed to avoid competition with each other. I remember feeling a little put out by this statement (a sure sign that my little ego was in charge) and I spoke to him after the talk. I told him that I came from a large family and that I had spent most of my childhood competing with my siblings in sports and school. I told him that this competitive existence prepared me well for the real world and that I was able to be successful since I knew how to distinguish myself. Anyway, you get the idea. So after going on like this for a while, I took a breath and waited for his affirmation that clearly, I was an exception to his statement. He looked at me kindly and said, "I'm sorry, you have a long way to go." My jaw dropped as he turned away.

Jesus tells us in the sixth chapter of Luke's gospel to be compassionate as your Father God is compassionate. What does this mean? God being God, there is absolutely no competition between God and human beings – it's absurd to even consider. God in his infinite power competes with no one, ever. Now God could simply observe us from afar, chuckling at our antics much as we chuckle at the antics of our pet dogs, but that's not what God does. God enters into our pain, our suffering, our challenges, in a real way, in a way that we call compassion. Compassion, at its root, is a word that means "to suffer with". How do we know that God is like this? Check out his son, Jesus. Jesus is God's visible sign of compassion.

Note how Jesus exhibits compassion. He first of all makes himself available to the hurting, the hungry, the poor. He is *present* to them. But what distinguishes Jesus is that he is often "moved with compassion", a phrase in the Gospels that is more literally translated as "moved at the gut level" when presented with someone in need. The blind, the lepers, the widow at Nain, the hungry thousands – they each move Jesus at the gut level. It seems that his miraculous cures flow almost naturally from his guts, from who he is on the inside, from his divine source. This is God's own compassion embodied. We are called to show the same compassion! How?

The rich man in the story got rich somehow. It is likely that he made some shrewd moves, some great deals, and distinguished himself. He was a winner. He competed well. At some gut level, having a poor beggar at his door was an affirmation of his worth, a nice reminder that he was better than most. He had made it. As hard as it is, we need to shut off the need to distinguish ourselves, to find validation in our ego drive, to be known by our trophies. Ironically, by distinguishing ourselves, we actually *separate* ourselves from the body of Christ, from the vine itself, from the true source of peace and love.

The key to compassion is presence. Not fixing problems, not giving money, not voting for a particular candidate. Presence. Jesus is God present to us. We are likewise the presence of Jesus to others. We are called to visit the sick, the imprisoned, the homeless, the ignorant, the hungry and thirsty. From our presence, the right thing to do will become apparent. It may be as easy as providing a meal. It may be as hard as taking someone into our home. From presence modeled after our Father God, the creative and healing result will naturally occur. You'll know what to do – once you're there.

Let me give you an example. A few years ago, a friend called, she was distraught. Her mother, ravaged by Alzheimer's, was dying in a nursing home and they couldn't find a priest. Could we help? Katie and I rushed to the Church, picked up some consecrated hosts in a little container called a pix, and drove to the nursing home. We walked into the room where the family was gathered around Mom's bedside. She was obviously out of it, but very agitated, writhing and moaning under the covers. It was distressing to see her like this, and the family was emotionally wrung out. So we began to pray the Communion Service together and I wondered what good it was doing. Then the daughter did something that startled me. As we distributed communion, she took the pix from my hand, with a host still inside, made the sign of the cross, and gently placed the pix on her mother's chest. Immediately, the woman stopped thrashing and calmed down, as if a storm had passed or she was being held closely, on the inside. Presence, compassion, peace.

In Matthew's gospel, at the birth of Jesus, we are told that Jesus fulfills the prophet Isaiah's words that the savior will be born of a virgin and be called Emanuel. Do you know what Emanuel means? "God is with us." Presence, compassion, peace.

Chapter 12 – Bearing Witness

Most of us find it challenging enough to be authentic followers of Christ. We struggle to maintain a prayer life, to immerse ourselves in Scripture, to just get to Mass on Sunday. But the reality is that we're invited to do so much more. Our Christian identity must permeate our votes, how we spend money, our political stance, our understanding of freedom, our response to aggression – all of it! As St. John so aptly puts it, "If anyone says, 'I love God,' but hates his brother, he is a liar…" (1 John 4:20) Harsh words, yes, but claiming to follow Christ is not something testified lightly. At the end of our days, we want Christ to say, "I know you!"

The Role of Government

Scripture Referenced: Matthew 22:15-21

> Knowing their malice, Jesus said, "Why are you testing me, you hypocrites? Show me the coin that pays the census tax." Then they handed him the Roman coin. He said to them, "Whose image is this and whose inscription?" They replied, "Caesar's." At that he said to them, "Then repay to Caesar what belongs to Caesar and to God what belongs to God."

It's amazing to me how utterly relevant today's gospel reading is in today's hyper-political world. As you well know, anyone in a political role, or it seems, any public role, is often forced into the exact same no-win choice that Jesus faced. Whether it's the secular press in today's world or the Pharisees at the time of Jesus, the question asked is specific and meant to trap the responder into an answer that will label the person as liberal or a conservative, or a hawk or a pacifist, or a winner or a loser. And how does Jesus respond to this game? He refuses to play.

The gospel is very clear that the Pharisees are trying to trap Jesus. Their question about the lawfulness of the tax puts Jesus on the spot. If he says the tax is unlawful, he'll be arrested by the Romans for advocating dissent. If he says the tax is lawful, he'll alienate 90% of his followers who hate the Roman rule and resent paying any taxes to Caesar. So Jesus responds with the enigmatic statement, "Repay to Caesar what belongs to Caesar and to God what belongs to God." This really doesn't answer their question, but instead muddies the water. Jesus is saying, in effect, that they're asking the wrong question. It's not black and white – it's much more subtle. We can certainly learn from this approach.

It may be a sign of our times that every thing and every person needs to be put into a simple box. I think the reason is that the world is so big and confusing that we hunger for simplicity and clarity. If a member of the press can do that for us through an insightful question, then we can sigh, relax, and say to ourselves, "Aha, I knew that person was a 'fill in the blank.' Now I can dismiss what he says in the future because I know what camp he's in." I don't know about you, but when someone tosses a label onto me, I get a little upset. Because the reality is that sometimes I'm a liberal, sometimes a conservative, sometimes a hawk, sometimes a dove, sometimes a winner, and sometimes a loser. It's complicated, and I don't like playing the label game.

When Jesus says to repay to Caesar what is Caesar's and to God what belongs to God, it begs the question, "How do you know what is Caesar's and what is God's?" Great question! Not an easy answer. From our first reading, Isaiah makes the point that Cyrus, a pagan ruler, is actually following the will of God, even though he doesn't know it! God is above everything and everybody. The little illusions of power that people have here on earth are just that, illusions. But at the same time, it appears that God does allow for institutions and governments to assume some earthly power. Is there a pecking order implied here? I think so. It goes like this:

God is first. He has all the power and has had all of the power throughout all time. If you believe in God, you have to believe that this is true. So what is second in line? Some might say that the government is next in power. Some might say, no, it's the Church that is next in power. The reality is that the Church and the State have been in tension for much of the past 2,000 years over this precise question. It has only been since 1870 that the Catholic Church completely removed itself from civic rule. But more to the point, separation of Church and State was not officially promulgated by the Catholic Church until 1965 in Vatican II's Declaration on Religious Liberty. The document proclaims "It is wrong for a public authority to compel its citizens by force or fear or any other means to profess or repudiate any religion." So everything is settled right? Not exactly!

Although the role of good government is to foster the safety, health, and well-being of all of its citizens, i.e., the "common good", it is just as possible for moral lines to be crossed in the name of good government. In some cases, this is obvious, as in the question of slavery in the mid-19th century or civil rights in the 1960's. Many, many good Christian men and women examined the issues carefully and determined that the government was violating God's law in upholding slavery and segregation. They protested, they spoke out, they marched, and ultimately these unjust laws were changed. This is how it should be.

Are there issues today that fall into this same camp? Many good Christian men and women would say, "Yes!" I'm not going to go into all of them today – just read the newspaper to see what the current focus happens to be. Many other people would prefer not to hear about these issues at all and simply refuse to discuss them. In light of today's Gospel, what is the right stance?

Start with the given – we are God's people first. Discerning the will of God takes prayer, study, and more prayer. Learn from those who are wisdom leaders in our Church. Open your eyes, open your ears, and ask the difficult questions. Pay attention to the stirrings in your heart. Speak out if you are moved to do so. But more than anything else, when you speak out, speak out with love. This part is often overlooked. A screaming match simply produces two hoarse people. Do not demonize those who disagree with you. Before long, demonizing people can lead to dehumanizing people and if someone is seen as less than human, then it's an easy step to war and extermination. Look at Syria. Look at Iraq. Look at the sorry history of wars fought for religion. Good religion always seeks peace. Never believe anyone who says that they are fighting for a particular religion. They're kidding themselves, to the sorry detriment of us all.

Pope Francis has spoken frequently about how the Church engages in the difficult social issues of the day. His advice is well worth remembering. You can't convince people of anything by yelling at them or wagging your finger in their faces. First, you need to attract them to your way of life, your Christian stance in the world. They need to see through your actions that Jesus Christ is paramount in your life, and that this has great implications on how you see the world. If they are impressed with you as a person, they will listen to your words. Look at Blessed Mother Teresa – she didn't get to address the United Nations because she was a Catholic nun. She got to speak to the rulers of the world because of the moral authority she brought to the table. Every poor soul she ministered to in India gave her a measure of respect in the eyes of the world. They recognized her love, since everyone knows love, and so she stood, upheld by the love of God, and told the world what she thought about social issues like abortion. The world paid attention.

Remember that we are members of Christ's kingdom by our baptism. Our allegiance is to Him first. Follow Jesus and the world will take notice. Follow Jesus and your words will be inspired by the Holy Spirit. Then render unto Caesar what is Caesar's and to God what is God's.

Responsible Voting

Scripture Referenced: 1 Corinthians 10:16-17

> Brothers and sisters: The cup of blessing that we bless, is it not a participation in the blood of Christ? The bread that we break, is it not a participation in the body of Christ? Because the loaf of bread is one, we, though many, are one body, for we all partake of the one loaf.

It seems fitting on this holy feast of the Body and Blood of Christ to acknowledge two realities. The first is that we are a Eucharistic people (Eucharist meaning thanksgiving), and therefore always in a grateful mode, grateful for life, for love, for peace through a faith that comforts and sustains us. The second reality is that we need to see ourselves, as St. Paul writes, as the body of Christ acting in this world. We are all gifted people, and the Holy Spirit invigorates our gifts to the glory of God.

As we're all aware, we're in an election year. Many of you have asked for guidance from the St. James clergy and staff as to how to respond to the challenges that seem to arise almost daily with respect to issues of birth control, abortion, marriage, capital punishment, immigration, economic crisis and perceived attacks on religious freedom. How do we make manifest our dual heritage as Catholics and as American citizens? These are important questions, and we'd like to help you address them in a constructive way while keeping in mind Jesus' one commandment to us: *Love one another*.

We are *all* called to bear witness to our Christian values in public life, but not in the same way. The role of the clergy is to teach, form, and encourage the action of the lay baptized. Pope Benedict, however, points out in his encyclical *Deus Caritas Est* that "the *direct duty* to work for a just ordering of society is proper to the *lay faithful*." Another way of putting it is to say that the clergy lead from the center, helping the lay faithful to turn around and face the world out there, to speak the truth in all walks and ways of life. Although church officials are prohibited from engaging in partisan politics, it doesn't mean that we can't help channel the energy of the Body of Christ to act in a very public way.

How does the Body of Christ respond? Our Body of parishioners have many different gifts, and each is called to perhaps a different way of responding to these challenging times. Some respond by engaging in charity to the downtrodden and marginalized, illustrating the reality that we are known by our love for each other. Others respond by community organizing, helping people help themselves, showing our engagement in the world in a positive, Christian way. Others respond by organizing prayer groups and healing ministries to call on the power of the Holy Spirit. Still others take part by engaging our government and political leaders through letter campaigns, marches, and media responses. All of these activities are appropriate, often powerful responses. No one of these is preferable to the other, since no one part of the Body of Christ is better than another. It's the action of the entire Body that changes the world.

Like the rest of the country our community is divided on how to approach many of our hot button issues. At the Last Supper Jesus prayed that his disciples may be one. Please understand that our role as your clergy and staff is to maintain the communion, not to create divisions. Above all, to paraphrase St. Paul, if we have faith to move mountains and hand our bodies over to any cause *and lack love*, we are simply noisy gongs. Charity, which challenges us to treat our enemies with the same loving forgiveness as we treat our own kind, is the highest virtue. This is the hallmark of our Catholic faith, and how indeed we are ultimately measured. It was the great Saint Augustine who wrote: "In essentials, unity; in doubtful matters, liberty; in all things, charity."

When I was a teenager growing up, listening to the radio for my favorite song, one of the DJ's favorite tag lines was, "The hits keep on coming!" As a faithful Catholic in today's world, I can relate to that statement, can't you? The hits keep on coming. But I am also a person of faith and the knowledge that Jesus Christ has already conquered Satan, has already conquered the world, has already redeemed us. It doesn't mean that world is hunky-dory, but it does mean that the Spirit is alive and well and acting in ways that may surprise us. People of faith, hope, and charity are optimistic people. Our God is an awesome God. Do you trust Him? Do you believe in the new covenant? God certainly believes in you!

As the election approaches, the level of rhetoric will rise. People will say outrageous things, and worse yet, tell you what a "good" Catholic should do. How do you respond? The key is to be educated on the issues, listen to our bishops, pray for guidance from the Holy Spirit, and follow the best part of who you are, the true self that God has formed in you. This is the essence of what it means to form a good conscience. I think it all comes down to two words of advice: listen and love. Listen carefully and love extravagantly. You can't go wrong with that approach. Let's pray for our country, our leaders both secular and religious, and each other in the coming months. May we all be one.

Open Your Heart to Life

Scripture Referenced: Habakkuk 1:2-3; 2:2-4

> How long, O Lord? I cry for help but you do not listen! I cry out to you, "Violence!" but you do not intervene. Why do you let me see ruin; why must I look at misery? Destruction and violence are before me; there is strife, and clamorous discord.

Today is Respect Life Sunday, a day that we are asked by Pope Francis to "open our hearts to life". Our readings today certainly suit this message, but perhaps in a way you may not immediately notice. Those of us who advocate the pro-life position in our Church, particularly with respect to abortion, probably feel much like our friend Habakkuk in today's first reading. He complains with some heat, "How long, O Lord? I cry for help but you do not listen! I cry out to you, "Violence!" but you do not intervene." It can get pretty discouraging at times, can't it? I remember marching a pro-life picket line some years back, and it was interesting to see the reaction of the people who drove by. Some were supportive, with thumbs up and cheers, and others were derisive and rude, but the vast majority were simply going about their business without so much as a blink. I kind of felt like Habakkuk that day. How long, O Lord, until people listen?

Note the Lord's answer at the end of the reading. Habakkuk hears the Lord speak in very reassuring words. "For the vision still has its time…and will not disappoint; if it delays, wait for it, it will surely come…" So, is it coming? Or not?

Some good news. Abortions have dropped 25% over the past 20 years. State sponsored executions have dropped over 50% in the past 14 years. Progress is indeed being made. But progress is slow. We still saw about 1.2 million abortions last year. California has the highest number of inmates on death row in the nation, each one costing us over $1 million per year. Euthanasia, deceptively marketed as "mercy killing," seems to come up for a vote every November somewhere in the nation. The common thread is what our Bishops call the "culture of death," the notion that the only path out of a difficult, painful problem is to kill the source. Unwanted pregnancy, dangerous felon, old person in pain – just kill the problem. Literally.

Many of us ask the question, "Who are these people getting abortions? Who are these people on death row? Who are these old people in pain?" I'll tell you who they are. Poor people of color. Black women in poverty have nearly 5 times the abortion rate of white women; and Hispanic women in poverty are nearly 3 times more likely to have an abortion than a white woman. The death row population is disproportionately black, and the often repeated gibe is that you won't ever find a rich man on death row. The poor elderly get the worst nursing home care of anyone, bar none.

Many of us struggle with the concept that a death row inmate is as loved by God as a baby in the womb, but this is exactly true! Life is life is life, and our God has made it very clear through the actions of Jesus that every life has dignity and value, especially if you're widowed, orphaned, poor, a sinner, blind, leprous, and outside of society. The very people who are the purveyors of abortion and state sponsored execution are the very ones that Jesus sought out. We are asked to do the same. If this challenge puzzles and dismays you, you're in good company. Look at the very words the apostles say to Jesus today. You can picture them throwing up their hands in exasperation and saying to Jesus, "Well, if you want us to do all of that, *increase our faith*!" Increase our faith.

I'll bet every one of us has had that prayer on our lips at some time in our life. It's usually when we're frustrated at things not going in the direction we want, or we look at a really holy person and think, "That person has a lot more faith than I do." But Jesus doesn't buy into this faith "accounting system". You see, it's not a matter of how much faith you have. Faith is not a commodity, a measurable substance. He makes the point that faith the size of a mustard seed, smaller than that sesame seed on your Big Mac, is more than enough to make miracles happen, to have trees fly through the air. He exaggerates the image to help us understand that faith is not something you *acquire* or *get* and then decide to *use.* Faith is inextricably bound up in two related traits – *trust* and *cooperation.* To have faith is to *trust* that God is utterly in command of the situation, even if we don't see how it will pan out. You see, it's not up to us to fix the world by ourselves. That's completely ridiculous. The apostles were making that exact mistake. Well, Lord, if you want us to do what you do, you'll need to give us a whole ton of magic sauce. No, all you need is a kernel of trust, an acknowledgement of the optimism embedded in the good news that Jesus has already won the battle against evil. Faith means that *we know that to be true*. We can't lose because God has already won.

But wait a minute, you might say. It sure doesn't look like victory out there. And you're absolutely right. Why not? The simple short answer is that not everyone is aware of the good news. It's hidden in plain sight. It remains hidden because people who have that kernel of faith, that unerring trust in God, are not always buying into the second element of faith that is required, that element being *cooperation*. Jesus illustrates this point with the story of the servant. The servant simply does his job – nothing more, nothing less – and that is sufficient for God. Note that the servant isn't running things at the household, nor is he making strategic decisions, nor is he laying claim to the fruits of the household. He simply *cooperates* with the vision of the owner. He listens, he acts, and he does so without any expectation of reward. He trusts that the owner will take care of him, and he cooperates by performing the simple tasks asked of him. The servant, in short, has *faith*.

How does this play out in real life? Pope Francis has asked the Church to stop and think about the impression we give to the world. We may think we're being people of faith, but if we're acting as if the world needs to line up with my way of thinking, with my agenda, with my recipe for peace and justice, we may need to stop and think. Is it working? Is the world becoming more Christianized? Is the kingdom coming? Are people flooding our churches, clamoring to join the body of Christ? Maybe it's time to stop and look and *listen*. Just like those old-fashioned train crossing signs – stop, look, and listen.

Let me give you an example. You heard me say that the preponderance of abortions occurs among poor women of color. How do you address this issue? A very typical strategy is to hold a prayer vigil at an abortion clinic in a poor part of San Diego. Or conduct a march down the main street. There's nothing wrong with these strategies – they might indeed cause a woman considering an abortion to rethink that option. But are there other strategies and approaches? Yes, there are. Pope Francis says that the Church should be more like a field hospital. If a person is bleeding profusely, or has a broken leg, we don't ask how often they brush their teeth, or whether they eat enough spinach. We address their wounds first, get those under control, and then we can speak to matters of lifestyle and moral choices.

You want to help curb abortions? Maybe you need to volunteer at a pregnancy clinic in Southeast San Diego. Maybe you need to talk to some of the people on the streets, the local community organizers who are advocating for better housing, better jobs, and better health care options for the poor. Maybe you need to ask them what is the best way to help right here, right now. Because, brothers and sisters, a moral issue gets *compromised* by hunger, homelessness, and despair. By eliminating the circumstances that nudge someone toward such a horrible choice as abortion, we allow them to hear the moral authority we quietly advocate. Do you see how that works? Poverty, homelessness, and despair are all occasions for sin. The solution is both/and. We need to educate people who *should* listen, and we need to help broken people get to a place where they're *able* to listen.

When we have faith the size of a mustard seed, we have trust in God, and if we trust God, we trust in the voice of the Spirit of God. The Spirit calls us to action, to cooperate, and to cooperate with God means that we listen, pray, and form a plan. We are *intentional*. When I go into the prison three weeks from now for the Kairos weekend, do you think that we only invite the inmates who are the best behaved? No. At least half of those we invite are the worst of the worst. We invite the gang leaders, the shot callers, the lifers, the murderers, the rapists, the child killers and the psychopaths. Intentionally. The only reason we dare to assemble such a rogue's gallery is because we have trust in God. A kernel of faith, a little trust, some cooperation, a few cookies, and look out! The dead come alive!

Open your heart to life. You can do this. You have all of the faith you need. Jesus shows the way. Why did he eat with sinners, prostitutes, and tax collectors? He sought them out! He was intentional. He trusted in his Father, he cooperated with the Spirit. He challenged and healed everyone he touched. And everywhere he went, life blossomed in abundance. That's why we respect life – it's at the heart of everything Jesus did. Pope Francis asks us to be intentional in bringing the healing message of Jesus to the world, and the only way that happens is if we open our hearts to life. All life, good, bad, and ugly. The only question left is, "If today you hear God's voice, will you harden your heart?"

Just a Little Bit More

Scripture Referenced: Luke 12:13-21

> [Jesus] said to the crowd, "Take care to guard against all greed, for though one may be rich, one's life does not consist of possessions."

Today's gospel is a tough one for us. It's one of several passages in Luke that rail against the inherent danger of wealth. It's not surprising. Luke wrote his gospel for an audience made up largely of Gentile converts, many of whom were quite wealthy. These new Christians were trying to figure out how to best follow Jesus and Luke pulls no punches. Luke 18:24: "How hard it is for those who have wealth to enter the kingdom of God!" It's one thing to parse the message of Jesus and plaintively ask, "Does this really apply to me? Do I misunderstand the context?" Sorry, no way out. There's something contradictory at a core level between love of God and material possessions.

So full disclosure. I have money. In the eyes of 90% of the world, I have a lot of money. I'm very uneasy about having this money on the one hand, and very comforted to have it on the other. As much as I'd like to say that I trust God to take care of me, the reality is that I would rather take care of myself. After all, I've been well-trained in the capitalism game and I can play it as well as anyone. And yet, I pray to God that somehow I can have Him in my life at the same time. I'm trying to work both sides of the street. I am a contradiction bordering on hypocrisy, dancing around the edges of commitment, and terrified to take the plunge into fully following Jesus. Sound familiar?

When I started my career back in the early 80's, I remember feeling that I was behind. I had spent four plus years in graduate school, was married with a son, and I was driven to start making something of myself, that is, to start making as much money as possible as fast as I could. In the next ten years, I scrambled. I looked for a new job every two years, certain that it was just a matter of time and effort and a little luck. The luck came in the form of a job offer in San Diego in the mid-80's, and things began to blossom. I worked very hard and I did quite well. I finally began to actually save some money. I remember thinking that I was finally getting it done, was finally catching up to this mythical level of accomplishment, and it was time to eat, drink and be merry. But another part of me was not buying into this definition of happiness. There must be another way.

The sin of the rich fool in today's gospel is not that he has money. The sin is that he has no concept of what it means to have enough. This is the key question. How much is enough for you? I've heard many responses from many thoughtful, Godly people to this question. One typical answer is, "Enough means never having to burden my children or society with having to take care of me when I'm old." Another answer is, "Enough means to see that my kids never have to worry about money like I did." Another answer is, "Enough means freedom to do what God wants me to do, and not count the cost." These are all great answers, aren't they? My favorite answer, however, is the simplest and most honest answer I've ever heard to this question. How much is enough? "Just a little bit more."

You see, all of these answers share a common thread. They give God no credit for our wealth, and they convey the false notion that we are in control. Even if our goal is a lofty one – to give away all that we have at some indeterminate point in the future, it still puts us in the driver's seat, doesn't it? And oh, what cost has been incurred in this crazy endeavor? The cost in time, in talent wasted, in suffering by our neighbor because we have ignored them on our journey up the ladder? How do we begin to wake up? Arthur Simon writes in his wonderful book *How Much is Enough?* that we're all suffering from the disease of affluenza!

Let's say you're feeling a little squirmy in your seat about who exactly you serve. Or, maybe you're feeling a bit defensive. After all, you've worked hard for your money. You get lots of positive vibes from that weekly peek at the pile. People respect you. But I'll bet that there's some uneasiness too. Perhaps you've felt the sting of the cruel master named money. Maybe you've made a lot of money and would like to forge a different relationship with wealth. Or maybe you're on the way up the wealth ladder and not feeling altogether positive about this climb. So now that we're all depressed, what next?

Here's some really good news. Money makes a terrible master, but a magnificent servant! That's right. The key to this is to recognize that money, like everything else good that makes you who you are, is also a gift from God. The question to ask is not how much is enough, but how to use this gift of money-making in the service of God's will. It's not about feeling guilty because you have money, it's about seeing money as a tool, a means to bring about God's kingdom in some constructive way. Three thoughts need to be entertained going forward. How to make money, how to spend money, and how to share money. If you have young kids, start this conversation early in life. If you're on the corporate ladder to wild success, put a sign on your bulletin board: *Make, spend, share*. All three need to be considered. If you're at the end of your career and thinking about the size of your barn, take steps now to ensure that a share of your wealth goes to a needed charity when you check out. Don't worry so much about your kids and grandkids. An inheritance from you will not be spent the way you want it to anyway – pretty much guaranteed. Make sure your gift works for God in the best possible way.

I remember when I was 10 years old, tucked into bed one night, pondering my life. It certainly wasn't a deep dive – goodness sake, I was just barely on the path. But God gave me a graced moment that has always stayed with me. That night, lying in bed, I thought about what I had. I had a roof over my head, food in my belly, a loving family, a hand-me-down bicycle, and a baseball glove. It occurred to me with perfect clarity and enduring satisfaction that I had all a boy could want. God gave me the grace of gratitude, and oh, what a wonderful grace. You see, brothers and sisters, what tames greed is gratitude. What tames spending is sharing. You have the opportunity to put God first and money second, to put yourself in the service of God and money in service of God through you. This is how you answer the question, "how much is enough?" As much as God needs from sharing our gifts.

Maybe it never occurred to you that the skill of making money is a gift from God. Yes, you are the key to that gift being carried out, as much as a great singer has to actually sing the song, or a great writer to overcome the panic of a blank page. You are indeed in charge of your gift. But you can misuse that gift horribly. A singer can sing songs filled with obscenities and hatred. A writer can weave words that cause pain and depression in their readers, or break down a person's life with gossip and attacks. If you have the gift of money-making, it is as much a matter of how you make it as how you spend it. Remember the three guidelines: make, spend, share. All of these are necessary aspects of what it means to aspire to or have wealth.

Now what about those of you out there who struggle to make ends meet? I guess you're off the hook today, eh? Sorry, no. The sin that Jesus is addressing is *greed.* Those who have money are much more susceptible to this disease than those who don't, but I have indeed met many people who are poor and greedy. It's no prettier a picture than rich and greedy because it's all relative. Remember the antidote to greed is gratitude. So the next time the stock market ticks up, say thank you, Lord, and figure out a way to share the good fortune. The next time the stock market goes down, say thank you, Lord for allowing me the perspective to know that I'll always have enough if I have you in my life.

The Gospel today is indeed challenging. I invite you at some point this week, perhaps as you're playing the money game, to stop and reread it. Easy to remember: Luke 12:13-21. If you have trouble with all of that, just think Luke 12-13. Last year – this year. *Make-spend-share*! Peace.

The Third Way

Scripture Referenced: Matthew 5:38-48

> Jesus said to his disciples: " When someone strikes you on your right cheek, turn the other one as well. If anyone wants to go to law with you over your tunic, hand over your cloak as well. Should anyone press you into service for one mile, go for two miles."

In these brief 10 verses from Matthew's gospel, we hear some of the most often quoted sayings of Jesus. Some Sundays it's hard to figure out what the theme should be – but today, there are too many themes! However, there is an overriding similarity in one respect today, and that is this: virtually every one of these sayings is misunderstood! Let's start with the first section on how to deal with aggression.

As human beings we, like many of our animal relatives, have built-in responses to aggressive behavior. These responses can be seen in the wild if you watch Animal Planet or some similar nature show. An animal under attack will perform one of two actions – either fight or run for the hills. Right? Fight or flight. Are we any different? Jesus says, yes, we are. There's a *third* way. Then he gives three examples of the third way to respond to aggression.

When someone strikes you on the right cheek, turn the other one as well. That sounds quite submissive doesn't it? But we miss the key point if we read this too quickly. *The right cheek.* For someone to strike you on your right cheek, the aggressor would have to either hit you with his left hand (unlikely) or strike you a backhanded blow with his right hand. In Jesus' time, the way you disciplined a slave was to backhand a slap to the slave's right cheek. When you turn the other cheek, you are inviting the aggressor to strike you with an open palm. The open palm slap was the way you disciplined a child, a family member, and it was more like a light spank than a blow. What you are doing in essence, by offering the left cheek, is shaming the aggressor into considering that you are just as important as one of his own children. In a sense, you embarrass him into considering a different, non-violent response.

If anyone wants to go to law with you over your tunic, hand over your cloak as well. Again, this sounds quite submissive, but read it carefully. The tunic was basically your underwear. If someone is suing you for your tunic, that means that they are going after your last penny in their zeal to bring you down. Do you fight in court? Or do you jump bail? Jesus advocates, like before, a third way that turns the tables on your aggressor. As shocking as it sounds, Jesus is telling his audience to not only give the guy your underwear, but your cloak as well. This leaves you quite naked, standing there in front of the judges and all the people of the court. Your willingness to go to the extreme uncovers the utter greed of your aggressor, and it is he who must shamefacedly hand you back your clothes! Because by law, you couldn't take a man's clothes. So who's laughing now?

Should someone press you into service for one mile, go for two miles. At the time of Jesus, a Roman soldier, by law, could demand your assistance in carrying something for him at any time. This practice was particularly galling, for it expressed the dominance of Rome in a blatant way, by enslaving anyone they wanted, whenever they pleased. But the law also stipulated that the soldier could only have your assistance for *one mile* and that was it. So what is Jesus saying? Go two miles! The second mile is your free will, and the soldier would be quite embarrassed because he didn't want to break Roman law. He would have to beg you to please stop helping him! The third way.

Note that none of these responses to aggression involve a return of aggression. They are subtle and involve shaming the aggressor into seeing you as a human being, a child of God's family. This third way is the backbone of non-violent protest, as carried out by Gandhi and Martin Luther King, Jr. Shaming the aggressor is very powerful medicine, and very hard to do. Our culture wants us always to fight back, sword to sword, bomb to bomb, vengeance forever following on violence. Does this mean that aggression is never warranted? No, it doesn't. If one can only save one's life through an aggressive act in response to aggression, then that act is justified. But the examples Jesus gives are not life-threatening. They're everyday situations that we're bound to encounter at some time, and our challenge is to always consider a third way.

That third way is often called the *high road.* And this is the focus of the next section of the gospel reading. *Love your enemies, pray for those who persecute you.* Why? *That you may be children of your heavenly Father, for he makes his sun rise on the bad and the good, and causes rain to fall on the just and the unjust.* Think about that for a moment. What Jesus is saying here is that no one is utterly good and no one is utterly bad either. If Father God treats his created universe in such an even-handed way, we have no right to second guess him. Everyone is redeemable, everyone is worthy of existence. No one can claim to be always and everywhere worthy, and no one, *by our judgment*, is completely unworthy. If we are children of the Father, we trust the Father to make everything right, not in our time, but in His. Taking this view, this position from the high road, allows us to shake off insults and injury, since we can be completely certain that we don't have the full picture on anyone, especially on that someone who just now cut you off on the freeway. We assume that the person is just being a complete idiot, when the reality is that they have a screaming child bleeding all over the backseat from a gaping wound and he's trying to get to the hospital. Do you know for sure which reality it is? Idiot or life saver? You know what? It's better to assume life saver. A lot less stressful. Take the high road.

And finally, we have that cringe-worthy statement at the end of the reading. *So be perfect, just as your heavenly Father is perfect.* Gee, thanks for that little challenge, Jesus. Right. Just be like God. That phrase goes in one ear and is very quickly tossed out the other ear. Again, misunderstood, and simply because of an unfortunate translation. The word *perfect* here is from the Greek word *teleios*, which does not mean perfect in the sense of flawless or pure, but perfect in the sense of *rightness of purpose*. What Jesus is challenging us to do here is to become the heart of who we are. Inside. The fullest expression of you in your unique qualities and humanity. As St. Irenaeus said, "The glory of God is man fully alive." So, the proper translation of this little sentence is actually: "Be fully alive, just as your heavenly Father is fully alive." What a different sense! Can you feel the difference?

What is standing in your way of becoming fully alive? A hard question. St. Paul gives us a clue. "If anyone among you considers himself wise in this age, let him become a fool, so as to become wise." In other words, as soon as you begin to think that you have the answers, stop kidding yourself. Laugh like a fool, and try again. God is immensely beyond us, and we have no right to speak for Him. We can only try to be as inclusive, as loving, as forgiving, and as merciful as He surely is. And even then, we've only scratched the surface.

Now for the homework. I want you to think about a situation that occurred to you recently that had you facing an aggressor. Not violent or life threatening, but just an annoying or rude person. Perhaps someone in the grocery store, or a neighbor, or my favorite, a person in the airport being a complete jerk, cutting in line. Your instinct is to act aggressively right back at them, isn't it? Maybe you did. Think of a third way. What could you have said or done that would have changed the situation in such a way that the aggressor would be walking away, maybe a little shame-faced, lesson learned? Let's be creative and become fully alive, shall we?

Freedom

Scripture Referenced: Matthew 11:25-30

> At that time Jesus exclaimed, "Come to me, all you who labor and are burdened, and I will give you rest. Take my yoke upon you and learn from me, for I am meek and humble of heart; and you will find rest for yourselves. For my yoke is easy, and my burden light."

It seems appropriate on this Fourth of July holiday weekend that we would hear these words of Jesus. *Come to me, all you who labor and are burdened, and I will give you rest.* If you go to New York City and visit the Statue of Liberty, you'll see similar words, written by the poet Emma Lazarus. *Give me your tired, your poor, your huddled masses yearning to breathe free. The wretched refuse of your teaming shore. Send these, the homeless, tempest-tossed to me, I lift my lamp beside the golden door!* I suspect Emma had some familiarity with today's excerpt from Matthew, since the sentiment is almost exactly the same.

But I invite you to consider – is the notion of freedom and liberty that we embrace as a nation the same notion of freedom and liberty that Jesus advocates? Are we indeed talking about the same thing? Like you, I love my Church. Like you, I love my country. It's so tempting to find a way to make these loves coincide, to somehow mix patriotism and Christianity. Is it possible to do so? Would Jesus approve? Does he celebrate the Fourth of July?

If you examine the history of the United States, you'll find freedom expressed as a great ideal, a driving notion that existed from the beginning. The very reason the Declaration of Independence was written in the first place was to express the notion of freedom – freedom from tyranny, unjust laws, invasive troops, and other complaints of a people who were under the control of an outside power. We fought for this freedom, and in the years to come, we strove mightily as a nation to do the same for other oppressed people, sometimes successfully, sometimes not. Advocating freedom from oppression and encouraging self-rule continue to be driving factors in our debate with the world. I'm very proud of America's desire to do this, despite setbacks and challenges and a cynical world that questions our every motive. The torch continues to burn brightly – ask any immigrant who hungers to join us.

But what about Jesus? Is he on board with this? Does he approve of this defining American ideal? Jesus, the Son of God, is the perfect human icon – the very image of God in the flesh. Does God have a special place in his heart for us Americans? In blunt terms, is God on our side?

I'm being a little hyperbolic here, of course, putting the question in just this way. We know that Jesus himself lived as a person in an oppressed land, completely at the mercy of a tyrannical power. From the evidence of the gospels, Jesus never advocates a violent overthrow of the Romans, despite being goaded to express this desire. However, at the same time, Jesus proclaims loudly his desire to free the captive and set the world aright, as expressed in the marvelous image of the Kingdom of God. There's no doubt that Jesus would approve of the great ideal of political freedom. But at that same time, Jesus would roundly reject the notion that God is on any one country's side. And this is where we need to reflect in a mature and thoughtful way. I think Jesus would say to us Americans that we are on the right track, but we have so much further to go, so much more to evolve to as a nation. In what ways, you may ask?

Consider that in the words and actions of Jesus, the notion of freedom is not simply political. In the eyes of Jesus, freedom is not simply freedom *from* tyranny, but freedom *for* the virtues of the Kingdom. To Jesus, freedom is a detachment from the false gods of material goods, power, and prestige, and an embrace of beauty, goodness, and truth. Jesus' notion of freedom is a personal choice to convert, to move one's mind to the greater goods, the greater virtues, and follow a path that is radically different from the usual way the world solves problems. To Jesus, freedom is more about forgiveness and awareness than it is about what government is in power. In short, Jesus wants to draw us deeper and wider and more embracing than the limiting notions of freedom as expressed by politicians. Jesus is saying, "Keep coming, don't stop, don't rest here. There's so much more to freedom than political borders and armies and petty tyrants!"

I hope you can see, brothers and sisters, that if you stop at patriotism, you're missing a big part of the journey. For the reality is that at some point in your life, if it hasn't happened already, you will find yourself in a position of weakness, of little or no control. It is inevitable, every one of us will face this critical juncture, for this is the precise definition of death – the final loss of our ego, the dawning realization that we are facing the end of our lives, that our *physical* freedom is ending. At that point of utter physical powerlessness, the freedom that Jesus offers becomes abundantly clear. For He says, "Come to me. You've been laboring hard, trying to be like God, taking on all of the burdens of the world. Stop. *Come to me.* I'm the source of rest and peace. I'm the one who is God. You don't need to be." Jesus is the icon of true freedom.

He goes on to say, "Take my yoke upon you and learn from me." In other words, let's do this world changing stuff together, and let Jesus be the one doing the leading, not some politician. So what does this mean on a practical basis? A few thoughts to consider:

- Try to avoid "us versus them" simplifications. Remember that God is radically inclusive, raining his goodness on the just and the unjust. This is a very difficult concept for our human brains to understand, but very important that we try. Why would God treat the world this way?
- God always favors the poor and the downtrodden. The entire Bible seems to emphasize that God not only favors the little ones, he goes out of his way to pick them for important tasks. What does this say about who are heroes are? Or who they should be?
- God always works from the inside out. In other words, what he wants is a personal choice for Him, not an imposed set of rules and loyalty oaths. Accepting God in our hearts is the ultimate source of all freedom, for from this awareness of God's unconditional love, we are truly free, regardless of how and where we live. That kind of inner freedom is the truly priceless pearl, the treasure that cannot be destroyed. Have you made that personal choice for God?

- Don't waste the gift of political freedom we've been given! We are able to speak our minds, celebrate what's right, denounce evil, and advocate for the ideals that define the Kingdom of God. Not everyone in the world can do that.

This weekend we celebrate with fireworks. We celebrate freedom, *political* freedom. Enjoy it – it's a great holiday, one of my favorites. But don't stop here. Jesus invites us to a much deeper freedom, a freedom that goes well beyond political freedom to an abiding freedom, a freedom not simply *from* burdens, but *for* the relationship of your life. Now that's worth a celebration!

Make Space for God

Scripture Referenced: James 3:16-4:3

> Where do the wars and where do the conflicts among you come from? Is it not from your passions that make war within your members? You covet but do not possess. You kill and envy but you cannot obtain; you fight and wage war. You do not possess because you do not ask. You ask but you do not receive, because you ask wrongly, to spend it on your passions.

We've been reading from the letter of St. James this past month and it's always interesting to me to ask the question, "Who was this guy? Who is St. James, the author of this letter?" There are actually *five* people in the New Testament that have the name James. Let's examine each one:

- There was James the father of Judas, one of the twelve (not Judas Iscariot – people sometimes forget that there are two apostles named Judas). Not a likely candidate to write this letter.
- There was James, the son of Alphaeus, one of the twelve, of which nothing whatever is known.
- There is a mention of James the *Younger* in Mark's gospel, who may be the same as James, the son of Alphaeus. Again, nothing is known of this James.
- There is James, the brother of John, one of Zebedee's sons, also a member of the twelve. He is much better known, and always appears on the scene with his brother John. He was clearly one of Jesus' favorites, and was martyred a mere 11 years after the death of Jesus. This James is our parish patron saint, but he couldn't have written this letter, alas, because he died too early to have been the author.
- So who's left? In Mark and Matthew's gospel, we hear of James, the brother of Jesus. The term *brother* is problematic of course, but most Catholic theologians presume that James is either a cousin of Jesus or a step-brother. He is not one of the twelve, and you may recall that in Mark's gospel, the family of Jesus,

including this James, was quite concerned about Jesus – even trying to get Jesus under control at one point. But something interesting happens after the resurrection. James, it clearly states in Acts, has become the leader of the Jerusalem Christians. Why the about face? Paul gives us a tantalizing hint. In the letter to the Corinthians, he says that Jesus was seen by James. Something special happened at that point, and James went from an onlooker to a leader. The Catholic Church has definitively linked the author of this letter to this particular James, the brother of Jesus, since at least the third century.

The letter of James has always been an important part of the New Testament in the Catholic tradition, but not so much in the Protestant. Martin Luther did not see much value in this letter and advocated that it be dropped from the Bible along with Revelation, Hebrews, and Jude. The main reason why is that the letter of James barely mentions Christ and in Luther's eyes, it focuses far too much on ethical principles and far too little on the transformation needed by every human being to become a child of God. The biggest sticking point for Luther, however, is the section we read last week that "faith of itself, it if does not have works, is dead." Luther felt that faith was primary, and works were secondary, and James comes way too close to disagreeing with that philosophy.

So what does James have to say this week? How does it tie in with the theme of this Sunday? Like we hear many Sundays, the first two readings pose a question that the words of Jesus answer. Today the theme is aggressive ambition. Somehow we are wired to compete, to claw our way up in the world. This approach, although understandable at a base level, never leads to happiness and peace, no matter how hard we try. James says that where jealousy and selfish ambition exist, there is disorder and every foul practice. He goes on to ask the difficult questions – where do wars come from, where do conflicts come from? The answer? Our passions, our desire for only what we want, without considering for a moment that if we want something that badly, it probably isn't good for us! I'm reminded of a Robert Heinlein short story that depicted a utopian society who selected its leaders based on only two criteria. The first is that the person be eminently qualified to lead the country. The second criterion was that the person must have no desire to have the job at all!

But Jesus offers a third way, which is always the case. His criterion for leadership is quite disarming. If you want to be the first, you need to be the servant of everyone else. Not just the servant of fellow Republicans and Democrats, but the servant of even those people who cannot possibly pay you back, like little children. Ironically, Jesus goes on to say, this is the only way to truly experience God, the most powerful being in the universe. Can you hear how strange that sounds? I only see God when I am the servant of the most powerless in the land?

I'm sure that many of you have heard of the writer and theologian Henri Nouwen. He had it all at a young age. Fame, a professorship at a prestigious university, multiple books in his name, etc., etc. But Nouwen was desperately unhappy, asking the question we all have – where is God? It wasn't until Nouwen left it all and went to work at an institution for those with severe physical handicaps that the answer came. Somehow, Nouwen tell us, in working as the servant of the lowliest, we make space for God, and God fills that space in ways that will astound and move us.

This is one of the reasons that we deacons and other parish leaders keep coming to you with ideas about how you can play this servant role. It's a bit of a hard sell at one level, but I think that everyone has a desire to give, an immediate connection with the idea that giving pays off in many ways, both on the part of the receiver and most certainly on those who give. I don't know how many of you know the reputation of St. James, our parish, throughout the diocese. When I'm in a meeting with other clergy who I don't know and the inevitable question comes up – what parish are you from – my answer always prompts a reaction. St. James? Aren't you the parish that does all of that outreach and social ministry? Yes, I proudly respond, that's us.

No, we're far from perfect. We struggle with all of the same things every parish struggles with. We have money challenges, we have people with different ideas of what the parish should do and say, we have our conservative bloc and our liberal bloc, we have the ups and downs that any family experiences. But as long as we take the words of Jesus seriously and keep servanthood to the poor as a pillar of our community ethic, I for one will always be sure of our future. So if you've been sitting on the sidelines wondering how to get engaged, I invite you to join the family. Pick a ministry, pick a way to be of service – check the bulletin, call me, call any of the staff. We'll plug you in – Jesus needs more servants! More servant leaders. All of us.

Chapter 13 – Death and Resurrection

Despite the rapid advances in medical science, despite the care we give to our bodies and minds, despite our dogged insistence not to think about it, guess what? All of us will die someday. That reality terrifies many people, and even good Christian believers noticeably gulp when talking about impending death. Our belief is that Christ conquered death, which means what exactly? It means that there is more, that death is not the end, that something glorious awaits. Do you really believe that? Let's explore this topic in a bit more detail…

Fear of Dying

Scripture Referenced: John 10:27-30

> Jesus said: "My sheep hear my voice; I know them, and the follow me. I give them eternal life, and they shall never perish. No one can take them out of my hand. My father, who has given them to me, is greater than all, and no one can take them out of the Father's hand. The Father and I are one."

It's a psychological truism that all fear, at its root, is a fear of death. All of our anxieties, worries, and night terrors can be distilled in essence to a fear of death. We particularly fear our own deaths, of course, even though we know that day is inevitable. As Woody Allen said, "It's not that I'm afraid to die, it's just that, I don't want to be there when it happens!" You can relate to that feeling, I expect. As we navigate through the Easter Season, we are invited to ponder the meaning of the Resurrection, the simple affirmation that death is really nothing to fear at all. More than any other religious tradition in the world, Christianity emphasizes the reality of an afterlife, of a life beyond our earthly existence that is not only an improvement, but positively heavenly.

A couple of weeks ago, I was in the Boston area visiting my parents, who are now in their late 80's. They live in a retirement community, a campus of modern buildings connected by well-lit corridors, completely protected from the outside elements. There is a bowling alley, a small grocery store, a swimming pool, a theatre, a library, a chapel, and of course, a number of dining facilities. My siblings and I call it "the cruise ship" because you never have to leave and everyone gets fat. As my folks age, their physical limitations come to define their existence more and more, and as my Mom is suffering from mid-stage dementia, her world has become smaller and smaller. It's sad, of course, but they're not in any discomfort or pain, and it's very peaceful to visit them, unless they turn on the TV to ear-shattering volume. The unspoken elephant in the room, however, is the reality that there is only one more major step left in their lives, and that step is death.

There are two very important statements in our short Gospel this morning that bear repeating. Jesus says, "My sheep hear my voice; I know them, and they follow me." The other line at the end is even more striking. "The Father and I are one." We can get very theological here and launch into discussions of the triune God and Jesus as the second Person, but that's not necessary. A simpler message works just as well. Jesus is talking about relationships. His sheep, those who hear him, are known *by* and *know* Jesus. Likewise, Jesus is known *by* and *knows* the Father. The logic is straightforward. If you know Jesus, you know the Father. If the Father is eternal, then Jesus is eternal. If we are in relationship with Jesus, we are given eternal life and Jesus will hold you in the palm of his hand. What's there to be afraid of?

Being the dutiful son, I took my parents over to see the director of the facility to go over their financial situation. The director was very soothing and respectful, emphasizing that there was nothing to be concerned about and even if the money ran out, they would be assured of a place to live. The only suggestion she had was for my parents to pre-pay funeral service expenses so as not to burden any of us kids. My Dad winked and suggested that I head over to Home Depot and buy a shovel. That should do it! We all laughed, because after all, what is there to fear?

Now lest we kid ourselves, know that being in relationship with Jesus and by extension with the Father does not guarantee a peaceful life. The book of Revelation clearly calls out the reality of great distress, of hunger, thirst, and hot sun, of sorrow that leads to tears, and blood that is shed in the name of goodness. Many fundamentalist Christians parse the arcane language of Revelation, looking for hidden meanings in the fantastical visions of the author. Again, you don't have to go that deep to appreciate the stunning beauty of the simple line, "..the Lamb.. will shepherd them and lead them to springs of life-giving water, and God will wipe away every tear from their eyes." This strikingly maternal image is one of the most beautiful passages in the entire Bible. How can you fear death with this vision in your mind?

One of my Mom's favorite books is *Life After Life* by Raymond Moody. It came out in 1975 and was an instant classic, introducing the world to an apparently consistent near death experience as told by many, many people. There are many striking similarities among the accounts, many of which have become cultural references. Moving through a tunnel into a great light, the ongoing ability to see, hear, and experience sensations from a disconnected state, a great sense of peace and serenity – all of these seem quite common. In addition, two of the more consistent memories of people having such NDEs are:

- An intense feeling of unconditional love, forgiveness, and acceptance from this ineffable light
- Encountering other beings, including deceased relatives and friends

Whether you buy into the notion of near-death experiences or not, you can't deny that something is happening to these people that is very consistent with what I've been saying today. Relationships carry over from life to death, particularly relationships with other people and with God. The sense of God's great mercy and forgiveness is exactly what Jesus tells us – there's a greater power at work here than we expect or frankly deserve.

But what I find so interesting is how NDEs change the people who experience them. After having an NDE, people report the following:

- An increased belief in God
- Lack of fear of death, a sense of peace
- Sense that life is precious and should be embraced
- Life has a purpose well beyond the material world; in fact, stuff doesn't matter at all
- Tolerance, forgiveness, and compassion are substantially increased
- Friends and people are what truly matter

Death remains inevitable, of course. But wouldn't this world be a lot better if people really believed that the universe is truly benevolent? That love of people far outweighs love of things? That a relationship with Jesus is an exercise in living the promises of the kingdom on this side of death? Our earthly existence doesn't need to be painful, brutish, and short. It can be a taste of heaven. There's really nothing to fear at all.

Who is Saved?

Scripture Referenced: Luke 13:22-30

> Jesus said: "And people will come from the east and the west and from the north and the south and will recline at table in the kingdom of God. For behold, some are last who will be first, and some are first who will be last."

It seems like a simple question. "Lord, will only a few people be saved?" Jesus appears to sidestep the question with his cryptic answer about striving to enter through the narrow gate. But you can't mistake the meaning of the parable that ensues. It's quite clear that just because *you* know Jesus doesn't mean that *Jesus* knows you! And the wrap-up line is a little disturbing. "For behold, some are last who will be first, and some are first who will be last." Does he mean that all of us good church-going folks will be last in the kingdom of God?

Let's contrast this gospel with our first reading from Isaiah. Here a very different vision is proclaimed. The Lord, we are told, comes to gather nations of every language, coming to see His glory – clearly salvation is offered to everyone. They'll come to the Lord in every conceivable way, from all directions. It's a spectacular, all-embracing invitation – who could resist?

The older I get, the more I find the obituary section of the newspaper interesting. Lately, I've been tallying up how many of the obituaries mention any kind of a religious identification of the deceased. Some are quite effusive, with language like "she's now dancing in the arms of Jesus" or "his labors are over and the saints applaud this humble servant". Others mention nothing about religion at all, but still seem to indicate a person who cares about others, perhaps through membership in service organizations. And still others are so superficial that you want to cringe. I hope my obituary mentions a bit more than "he was a lifelong Chargers fan". I already know what *his* afterlife is going to be like!

Is it easy to get into heaven? Or is it hard? Will everyone get in? Or only a few? What happens to everyone who doesn't make it in? What's going to happen to you?

Let's clear up a few misconceptions. What are the three different options that await us when we die? (It's not a trick question!) Yes, heaven, hell, and purgatory. We tend to think of these as "places", or locations in some vague cosmological universe. After all, we are bound by place and time, so it's logical that we would similarly think of the afterlife in the same terms. But that's not what the Church teaches. In painstaking language, the Church defines heaven as "…the ultimate end and fulfillment of the deepest human longings, the state of supreme, definitive happiness." (CCC 1024) So note that heaven is a "state of being". Hell is described as a "freely chosen eternal separation from communion with God." Another "state of being" rather than a place. And finally, purgatory is defined as a *process* of purification, which is entirely different from hell.

What is striking to me about these definitions is how little they tell us! It's not that the Church is hiding anything, it's that no one really knows for sure what these states are like, so the Church takes what it can from Scripture and the writings of some very astute theologians and opts to say as little as possible. Of course, that doesn't stop people from speculating, and there are many fascinating theories floating around about the nature of heaven, hell, and purgatory. The near-death experiences of many people have added mountains of literature on the topic. It seems the best way to have a best-selling book these days is to have a near-death experience and write about it. It also helps if you're either a brain surgeon or a four-year old, but I digress. Quite frankly, I'm a sucker for these books just like everyone else, because I'd like to know what my options are at the end of this life, and have some inkling of how to behave! Is there a trick question? Do you go into the light or not?

What *can* be said? Let's go back to my earlier questions. Is it easy to get into the kingdom of heaven? Or is it hard? From Isaiah's reading earlier, we can devise that God is absolutely offering heaven to everyone, wherever they live, what language they speak, even what religion they profess. The teachings of Jesus, however, stress that accepting this offer is not simply a matter of saying that yes, I want to be saved. There are implications, decisions, conversions that must occur. You might want to be saved, but if you continue leading a life that demonstrates a disdain for God and his people, then you've made your decision. I want to stress this point because it's often missed. Judgment at the end of our lives is not about what we believe or claim to believe, it's about our actions. Matthew 25 makes this point very clearly – the sheep and the goats both call Jesus "Lord". You can look it up. Having a Catholic label no more guarantees salvation than being labeled an atheist guarantees hell. They key to entry into heaven is in many ways so obvious that it's hardly worth saying. To guarantee heaven, act like a citizen of heaven while you're here on earth.

But what about hell? The Church clearly states that "God predestines no one to go to hell." (CCC 1037) In fact, to this day, the Church has never stated that any particular person is definitively in hell. That doesn't stop the rest of us from saying so, of course, and we have lots of likely candidates in our collective mind. We certainly do love to play judge, don't we? So is anyone in hell or not? Remember what I said earlier. Hell is not a place that God throws people who are bad, despite the dramatic depictions of Michelangelo and other artists. Hell is a *choice* that each individual makes. You might wonder why anyone would make such a choice, and I'll bet that if you asked 100 people at random if they would choose hell over heaven, I can't imagine a single sober person saying they prefer hell. But again, words are just words. Actions are what count, and a life of actions that repel God simply self-select the person to an eternity of the same choices. A life of hell freely chosen and acted out here simply leads to the same. To guarantee hell, act like a citizen of hell while you're here on earth.

Then there's purgatory. There's no mention of purgatory in the Scriptures. Jesus never talks about it. Where did this come from? The Church formulated the doctrine of purgatory in the 15th and 16th centuries to answer the observation that the vast majority of people then, as of now, are not citizens of heaven nor citizens of hell, but muddle about in the middle. Clearly, very few of us are saintly all of the time, and even the worst criminals seem to have a spark of goodness in them. God's mercy is something we all count on, but at the same time, we know that God is a just judge. Our actions have implications, even if we are sorry for our sins. How is all of this reconciled? Purgatory is defined as a "process", a cleansing, a purging of the soul. When I was a little kid, the nuns used to talk about our souls being stained by sin. Inevitably, all of us boys would look at our shirts and pants and assume we had lots of purgatory in front of us, as opposed to our spotless girl classmates. But in all seriousness, there is a certain logic to the Church's teaching, even if the details of purgatory are left to our imagination.

This Church teaching on purgatory proved quite popular at the time it was released in 1439, and it led to some of the most severe abuses in the Church's history. People assumed that you could rate your life and assign a length of purgatory time for each sin committed, which sounds like a silly parlor game until you realized that people took it very seriously. Whole books were written that depicted time in purgatory by each sin, and what you needed to do to erase this time by various good acts of atonement. One bad assumption led to another and soon the Church began to "indulge" people by erasing their purgatory time if they performed some wonderful charitable action, like say, giving a bunch of money to the Pope so that he could build St. Peter's Cathedral. You know what happened next. A young priest named Martin Luther found this whole business distasteful and utterly wrong-headed, and the rest is Protestant history.

The doctrine of purgatory remains, however, as do indulgences, although they are no longer for sale. The simple teaching today is much more to the point. We are invited to pray for those in the process of purgatory, because somehow that matters, somehow that loving connection with our world makes a difference, that somehow our actions here on earth make a difference in the afterlife. Interesting and consistent, isn't it?

We can listen to Jesus' words today and feel threatened or uneasy. I hope you don't. If you're leading a life of intentional action to bring forth the Kingdom of God here and now, in whatever way, small or large, that you can, please don't worry. There are no trick questions on the final exam. Believe in the mercy of God, be happy that our fellow human beings aren't the judges, and life as loving a life as you can. Whether I'm first in line at the banquet or last in line at the banquet, I'm still going to the banquet! I'll see you there...

The Nature of Evil

Scripture Referenced: Acts 1:1-11

> While they were looking intently at the sky as he was going, suddenly two men dressed in white garments stood beside them. They said, "Men of Galilee, why are you standing there looking up at the sky? This Jesus who has been taken up from you into heaven will return in the same way as you have seen him going into heaven."

One of the most frustrating parts of being a believing Christian is how to deal with the cold reality of suffering – either suffering we endure or the suffering of a loved one. Suffering, especially if that suffering seems to be arbitrary or particularly cruel is such a frustrating topic that it even has its own special name - *theodicy*. Theodicy is the study of evil in the context of a supernatural, omnipotent God. Evil and God. How are these reconciled? As many philosophers have pointed out, the problem of evil is the root cause of atheism. Just like the apostles, in the face of evil, we're all looking around wondering where God is? Where did Jesus go? Doesn't he care about our problems? We're looking up at the sky asking the question why?

For purposes of this homily, let's distinguish two kinds of evil: natural evil and moral evil. Natural evil (or *physical* evil) can be seen to come from the operation of the universe itself, most clearly seen in natural disasters such as earthquakes and wildfires. The animal pecking order is often seen as a distressing reality – why do we have predator animals feeding on other creatures? Moral evil, on the other hand, is always a result of choices made by intelligent, free persons. As such, according to the *Cathechism of the Catholic Church*, it is incommensurably more harmful than physical evil. (CCC 311)

The distressing fact is that evil exists in a God-created world. Could God have created a world without evil? Wouldn't this be better, all things considered? If God is truly omnipotent, why can't he create a universe containing free creatures who do moral good but no moral evil? Theologian Alvin Plantinga answers that our perfect God creates creatures who are perfectly free. Perfect freedom means that we can sometimes choose good and sometimes choose evil. Furthermore, since God cannot contradict His own perfection, God is both omnipotent and yet unable to deny his creatures their free will option to choose evil. Ironically, not only is our current universe possible, it is the only possible world God can create in His perfection!

C.S. Lewis would agree: "Exclude the possibility of suffering which the order of nature and the existence of free will involve, and you find that you have excluded life itself." In other words, the very nature of our existence as creatures with free will necessitates the existence of evil. To be "redeemed" simply means we share a partial knowledge of God, so we are able to choose the good act more often than the evil act. Only Jesus, who is fully God and fully man, can navigate the universe without falling into sin. But Jesus also had the free will at all times to select the evil option, and it cannot have been an easy choice in every instance!

But how do we understand the problem of "natural evil," the seemingly random occurrence of natural disasters such as rockslides and floods, or perhaps the all too evident violence in the animal world? Why would a good, omnipotent God allow these things to happen? Going back to the notion that God creates us, His human creatures, with perfect freedom, it is clear that God has given us the ability to make a significant impact on the operation of the universe. In essence, we can share in God's creative work or we can destroy God's creative work.

The only way mankind can acquire knowledge of good and evil is by observing the state of the universe. Consider a person who is considering whether to cross a frozen river by walking on the ice. He notices a deer step out onto the ice and get halfway across the river. The ice gives way, and the deer falls into the stream and drowns. The person now knows the danger of thin ice and takes steps to cross the river by some other means, perhaps by using a fallen tree as a bridge. He also knows that other people coming up behind him will be faced with the same dilemma. As a matter of moral good, he erects a sign that says "Danger – use tree to cross." Or, if he chooses, he can put up a sign that says, "Short cut – cross the ice." Or, he can do nothing at all and by his negligence fail to warn them. The point is that the person's free will to choose moral good or moral evil is formed by the experience of nature. Man learns by observing and making inferences to his own experiences and those that have happened to others in the past. The bottom line is that nature is our teacher and offers us an opportunity, perhaps an obligation, to help each other avoid these problems.

When we witness a truly horrible natural disaster, there are usually three different reactions, have you noticed? One reaction is to leap into action to help the survivors, providing medical attention, shelter, food, and other basic needs. Another reaction is anger at God for allowing such a thing to happen, usually accompanied with much head-shaking and sadness. The third reaction is to take a step back and ask, "How do we avoid this in the future? What can we do to minimize or eliminate such a disastrous outcome?" Which of these reactions is God encouraging us to follow? If you said one and three, you're absolutely on the right track. Exercising free will properly is not simply avoiding evil. Free will also challenges us to respond to evil and suffering in a God-like way.

Free will is a two-edged sword. It is a fine gift with enormous implications for ourselves and others. Jesus leaves his disciples standing there, uncertain and puzzled. As you know, next week we celebrate Pentecost and the coming of the Holy Spirit, who infuses their frightened souls with the energy to move out, to act, to make a difference in re-molding God's universe to the perfection God would like. We are poised on the same hill top it seems, wondering what we should do next. As this week unfolds, ask the Lord to put some ideas in your mind about how to exercise that free will you have. Perhaps a ministry you've been considering, or a charity, or a call to respond to something that really bothers you about the world "out there". So here's a tip. As you monitor your media intake this week, be it from television or newspaper or magazines, take stock of which stories really grab your attention, especially if there seems to be an element of evil or suffering embedded within. (You don't have to look very far to find these stories, by the way!) Do you think the Holy Spirit is calling you to pay attention? What God-like action may be coming to your consciousness? Pray on it.

If you want to test your response, try this exercise.
Since God is on our side, I think I should do the following.
Then say,
However, since my aim is to be on *God's side*, I think I should do this instead. Then do the second thing.

Queen of the Sheep

Scripture Referenced: Matthew 25: 31-46

> Then the righteous will answer him and say, "Lord, when did we see you hungry and feed you, or thirsty and give you a drink? When did we see you a stranger and welcome you, or naked and clothe you? When did we see you ill or in prison, and visit you?" And the king will say to them in reply, "Amen, I say to you, whatever you did for one of the least brothers of mine, you did for me."

As I think I've mentioned before, Christ the King is a relatively recent feast in our Catholic calendar. It started in 1925, when Pope Pius XI, alarmed by the rise of fascism in Europe, decided to remind Catholics across the world that there is only ONE person who deserves our absolute devotion and obedience, and that of course, is Jesus Christ. Apparently, the message didn't resonate with Mussolini and Hitler, both baptized Catholics, alas. And the last I checked, dictators are still around, so I guess we continue to need the message of this feast over and over again. But the message today is not about political systems. It's about something much deeper.

The readings chosen for the feast day this year (Cycle A) are really quite striking. All three have a certain "cosmic" nature to them, as befits the end of the Church year. The first reading has Ezekiel speaking for God in a very direct way. Did you notice how personal the words are and how each sentence starts with the pronoun "I"? God is talking here! I myself will look after the sheep. I myself will give them rest. The lost I will seek out, the strayed I will bring back, the injured I will bind up, the sick I will heal… This is a very active, very involved God, not some lofty distant guy with a white beard. God is among us to the fullest extent. Do you believe that?

As most of you know, my Mom passed away last month. She was a woman filled with faith, but also struggled with fear. She wasn't afraid of death per se; but she was afraid of dying. She was quite devoted to Jesus, and she was afraid that Jesus would ask her to suffer as He did, perhaps as the final test of her devotion. We talked about this more than once in the past several years, and one day I said to her, "Mom, you need to bring these fears to Jesus. Let Him tell you His plans for you."

The second reading from Paul's letter to the Corinthians is one of the most profound theological insights in the Bible. In a very carefully constructed logical flow, Paul lays out how Jesus fits in the big picture. Humankind brought death to the world through our stubborn insistence on being little gods. God's solution? Introduce into the world God's son, Jesus, fully human and fully divine, to reclaim life, defeat death, and show us the way back to God. Christ, through his resurrection, is the first one to go through the full cycle, from birth to death to resurrection. We, Christ's followers, can expect the same, quote "at his coming", which means sometime soon, but not yet. This is uncomfortable for us, isn't it? No one wants to wait. Let's get rid of all of these sovereignties, authorities, and powers and put those enemies under his feet. Won't that be grand? But….not yet. The easy to miss sub-context of this passage is the very important understanding that Christ is the key to all of this happening. He is God's chosen one, the one who is going to bring this world conversion to fruition. Look to Jesus if you want to know the way.

Mom took her fears to Jesus. She prayed fervently and frequently. In her later years, Mom began to use a method of prayer that I have used myself. She kept a diary where she would write her prayers to Jesus on the left page, pause a few moments, and then write Jesus' answer on the right page. You may be a little puzzled by this approach – logically speaking. How does this work? It's surprisingly simple. When you write down Jesus' answer, the key is to simply write what comes to your mind and heart. Don't edit it, just write it down. Let it flow through you. Suspend the judge in your head, suspend the control room. Just let it come. At first, it will feel stilted as your brain interferes, but stick with it and relax. You will definitely find a surprise or two. I spoke to Mom after one of these sessions one day after our prior conversations about death, and she was all smiles. What? I asked. She whispered to me, "Jesus is going to go easy on me." I laughed with her. Of course he would, she was one of the sheep.

The gospel reading is famous for its quite striking imagery. Sheep and goats, as simple to tell apart in Jesus time as we can separate dogs and cats today. There's two rather interesting points that stand out in this reading. First of all, what seems to be important to Christ the judge is simple acts of kindness. There isn't much about saving the world through some dramatic effort, or fighting off the foes of Christianity. It's about sharing food, sharing drink. It's about welcoming strangers and clothing shivering people. It's about caring for the sick and not forgetting the prisoner. It's really quite simple. The second point is even more subtle. A sheep does these things without even thinking about it much. They just do. And what condemns the goats? Also just as simple. The goats are not evil dictators, or terrorists, or crooked politicians – *necessarily* – but what sets the goats apart is their simple, everyday selfishness. They simply don't share, don't welcome, don't care, don't visit. And like the sheep ironically, they don't think about it much, if at all. In fact, they're quite surprised when they turn out to be goats and lose eternity. This is the insidiousness of evil – it turns otherwise caring, thoughtful people into self-centered folks who, when asked to do anything for others, simply say no.

My Mom, quite simply, was always yes. She put herself, quite intentionally, at the service of others in an ego-less way. She worked at an office for several years, and whenever anything went wrong, from a clogged toilet to a customer complaint, her first comment was always, "It was probably something I did!" It became a standing joke in the firm, but in this simple acceptance of blame, mostly unwarranted, every little problem stayed little. It was a happy place to work, and here, 25 years after her retirement, they all came to her funeral. She was the queen of the sheep, and I think Jesus gave her everything she asked for. It was personal.

Did my Mom suffer a lot in the end? From my vantage point, I would say no, but dying is always a hard process. She lost direct awareness of her surroundings on Monday, went into a coma by Wednesday, and died on Friday. The direct cause was congestive heart failure, and my sisters acknowledge being disturbed by her ragged, painful sounding breathing toward the end. But Mom was not conscious, and I don't think she suffered in any substantial way. Jesus took her home as he promised he would. A simple end to a simple life of caring.

Following Jesus is not hard to do. We can overstress about worthiness and right behavior and following the rules. Please refrain from that tendency for a bit and focus on the simple things. When your heart reaches out to someone in need, do you shut it down or think it through? Do you run or do you act? I think we get wrapped up in all or nothing thinking. Maybe it's a simple gesture, a small amount of money or an hour of donated time. Those pledge cards you received last week, hint hint, are a great place to start. Think of them as sheep time.

And, most importantly, get to know the shepherd. Jesus really wants to know how you tick, your hopes, your fears, your frustrations and your joys. Don't hold it inside. Prayer is a dialog, a two way conversation. Ask, rage, laugh, wonder, demand – it's okay. But for every minute of asking, spend 2 minutes listening. One mouth, two ears. When you hear the shepherd's voice often enough, you'll know who to follow.

Can I hear a "Baaaaaa-men"? Perfect!

Miracles

Scripture Referenced: John 2:1-11

> When the wine ran short, the mother of Jesus said to him, "They have no wine." And Jesus said to her, "Woman, how does your concern affect me? My hour has not yet come." His mother said to the servers, "Do whatever he tells you."

Everyone loves a miracle! The seemingly impossible happens. From hopelessness, hope. From sure death, life. From sickness, health. From lack and emptiness, abundance. Have you ever seen a miracle? Seriously – have you seen a miracle? Let's define our terms carefully, shall we? What is a miracle? A miracle, according to the dictionary, is an effect or extraordinary event in the physical world that surpasses all known human or natural powers and is ascribed to a supernatural cause. So notice in this definition that a miracle is somewhat of an interpreted event. It surpasses all *known* human or natural powers. So, a person from the 16th century dropping into our world would see miracles everywhere he looked – electricity, cars, television, airplanes, running water. It would all be miraculous from his point of view. As science has progressed in our time, many things we would normally see as miraculous are explainable and clear to our sophisticated brains. It would seem that the age of miracles has ended. Or has it?

The miracle at Cana is remarkable for a number of reasons. Let's look a little closer, shall we? First of all, note that very few people know that a miracle has happened at all! Jesus, Mary, the apostles, and the servers are in on the event – no one else seems to be. Secondly, the nature of the miracle is absurd in its *excess*. Note that Jesus doesn't just whip up a few extra wineskins to get through the rest of the reception. No, he takes six stone jars each holding 25 gallons of water and promptly comes up with 150 *gallons* of prime wine. That's 757 bottles of wine (I did the math the other night). 63 *cases* of wine. Why did he do that? Mary had simply informed him that they had no wine. She didn't tell him what to do – but even in his reluctance to do anything, he ended up doing a lot – much more than expected. Hold that thought.

John's gospel, the *onion* gospel I call it, has layers and layers of meaning. To John, miracles aren't unexplainable events, they are *signs*. Signs are pointers, meaningful in their own right, always showing us more than what appears on the outside. To John, this miracle is a sign that shows many different elements of Jesus. It shows that Jesus is obedient – yes, to his Mom, but more importantly, to the situation. We're not sure why he seemed reluctant to act – perhaps he saw more nuance in the situation than Mary did – but he took his mother's observation and decided that he had to act. So he did, and in this action, he demonstrated the love of God in a simple yet profound way. He took ceremonial washing jars, a symbol of Judaism, and turned these glorified wash basins into containers of great wealth. Wine was costly to make and incredibly valuable since it was used to make water drinkable in a region where water was brackish and unhealthy. Jesus not only made the water drinkable, he made it the best wine possible. The sign is clear – God doesn't do things in half measures – it's all big, it's all abundant, it's all more than expected. As the song says, "our God is an awesome God". And finally, in a toss-away line at the end of the reading, we hear that due to this event, the disciples began to believe in him. Miracles, signs, lead to faith, lead to awareness, lead to God.

If you look at many of the other miracles of Jesus, you see similar patterns. Jesus calming the storm – an action witnessed only by the disciples, but clearly impressive, and a sign that led to more faith among his blockheaded followers. The healing miracles all have deeper meaning if we look closely. Many of the healed are lepers, not because leprosy is imminently deadly, but because leprosy broke human relationships by isolating the sufferer. The miracle not only cured the leper, but brought the person back into family and society. The leper is led back to love, which always means back to God.

So again I ask you – have you ever seen a miracle? You may not have witnessed an extraordinary event that defied the law of nature, but if you have seen the result of the miracle, then you're close enough. If you have seen a person come to faith due to an outside agency, if you have seen a person accept love where to that point he would not, if you have seen a person receive an abundance of grace that changed them, then you have seem a miracle. Remember, miracles, then as now, are not seen by everyone. One of the gifts of the spiritual journey is seeing miracles, again and again and again. I have. Have you?

There was a man on his death bed who refused to have a priest hear his confession because he had been away from the Church for the last 50 years and God couldn't possible want him back. His daughter finally asked if a priest could simply come by and anoint him. After days of gentle persuasion, he finally agreed. The priest came, anointed him, and at the last amen, the man passed away. The daughter was sad that he had not been to confession, but I gently reminded her that the Rite for the Sacrament of the Sick includes absolution for the person being anointed. Her eyes opened in wonder. "So, I guess I tricked him into the arms of God!" No, I said with a smile, you simply facilitated a miracle.

One of the persons who saw miracles was St. Paul. He saw the miracle of the Corinthian people coming into knowledge of the Spirit. But they continued to squabble among themselves, arguing which gift was the greatest. It's as absurd as arguing which miracle of Jesus was the greatest. You see, in the end, every time the Spirit of God enters into us, a little miracle happens. The nascent gift that we have is watered and nourished. What seems to be a simple skill, perhaps speaking in public, becomes imbued with God's grace and miraculously, a preacher is born. What starts as an ability to read the mood and physical aura of a person becomes a gift of discernment and healing. What begins as a love of learning becomes a love of teaching and a miraculous power to drive off ignorance and enable people to walk proudly in a new job. These are miracles – not because something spectacular happens – but because something deeper occurs. Where there was nothing, there is now something. Where there is just a little spark, there is now a burning fire. What's the common thread? These gifts, these charisms, are signs of God's action in the world through each of us. In such signs and gifts, God reveals his glory and people begin to believe. It's happening all of the time.

The bottom line is that each and every one of you is a miracle about to happen. Do you see that reality? Every one of you has a gift or two or three that are just waiting to blossom into manifestations of the Spirit. Your gift, when expressed, will bring people to God. Explore your giftedness. Ask your loved ones what gift they see in you – that's a hint at the spark. Ask the Spirit to use your gift for the glory of God. Then look out- miracles are coming up. You're in for a treat…

The Resurrection Specialist

Scripture Referenced: Mark 16:1-7

> He said to them, "Do not be amazed! You seek Jesus of Nazareth, the crucified. He has been raised; he is not here. Behold the place where they laid him. But go and tell his disciples and Peter, 'He is going before you to Galilee; there you will see him, as he told you.'"

How many of you have been to the Holy Land? I certainly hope that part of that experience for you was a visit to the Church of the Holy Sepulcher in Jerusalem, which was built at the original site of Golgotha, a stone quarry, the place of crucifixions in Roman times, the place where Jesus was put to death. When you enter the Church, the crucifixion site is to your right, up a narrow staircase to the top of the rock called the skull, a piece of granite that was unsuitable for quarrying, but positioned perfectly outside the city gates as a place of execution. Anyone arriving or leaving the city gates must walk right past this gruesome rock, and be reminded that the Romans were very much in charge, thank you. When you come to the top of the rock, you can reach through a hole in the floor and touch the worn groove in the rock where the cross was jammed, as cold and hard a place as you can imagine, even to this day.

As you come down from Calvary, back to the floor of the Church, over to the left near the entrance is a large canopied structure, perhaps 20 feet high, and only large enough to hold about six people at a time. As you enter, you must duck your head and go down about 3 steps. There, in front of you, backed by candles, is a low stone slab, the traditional place where the body of Jesus was lain. It is, just as the scriptures tell us, "near the place where Jesus was crucified", and other tombs can be found in caves that branch out under the Church. This simple stone slab feels utterly authentic, easy to imagine as "the place where they laid him." My point in describing this place in Jerusalem? *It exists*. There is a reality to this story we hear spoken of today, a reality of geography, topography, and significance. The story of Good Friday is completely historical and plausible. You can check it out for yourselves.

But what about Easter Sunday? The resurrection event is miraculous, a direct interference by the God of creation into a world governed by the natural laws that He created. This resurrection is hard to imagine, hard for us to visualize, hard for many of us to believe. Did God really do that? Did God really do that?

I've got news for you. God not only did that some 2000 years ago, he keeps doing it. He's been doing it ever since, and does it today. If God gave you his business card, it would say, **God**, in bold print of course, and beneath it in italics, *Resurrection Specialist*. Hmmm, you may think, interesting. Can you give me some examples of other resurrections you've orchestrated, God of the Universe? I'm not sure how God would answer you specifically, but I can give you a few examples.

There was a young man named Bill who found himself a slave to alcohol. Bill was racked with guilt, unable to control his cravings no matter how hard he tried, knowing that his path was the path to death, but unable to find a way out. Bill knew he was powerless over alcohol, that his life had become unmanageable. Then God stepped in. God brought Bill to the understanding that God could restore him to sanity if Bill simply turned over his will and life to the care of God. The resurrection plan worked, and Bill, in humble gratitude, spent the rest of his life helping others resurrect their lives of misery. Bill's program is called Alcoholics Anonymous, and it is probably the single most significant spiritual revelation of the 20th century. The Twelve Steps of AA is so effective that it has become the model for the treatment of every human disorder out there, from overeating to sexual addiction to gambling. Talk to any AA person with a 5 year sobriety token and you'll hear a resurrection story.

Three weeks ago, I was in the RJ Donovan state prison, assisting a group of Christian men of all denominations as we put on a retreat for 3 days. We ministered to 36 inmates who were locked in a death spiral of incarceration, release, crime, conviction, another incarceration, and so on. The retreat is called Kairos, and presents to the men a new way of looking at life, and introduces them to a God who unlike the fathers many of them have, actually loves and cares for them, who suffers with them in compassion, and as astonishing as it seems to them, actually forgives them even as the outside world does not. There is nothing about Kairos that gets these men out of prison any earlier, but to those who are eventually released, the recidivism rate drops from the typical 70 percent to less than 15 percent. Witnessing a Kairos weekend is like watching a master artist at work. From darkness, fear, and isolation, these men are given light, security, and a community of Christian brothers who walk the journey with them. The smiles on their faces tell you exactly what you suspect – these men have been resurrected.

OK, addicts and prisoners may not be groups you can entirely relate to, so let's bring it closer to home. Stop and think. Who needs a dose of resurrection in your life? Who is slowly dying or already dead? I don't mean in a physical sense necessarily. Think about it. Who is walking around in the grip of death? You know some – they're the ones who are in some form of despair. Perhaps they've lost jobs, lost children, lost money on a house. Perhaps they're battling an illness or a chronic disease. Perhaps they're just getting old and life is hard to deal with. But you can see on their faces that they're in a tomb. Perhaps that person in the tomb is you.

Easter celebrates resurrection! Jesus shows us the pattern – did you see it? Good Friday, Holy Saturday, Easter Sunday. Suffering, Reflection, Resurrection! The downward journey is apparently necessary to understand how much God wants to heal you, wants to work within your pain and brokenness, wants to let the light back in and pull you from darkness and despair. This is the promise of Resurrection. It's a gift – you can have it, you simply have to say *yes*. How do you say yes? Here's how:

- First of all, give your consent to God's invitation. This is important. You have free will. When you're ready, simply say to God, "Save me, Lord." Start there. It's right at the bottom of His business card under contact information: *Save me Lord.*
- Next, open your eyes, your ears, your senses to God's response. It won't happen as a lightning bolt – although it might – but in most people's experience, God responds to your *yes* with invitations and encouragement. It could be a phone call, a meeting that comes to your attention, an email that you wouldn't typically open, a friend or acquaintance who you haven't seen in a while. When it comes, don't blow it off as a coincidence or a random event. God is God, after all. What do you expect?

- You might feel a prompting to help someone else in need. Listen carefully. In my experience, the surest way to see the presence of God is through service to someone who is worse off than you are. God works from the margins in – from the edges to the center. God rarely if ever speaks through people in power. Don't get fooled – especially in an election year. Listen to God's voice in the powerless, to those with nothing to lose.
- Finally, seek a community in which to share your journey. We obviously hope you'll choose St. James, and we have much to offer you, but whatever you do, pick *some* place. An isolated Catholic is no Catholic at all. Find a community of faith and cling to it.

Brothers and sisters, Easter is about resurrection. It's real, it's available, it's been done in an amazing dramatic fashion, and it happens throughout the everyday life of millions of Christian believers who see, who hear, who are aware. You can have some, too – that's the promise of Easter!

Scripture Referenced

CPSIA information can be obtained
at www.ICGtesting.com
Printed in the USA
FSOW02n0515080316
17656FS